The Complete Book of
Aliens & Abductions

The Complete Book of
Aliens & Abductions

Jenny Randles

PIATKUS

Picture credits

Permission to use copyright material is gratefully acknowledged to the following:

Pages 13, 20, 22 [top], 24, 26, 30, 37, 39, 44, 61, 69, 75, 93, 96 [top left, bottom left and right], 102 [main and inset], 110, 114 and 137: Fortean Picture Library; *pages 22 [inset], 84, 86, 169:* Jenny Randles; *page 43:* Lisa Anders/Fortean Picture Library; *page 45:* Dennis Stacy/Fortean Picture Library; *pages 50 and 161:* Peter Brookesmith/Fortean Picture Library *[top]*; Ansen Seale/Fortean Picture Library *[bottom]*; *page 79:* Project Hessdalen/Fortean Picture Library; *page 125:* RKO Radio Pictures/The Kobal Collection *[top]*; Twentieth-Century Fox/The Kobal Collection *[bottom]*; *page 126:* Twentieth-Century Fox/The Kobal Collection *[top]*; Columbia/The Kobal Collection *[bottom]*; *page 128:* Columbia/The Kobal Collection; *page 134:* Janet and Colin Bord/Fortean Picture Library; *page 156:* Daniel L. Osborne, University of Alaska/Detlev Van Ravenswaay/Science Photo Library; *page 164:* NASA/Science Photo Library.

Whilst every effort has been made to trace all copyright holders, the publishers apologise to any holders not acknowledged.

First published in 1999 by
Judy Piatkus (Publishers) Ltd
5 Windmill Street, London W1P 1HF

The moral right of the author has been asserted

*A catalogue record for this book is available from
the British Library*

ISBN 0–7499–1956–6

Edited by Cecile Landau
Designed by Jerry Goldie Graphic Design

Typeset by Phoenix Photosetting, Chatham, Kent
Printed and bound in Great Britain by
Butler & Tanner Ltd, Frome, Somerset

CONTENTS

INTRODUCTION

We live in a world that is under siege by 'aliens'. It matters little whether these small, grey entities are 'real' in the sense that your next-door neighbour or your pet cat is real. All that counts is that these often terrifying episodes are shattering the mental health of large swathes of humanity, in what can only be described as a serious epidemic.

'I don't really know how to tell you this,' one recent letter began. 'You will think that I am mad . . . These awful things are happening to me. They really are. Aliens are coming for me as I lie in bed at night.'

There were pages of material like this, heart felt cries for help. The writer was a teenager living in the West of England. In letters and phone conversations throughout 1998, he urged me to help him find escape from this horror. His parents could not believe what he told them. The various doctors that they had sent him to see 'gave up' claiming – he alleged – 'They knew I was not mentally ill but what I told them was impossible. It was easier for them to pass me on to someone else.'

Who could come to the aid of this young man and free him from his obvious suffering? Could I, without medical or psychological training, get involved? Would my doing so help or hinder the situation? What if I explained that his nocturnal encounters with alien creatures were like the tales that thousands worldwide were reporting? Would this reassure him that his memories were true or would I inadvertently foster a delusion? Nobody can answer that pressing question. So instead most of us just run away.

Alan from Stirlingshire is another in the ever-growing tide of people, estimated by some as approaching several million, who suspect they may be alien abductees. He had first been in touch in 1990 to describe to me a series of events that seemed to involve physical attacks on his body when in a dreamlike state. After seeing huge public interest in aliens, through endless TV documentaries, best-selling books and tabloid headlines, he had begun to feel that his mind had buried awful memories of a similar kidnap. Perhaps he had been subjected to unspeakable medical experiments or taken away in some fantastic craft. There was no hard evidence for this, but such is the impact of a global belief system that it is all too easy to assemble oddities from your life into an abduction.

I responded cautiously to Alan, pointing out that one should not jump to conclusions. There are various possible scientific options for what might have been taking place. If he desperately needed to explore his story further then I offered to try and help.

When Alan wrote again several years later, he reported that he had 'told nobody [except me] what had happened'. This is common. Contrary to the idea often suggested by sceptics, abductees are not people seeking the limelight. In a study I made of 74 British cases (to 1995) only four witnesses were willing to talk in public and only another 15 had ventured details of their story even to close family members. The majority regard what has happened as a terrible secret never to be revealed. They feel tainted, blame themselves, are certain that nobody can possibly understand what has happened and that if they talk they will be locked away as a lunatic. The very last thing most of them want to do is tell the world via the next edition of Jerry Springer. As Alan continued, 'I quietly accepted that something terrifying and extremely odd had happened in my life ... then I tried to blot the experiences out altogether.' He failed. Nightmares kept haunting him, reliving his visions of alien contact. Far from being a heroic scene as in the movies, Alan's experience was horrific – more *ER* than *Close Encounters*. He desperately needed someone to help him come to terms with the trauma.

Perhaps he had been subjected to unspeakable medical experiments or taken away in some fantastic craft.

Of course, like so many facing this nightmare Alan had no idea where to turn. The phenomenon of alien abduction is an unwanted problem in search of a solution that makes any kind of sense. There are no practitioners who can wave a magic wand and make it go away. There are no easy answers as to how you can learn to live with the reality (or unreality, for we do not even know which of these words apply).

Many well-meaning people (from doctors to psychiatrists to UFOlogists) will offer aid in their own special way. But each will do so from a deeply loaded perspective and it is far from clear whether any such offers of help will be of long-term benefit or simply make matters worse. Those who probe alien abductions, from whatever direction, are quite literally messing around with people's minds. A doctor may feel qualified to do so, but will assume no reality for the experience. A UFOlogist will probably take the opposite stance but lack clinical expertise. The consequences of being wrong for either party are potentially disastrous and it is the witness who pays the price. It is time to call a halt to this despair.

For the sake of Alan, and all those who will undoubtedly become victims in the future, we must do more than we are doing right now. We have to find what is really going on. To do so we must suspend belief. The evidence must be allowed to dictate what steps we take.

Unfortunately, that is less easy than it sounds. Because thousands of seemingly sane, honest and clearly frightened people have claimed an alien abduction does not mean such things are really taking place. Nor, of course, does it mean that these people are deluded. So what in fact does it mean? Consider the following analogy, which may prove surprisingly appropriate.

The storyline gripped the nation for months during 1998 – Deirdre
Rachid was innocent. The entire 17 million-strong audience of British TV
series *Coronation Street* knew this. They had watched her fall under the spell
of a sinister con man who had pretended to be an airline pilot, then seen him
defraud a lot of money and blame her. Slowly Deirdre's world fell apart through
her arrest, police investigation, trial and imprisonment, while the real criminal
walked free convincing the courts that he had been cheated on by her.

Coronation Street is a remarkable TV show. It airs four nights a week, has
been on screen for almost 40 years and involves actors who often stay with the
show for decades. William Roache, who plays Deirdre's ex-husband and was
intimately bound-up in this plot, has grown on screen from being a college
student to a man now approaching his old-age pension. Even Anne Kirkbride,
the actress who plays the wronged woman, has been a cast member for a quarter
of a century. As a result this 'soap' – the most popular programme on any
channel in the UK – is a major part of life for about a third of the population.

Millions have seen characters in the series live and die, watched babies
be born and grow in front of their eyes into adults. Every detail of their lives is
followed. There can be few TV programmes worldwide that can match the emotional impact that this show has on a nation. Tens of thousands of people discuss
the lives of the characters as if they were real. They rarely stop to think of the
absurdity of this. Of course, deep down they appreciate the difference between
a soap and real life, but it evades them as they chat away. We often temporarily
suspend rational judgement to accept fictional characters into our lives.

Oddly this story may tell us a great deal about aliens. For after Deirdre
was wrongly jailed and millions had to watch her descent into mental torment,
it seemed as if the whole country began a campaign to see her released. The
'Free Deirdre' bandwagon took on such extraordinary life that it generated
front-page stories in the press, made the TV news alongside real accidents and
murders and even brought official statements of public support from the Prime
Minister, Tony Blair, and the Leader of the Opposition, William Hague. The
character suffered in prison (or rather inside a set within a TV studio) and the
actress portrayed her bitterness (whilst in truth being paid a large salary affording a lifestyle beyond the dreams of most entranced viewers). As this happened
the situation rapidly got out-of-hand.

Before long there were daring stunts by foolhardy fans, desperate to appeal
for Deirdre's release. Real people put their lives in danger to collect money for
a fighting fund to seek the freedom of this fictional character. Protest marches
took fans to the gates of a real prison at Risley in Cheshire, where they (quite
wrongly) assumed that their beloved Deirdre had been incarcerated.

On the day Deirdre was finally released Granada TV, who film the programme, received a cheque for £5,000 to help (Granada were informed) with
Deirdre's legal costs. A spokesman for the show stated that they had naturally

assumed that the cheque had been submitted as a joke. But the bank confirmed it was genuine and that the fan in question was not unduly wealthy. Someone had donated their savings to secure the freedom of an invented character who had never been near a real prison.

The phenomenon displayed by this case is fascinating. It shows that people can at times find it hard to see the dividing line between fact and fiction, or between real people and strongly portrayed characters. When the 'reality' of this storyline was reinforced in many subtle ways – notably the media blitz and statements from public figures – a few people were driven across that divide. In the end some reached the point where they genuinely found themselves unsure what was real and what was imaginary.

The lessons for the alien abduction mystery are clear. For it does not follow that something has to be a reality in order for it to be widely perceived as true or to produce a huge emotional impact. All that is necessary is that enough people talk, write and speculate about it as if it were true and that these discussions then gain widespread attention through today's mass-market media. Nobody can doubt that alien contact stories do this. You only have to open a newspaper, turn on a TV set, read a comic strip, watch a Hollywood movie or go into a toy store to see the hold that aliens have on our imagination.

If public fascination was directly proportional to the supporting evidence, then there would be no adulation for aliens. The mystique that has grown up around the belief that they exist creates assurance in millions that the evidence is strong. Too few seek to put the record straight and it is easy to see why. UFOlogists get the most attention and sell the most books and group subscriptions if they pander to the desire that aliens are out there. Since these things are what most UFOlogists want to believe in for themselves then the incentive to say differently is small. This belief, trust, delusion (call it what you will) brings the same resolution found in the Deirdre Rachid story – from the T-shirts to the protest marches demanding government action.

Often those who speak out to try to dispel the fallacies behind the alien abduction evidence are themselves motivated to do so. Scepticism is a belief system. These folk reject the whole mystery and protest about human gullibility. They fail to see that there is something odd taking place that still requires an explanation. Even if the sceptics are right to say that no aliens are landing in vast space fleets to kidnap a dustman from Basingstoke that does not mean that something truly weird is not taking place.

The idea that aliens are involved in the abduction mystery is a reasonable candidate for what might be happening. It deserves to be explored (and eliminated if possible) but is not the only option. Those who have studied the mystery think that new science will be learnt when we resolve what is going on. The simple answers (wishful thinking by pie-eyed dreamers, for example) are among the easiest to disprove by the accumulating evidence.

The result is that an enormous industry has grown up that effectively promotes a myth. That myth is not that alien abductions are real (for in many senses they are), nor that alien contact is possible (for scientifically that is more likely now than ever). Rather it is a myth that this possibility has become a certainty. It is so widely believed that a disturbing number of people do live their lives as if the alien abductors were every bit as real as Deirdre Rachid.

To prove that real aliens are interacting with our lives takes a lot more than book sales, tabloid journalism and impassioned pleas to end the 'cover up' on TV chat shows. It requires hard evidence and proof, rare luxuries in this field – perhaps for all too obvious reasons! Undoubtedly, there is an intriguing, even astounding mystery occurring in our midst. That thousands claim to have seen aliens all across the Western world is without dispute. But never forget that millions believed that they saw Deirdre Rachid in prison and responded remarkably to that 'reality'. What appears true and what actually is true are sometimes not the same thing.

This brings me to the purpose of this book. We need to assess the facts, such as we can understand them, evaluate all of the possible answers which have been theorised, and see if this can show the way forward. As the new millennium dawns, this is the perfect opportunity to review our approach to this baffling enigma. This book is intended to be a step in that direction. It will provide you with the cases, the global patterns, the way in which society has embraced abduction evidence and the subtle interactions that take place between fact and fiction. It will also give what I hope will be a useful reference source to the researchers or 'alien hunters' (see page 173). Finally, all major theories for what might lie behind the alien abduction phenomenon will be set out for you to consider.

I do not pretend that I know the truth about alien abductions. Anyone who tells you otherwise is fooling themselves. For too long we have been 'treading water' in our efforts to figure this out. Left to their own devices mysteries entertain us but do not get resolved. Indeed often those involved with their study subconsciously prefer to keep it that way because a resolution may put them out of a job!

> *UFOlogists get the most attention and sell the most books if they pander to the desire that aliens are out there.*

However, the alien phenomenon is too important for us to play games with or make selfish judgements about. It is affecting the mental health of our society. Perhaps beings from another reality truly are abducting humans. Or there may be an answer somewhat closer to home. But there will be an answer and we owe it to those who suffer in silence to go out there and find it.

Jenny Randles – Buxton, Derbyshire, January 1999

PART ONE

AN ALIEN HISTORY

I f you read most books about the UFO mystery, whether written by believers or by sceptics, they tend to agree on one thing. While sightings of 'flying saucers' were first made in 1947, the earliest reported abduction by their alien crew came in 1957. However, as with most convictions held about the subject this is a somewhat contentious opinion.

There are many claims by modern abductees that their encounters with aliens began when they were children.[1] This places their earliest recall as far back as the 1930s. Unfortunately, most have emerged through the rather doubtful means of regression hypnosis. More importantly, nearly all have been recorded since the abduction phenomenon became the subject of study in the 1970s. There do not appear to be good records to establish that decades-old abductions were described when they were happening let alone were documented in some verifiable way. No researchers appear to be seeking such evidence – for instance, in the form of diary records. They should be. Memory is fallible. It can – and does – adapt with time as psychologists have long proven.[2]

To establish that old cases are just like modern ones is critical, because it is the only way to be certain that the same phenomenon has been happening for centuries. We also need to know if the older event was in any way culturally dependent. The 1930s were beset by war, with modern technology and space travel years away. Those who contend that alien abductions are real should expect the format adopted by a 1939 abduction to show unmistakable comparisons with a case from 1999 – not just vague links, but the same kind of aliens using identical (futuristic) technology and behaving in the same kind of way. On the other hand, those who suspect that some weird mental phenomenon is at the heart of the abductions would expect case details to match the era from which they emerge. Cultural progress would be bound to leave its mark on the story. If, despite hundreds of abductees claiming decades-old abductions, no contemporary proof is available, then this will be an important negative finding. Many abductees record their experiences, for example through artwork. Surely some would have done so years ago?

A second way in which abductions may have a precedent comes from alien contacts that are not, strictly speaking abductions. A large number exist.[3] Again many of these sightings (over 100 as of 1999) were put on record *after* interest in UFOs began. However, almost none of these stories depend upon artificial means (such as hypnosis). They are consciously remembered and described. In some instances there is also documentation to prove that they were first reported at the time of the event, perhaps several decades prior to modern-style abduction reports.

Finally, we can also examine the evidence of folk-tales. These have been handed down across the centuries from every country on Earth and a surprising number appear to describe contact with strange beings. Of course, some folk-tales are just mythic stories passed through verbal communication like the parables in the Bible or the warnings parents issue to children about the 'bogeyman'. They can serve a useful purpose by scaring youngsters away from potentially hazardous places or teaching moral lessons.

Nevertheless, folklorists agree that at least a percentage are based on real stories – puzzling events that seemed at the time to have a supernatural explanation. Their telling and retelling became the ancient equivalent of an episode of a TV series like *Strange but True?*, setting them down and ensuring their survival by repetition. The key, as folklorists know, is to find what are apparently verifiable accounts that do possess testimonial support.[4]

So we can now look back in time to discover what precedents – if any – there are for the alien abduction story as we know it today. Watch closely as this book develops to see just how little has changed over 350 years.

> **The key is to find what are apparently verifiable accounts that do possess testimonial support.**

FAIRY STORIES?

Many cultures have old stories describing intelligent beings that reputedly co-exist with humans. Sometimes they are thought to inhabit what modern physicists might term a 'parallel reality', where time and space flow at rates different to those of the 'normal' world. Usually no presumptions are made as to the origin of these 'fairy-folk'. They simply appear when they choose to, toy with us, and then disappear back to the nether world from whence they came.

Of course, it is tempting to argue that these fairies were aliens, misinterpreted because our ancestors had no concept of the universe beyond. But that is no more likely than to suggest that today's aliens are fairies who have donned a topical guise.[5] The phrase used to denigrate alien contact – 'little green men' – is even taken from fairy lore where nature spirits wore green.[6]

1645: TAKEN AWAY

A teenage girl called Anne Jefferies had what appears to be a modern-style abduction in the year 1645. There is no doubt that an actual event took place. It was reported at the time to the Pitt family, for whom she worked as a servant. Later it was documented by the Bishop of Gloucester.

Jefferies worked in a large house at St Teath, Cornwall, and had long been fascinated by 'pixies', the small fairy-folk said by locals to inhabit the countryside. Sat outside knitting, she suddenly collapsed into what would now be recognised as an epileptic seizure, her body convulsing and her eyes fluttering as she lost consciousness. To most people she seemed 'possessed' and this led to subsequent accusations of witchcraft, when she displayed an apparent ability to predict future events in visions. She also claimed healing powers and altered her diet and lifestyle permanently because she believed the experience left her with a purpose to fulfil. She paid for this by spending several years in prison and after her release – perhaps wisely – declined to use her abilities or discuss her abduction again.

The Pitt family had found Anne in the garden some minutes after the attack began. She was writhing violently and they carried her into the house. By now she had partially recovered consciousness and was muttering details of an ongoing encounter with strange beings. It took some minutes for her to fully regain her senses and she was left debilitated for days. Although she had 'memory blocks' that prevented full recall, she later described an 'adventure' that occurred during her period of unconsciousness. Her account of a trip to another realm seems to involve a time distortion, as it would have taken longer to act out in real time than the duration of her seizure.

According to Anne's memory, she heard a strange noise and was approached by several small creatures in the garden who displayed an interest in her body, touching it and even kissing her. She felt dizzy, there was a swirling

Girl with fairies.

sensation and a feeling like needles being stuck in her body. Then all went black. Her next memory was of being in a strange, bright land, surrounded by golden buildings, flowers and several human-sized creatures who seemed fascinated by reproduction. Then a noise like 'a thousand flies buzzing about her' filled the air and all went black again. She then found herself back in Cornwall and was being carried into the house, but several 'pixies' were still surrounding her. None of the Pitt family could see these beings, although Anne claims they came into the house and exited through the window just before she fully awoke.

This fascinating case features so many aspects that now recur in modern abductions. Anne was a bright, artistic girl, prone to having what we call psychic experiences. She suffered a physical trauma that we might term an epileptic seizure, but during her periods of unconsciousness she had dreamlike 'sequences' linked by physiological symptoms involving buzzing noises and floating sensations. Anne clearly believed she did meet pixies and had a sexual rapport with them, but others present saw nothing – only a clearly distressed girl in an altered state of consciousness having physically travelled nowhere.

Five hundred years from now historians may view today's close encounters in the same way most of us interpret stories like that of Anne Jefferies (see page 13). Yet, the way in which many similar traditions emerge across the planet must hint at the possibility of some underlying reality, whatever we determine that to be.

Interestingly, our fairy image of tiny creatures wearing wings is from Victorian children's stories. In genuine sightings, they were only slightly smaller than humans, and physically similar. A typical description from a sighting in 1842 at cottages near Stowmarket, Suffolk, was of a being '3 feet high' that had a dress that 'sparkled as if with spangles'. There was a strange silence and stillness pervading the area.[7] Many alien reports are remarkably like this. Indeed there is an eerie consistency between both types of being. It is worth noting that such extensive parallels are cited by modern folklorists like Dr Eddie Bullard from the University of Indiana as one reason to take alien abductions as real events and not just myths. By that logic we could say the same of the intelligent 'fairy' beings who share this planet with us.

In countries where there do not appear to be alien abduction cases, some contact with 'little people' is reported.

Even more interesting is that in some countries where there do not appear to be modern alien abduction cases (about one-third of the world's population) some ongoing contact with 'little people' is reported. In Indonesia and Malaysia, for example, there are still sightings of the 'Bunian' – as their breed of 'elemental' is known (see page 61). Ahmad Jamaludin, a veterinary surgeon, has collected Bunian tales from what are often very poor villages, but searched in vain for alien abductions. He notes how these stories fill the same role. Do modern alien abductions only occur naturally where the death of old-style fairy lore makes them necessary? Yet Bunian cases involve kidnap, time distortion, even sexual adventures – all the 'modern' trappings.[8]

In one of his cases (Maswati Pilus in a rural village near Panang in Malaysia during June 1982) a young woman reported the sudden disappearance of all environmental sounds, as she entered what we would call an altered state of consciousness – a consistent opening gambit in abduction cases. A child-sized being then appeared and took her to a strange, bright land where she suffered memory blackouts and time distortions. When found by frantically searching relatives she was on the ground in a semi-conscious state, very close to the spot where she had first met the Bunian. According to her memory she had been 'abducted' to 'another realm', yet physically she had apparently remained where she was in an altered state of consciousness.

Is all this evidence that the alien abduction dates back into the dawn of history? Are we wrong to conclude that its contemporary technocratic disguise is its only form? Is it a mistake to give too much emphasis to this current, slightly modified, version of an old, old story simply because it suits our media-obsessed culture with its trappings of space and alien technology? We can only file these thoughts as clues to bear in mind.

1868: 'A WONDERFUL DREAM'

According to his notebook, council engineer Frederick William Birmingham had the following experience on the night of 25 July 1868. He found himself standing on the verandah of his cottage, overlooking what is now Parramatta Park near Sydney in New South Wales, Australia.

In his 'wonderful dream – a vision' Birmingham saw a craft cross the sky. This he calls 'an ark' that 'moved through the air in a zig-zag fashion' that then 'stopped, and descended some 20 feet or so as gently as a feather on the grass.' Stunned by this sight Birmingham then heard a voice coming into his mind. It explained 'that is a machine to go through the air' and asked 'Do you wish to enter upon it?' At his agreement Birmingham felt himself lifted upwards, floating. Once in the craft he stood in a room with a 'spirit' (seemingly a human). This being had a sheaf of papers containing mathematical formulae and told Birmingham 'it is absolutely necessary that you should know these things'. He sensed that this was a task he *must* perform. Birmingham reports that he stared at these papers but lost consciousness – or, as he assumed, 'fell, I suppose, into my usual sleeping state'. He awoke next morning – in bed – with his mind filled with this vivid set of images.

As a story this is a rich blend of Victoriana and space-age abduction lore. But it contains many aspects of the modern-day phenomenon, such as the task set by the aliens for the witness. Of course, it is clearly visionary in nature, not a real-world event. Like most abductions it features the out-of-body, floating sensations that merge reality with ESP and dream states.

British science fiction writer David Langford fooled many for years with his not dissimilar tale in a book called *An Account of a Meeting with Denizens of Another World*, purporting to be the journal of a Victorian cabinet maker from High Wycombe. He filled this saga with clues about its bogus nature, but few spotted them until Langford owned up. Even then some writers said his confession was the hoax![9]

However, there is little doubt that Birmingham's case is *not* a modern fake. Local research scientist and UFOlogist Bill Chalker has dug deep and traced the history of the journal recording it back to at least 1940 (thus pre-dating today's UFO culture). Here he discovered that it had already been handed down through the generations. The recorded details of the incident seem to be historically correct. The house still exists, and Chalker has visited the site. Most importantly there was a Frederick William Birmingham, a surveyor and engineer, who *did* live in Parramatta between 1868 and 1873. He died in 1893 apparently still obsessed with trying to understand the secret of 'the ark and its mysterious formulae'.[10]

1921: THE FIRST KIDNAP

One of the clearest features of modern alien abductions is the element of kidnap. The witness is forced to enter what is perceived to be a UFO against their will. Although very old cases such as that of Anne Jefferies (see page 13) include hints of this, it is extremely rare in any alien contact prior to 1957.

The first undeniable case is from the summer of 1921; although it was not reported until 33 years later in the form of an anonymous letter published by the respected French newspaper *Paris Match* (23 October 1954). The date is no accident. Late October 1954 was the height of the first known wave of alien sightings within the modern UFO context. Although there were reports across Europe, many of these first sightings occurred in France. The press coverage was obviously the stimulus for G.B. (as he termed himself) to contact the paper. However, while many of the then current stories featured aliens who attacked witnesses, no actual abductions were involved.

G.B. professed to have had his sighting on a hot afternoon in Marseilles, when he was just 8 years old. He was walking on the banks of the Canal du Nord playing in the 'moonscape' left behind after the recent war. As he did so 'two beings dressed in a kind of flexible diving suit sprang from among the acacia trees'. These suits were 'metallic' and the entities 'tall and very slender'. He was then 'dragged toward what I thought was a strangely shaped tank'. They carried him into this and he felt oddly unable to resist. Inside was a room with a 'flexible couch' and square or rectangular 'port holes'.

The stunned witness then reports that he 'started to cry'. An opening appeared in the roof of the vehicle and G.B. found himself 'back on the ground'. He was, however, much further from the place where he had been abducted and had to walk home for hours.

It is very difficult to evaluate such a case because for obvious reasons it was never investigated. But it has to be noted that several of the details mirror rather well (or too well) celebrated cases in the 1954 wave, in particular the reference to a 'diving suit' and the inability to resist the aliens. Also the tall, slender beings were one of two types (the other being dwarfs) that populated most of these 1954 sightings.[11]

It is possible the story was a hoax. But why set it so far back in time? If it *is* genuine it is the first known alien abduction to resemble modern accounts. Yet it has major differences. The fully conscious recall and very physical form of abduction – literally being carried into the UFO – are extremely uncommon. The Anne Jefferies case is much more like modern abduction reports with its memory block as to how she got to the 'strange' land. Indeed, nearly always,

1932: THE MAN WHO DID NOT COME HOME

One of the most amazing early abduction cases comes from France. It is told by Rose, a recently divorced 24-year-old mother. It occurred on the night of 10/11 April 1952, but partly describes events dating 20 years before then. Rose was staying with her grandparents in a country house near Nimes. Residing overnight in an outbuilding with her dogs she was awoken in the night by their growling at an unseen presence. Following them outside to another nearby stone building Rose came upon four beings. One appeared to be an ordinary human, but the other three were about 7 feet tall and with an oriental appearance. One carried a box around his neck held by straps and covered in buttons. The human acted as a go-between translating what the others said.

The man explained that he was a teacher. In 1932 he had met these aliens when they landed in a strange craft and they had urged him to go with them. Being without family ties he agreed and had since lived with the beings in a strange 'faraway world' where time passed much more slowly than in our reality. Although now 45 by Earth years he was still physically in his late 20s.

It was explained to Rose that the beings wanted some Earth literature to study, so she took them back to her room and handed over fashion magazines and a copy of Dumas's classic *The Count of Monte Cristo*. As a thank you she was informed that humans had been 'seeded' on Earth millions of years ago by these visitors (Earth being in effect a penal colony of banished cosmic citizens). Rose was invited to go with them, but refused to leave her 4-year-old child. However, they showed her their craft, which was grey and shaped like a straw hat. It floated in a gully several feet off the ground. They also demonstrated their ability to make objects such as rocks float and then dematerialise, apparently being 'teleported' into their ship.

Philosophical information was conveyed next. They claimed not to interfere in the 'Earth colony' and used an analogy of rats to justify this! Rats were infesting Rose's outhouse at the time and she had been thinking of killing them. The aliens advised her not to do so, but also not to feed them because they would then become dependent on humans. They must fend for themselves, just as humans had been left to do. Then the aliens had to go, because it was very tiring on Earth due to their size. Tall beings could indeed originate in a 'light gravity' environment and would find the relatively 'heavy' gravity of Earth very taxing. Would Rose know that? But if this *was* true then how did the abducted human cope when living in their 'low-G' world?

After her encounter, Rose was left with an intriguing legacy – an ability to have psychic experiences. She had visions of the future and telepathic messages she felt came to her from these beings.[12]

> *Nearly always, witnesses simply do not remember their mode of entry into a UFO, nor can they locate where they are taken.*

witnesses simply do not remember their mode of entry into a UFO, nor can they locate where they are taken. In fact the conclusion that they *do* arrive inside a UFO is often a surmise imposed after the fact. It could easily be one of UFOlogy's great mistakes!

1942: WARTIME MEMORIES

The war brought the first hint of modern-style UFO encounters. One case was reported to me by Eileen Arnold and took place in February 1942. Eileen has proved that she reported it briefly in 1975 to a famed international UFO group. They promptly wrote to say that she had seen a 'mother ship' with 'disc-type UFOs departing on some unknown mission'. I will not embarrass the group by naming them. But indoctrinating a witness into a belief system is all too common.

This case occurred in the busy High Street of Cheltenham. Eileen, then aged 26 and seven months pregnant, was returning from a routine doctor's appointment. It was a bright sunny afternoon and there was much traffic and people around. Eileen says that she was in an unusually 'sensitive' state of mind, on an emotional high. She was 'radiating out' thoughts and others passing seemed to be aware of this.

As she walked home Eileen also noticed a switch in her state of consciousness. The street and traffic around her vanished, all sounds disappeared and she became 'tuned in' to another reality. Suddenly a huge 'thing' appeared in the sky, low above the rooftops. It moved very slowly, but as time had now lost all meaning this was hard to judge. It was a large oval filled with light emerging from holes in the side and with quills like those of a porcupine on its edge. These also gave out light as they detached, one by one, moving into the sky. The whole process seemed to take ages, but lasted seconds only in real time.

This episode became a spiritually enlightening event that changed her life. The effects described by Eileen Arnold, signalling this inspirational state of consciousness, are very important to our understanding of these phenomena. I call them the 'Oz Factor' from the story about a young girl transported suddenly from our reality into the mythical reality of Oz. The state is very common in abduction events.

Following the incident Eileen had numerous 'psychic' experiences, involving premonitions and visions. Some provided messages that she believed were coming from 'other dimensional' entities and spoke of the beauty of life in other realms. Eileen became a teacher, to help others, and after years of educational service adopted the role of a psychic counsellor. Her two children have shared her lifestyle, her daughter, in particular, being artistically gifted and channelling 'higher realm' messages. In August 1975 (when 13) she and her mother had a second encounter when Eileen suddenly 'felt the urge' to go out onto the balcony of their home in the Malvern hills to watch an arrowhead object drift by. This again distorted the passage of time during its flight.

Seven months later in 1942, 27-year-old Albert Lancashire claims that he became the first true British abductee. He told me his story in 1975, although I was able to establish that he had talked of it a decade earlier. Albert was guarding a wartime sentry box at a secret radar site at Cresswell near Newbiggin-on-Sea, Northumbria. It was late evening in September 1942 and he was 'made' to go outside his box by a 'strange impulse to look at the sky' – another common indication that these contacts occur in an altered state of consciousness. Out over the North Sea was a large, dark mist surrounding a glowing light. Thinking this was some German weapon he was about to raise the alarm when a beam of yellow light from the cloud struck him. He recalls a floating sensation, then nothing until regaining awareness by the sentry box. There was no obvious time loss involved.

Albert grew, like many witnesses, through a period of psychic experience (apparitions and ESP) and told friends of his story in the form just described. He had by now attached a mystical godly connotation. Then, in October 1967, Britain experienced a wave of UFO sightings and some white lights in the sky appeared outside the signal box at Ashton-Under-Lyne where Albert now worked for the railways. Poltergeist effects struck Albert's home and he had a series of dreams or visions that awoke his memory. In these visions he saw

> *The episode became a spiritually enlightening event that changed her life.*

himself during the 1942 experience, waking in a strange room with a couch or bed and being in the presence of a woman of oriental appearance. There were also several 'pygmy men' and a human-sized being in a white suit. Albert now recalled being 'examined' on the bed by an entity wearing a surgeon's mask. But much of the rest of the experience remained unclear because of 'memory gaps'.

ARRIVAL OF THE FLYING SAUCERS

By coincidence, it was another witness called Arnold, 5,000 miles from Cheltenham, who ushered in the age of the 'flying saucer' on 24 June 1947. On that date Kenneth Arnold, private pilot and businessman, spotted a formation of crescent-shaped objects high above Mount Rainier in the Cascade Mountains in the USA. His verbal description caused a media sensation, even though Arnold believed he had seen some kind of secret US plane or prototype missile. In fact, he may well have seen distant military aircraft.[13]

In Arnold's haste to escape an impromptu press conference, he innocently misled an enterprising reporter. He described the UFOs as flying 'like saucers skipping across water'. The media thought the phrase too good to resist and called these craft 'flying saucers', thus implying that they were *shaped* like saucers. They definitely were not, but the media blitz led millions to keep a lookout for saucer-shaped objects. Unsurprisingly, many people quickly found them.

The media probably expected this to be a short-lived fascination, but it is very unlikely that UFOs suddenly appeared in 1947. All the evidence suggests that they have been reported in our skies as long as human beings have looked upwards. What the Arnold sighting did was foster a massive publicity campaign. The creation of the cute name firmly secured the mystery in popular imagination. The theory that the flying saucers were alien in origin did not enter public consciousness until after 1950, when the first UFOlogists began to accuse the American government of a cover-up of this news.

Kenneth Arnold with a drawing of the UFO he saw over Mount Rainier, 1947.

This case demonstrates superbly one crucial problem. Follow the logic. Arnold really saw crescent-shaped craft. These were misreported to the world as being 'saucers'. That error was not corrected and has been compounded by almost every science fiction movie and TV series since. Millions looked skyward and saw what Arnold reported, but not his crescents – *they saw the 'saucers' they were wrongly told to look out for*. This proves that expectation and conditioning shape the mystery. Such a vital lesson cannot be forgotten. In a 1987 study of several hundred of the best alien abduction cases, folklorist Dr Eddie Bullard found that 82 per cent involved aliens flying in *saucer-shaped* craft.[14] Yet if these shapes stem from a reporting error in 1947, then how real are the abductions that accompany them?

1951: IN SEARCH OF LITTLE MEN

One of the interesting features of alien encounters during the first decade of the flying saucer mystery is the almost total absence of the beings now universally associated with abductions – the so-called 'grays'. They are small with pasty skins, large heads, huge eyes and skeletal bodies. If such beings are engaged in a massive operation to abduct humans, they were once far more skilful at hiding their activities.

A new trend began in 1951 with what we might term 'voluntary abductions'. Keith Basterfield investigated an example involving a woman rounding-up cattle at her farm in Halidon, South Australia. In doing so she came upon a strange object on the ground, out of which emerged several figures dressed in silver suits and hoods. They seemed normal in both appearance and height, but invited her on board their craft. She willingly agreed and saw a room filled with equipment and consoles or computing devices. The beings explained that they knew many things about her life and after a friendly conversation they led her back to the ground, where she continued her work.[15]

Another fascinating case was reported by UFOlogist Ted Bloecher. On 19 June 1951, mechanic Joseph Matiszewski was in a meadow at lunchtime in Sonderborg, Denmark. A large oval landed nearby with a whistling noise and as he walked towards it he encountered an energy that 'paralysed' him. Joseph also noticed that nearby cows were similarly unable to move and all the birds had stopped singing – a classic 'Oz Factor' symptom. Four human-like beings with tanned skins were 'making repairs' on the craft.

One of the few signs of *small* entities came in August 1947 at Villa Santina in Italy (see page 74), when a prospector was rendered senseless by a light beam fired by some 'child-sized' beings. The witness was – as are so many alien abductees – visually creative and in his spare time wrote science fiction stories!

THE COSMIC BROTHERHOOD

A very strange split in the evidence becomes apparent by 1952. Up to then there were 10,000 UFO sightings on record, but less than 0.5 per cent involved alien beings. You could count on your fingers any that even hinted at abduction. Although there were a few reports of little men, most aliens were much more human. When witnesses inadvertently stumbled upon them, they rarely exhibited any desire for contact. Often witnesses were sidelined as an inconvenience, although most aliens were reported as friendly and there were stories in which invitations to step inside the UFO were being made.

None of this was recognised by the public or even by early UFO researchers (who published their first books in 1950 and formed groups in 1951). They were fighting to make their field seem legitimate, which was part of the thinking behind the switch to the more scientific-sounding term 'UFO' (unidentified flying object) – a USAF initiative – in 1952. But it was also why many UFOlogists had to be dragged kicking and screaming to take note of aliens.

The witness was – as are so many alien abductees – visually creative and in his spare time wrote science fiction stories!

Yet against this reluctance, a new type of case appeared between 1952 and 1956 that was especially influential. It involved friendly aliens and rides in their craft, achieved a lot of publicity, several best-selling

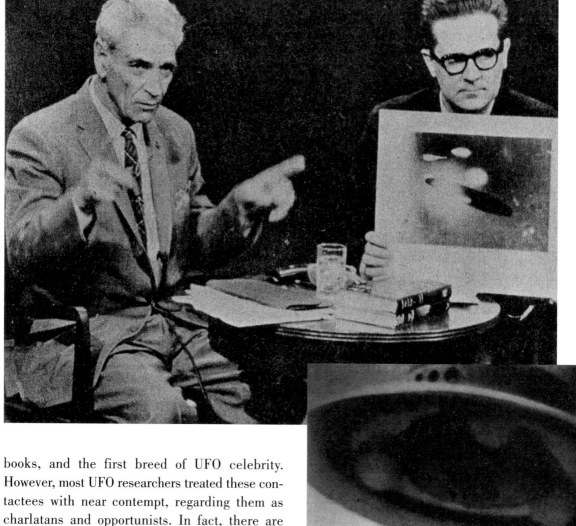

books, and the first breed of UFO celebrity. However, most UFO researchers treated these contactees with near contempt, regarding them as charlatans and opportunists. In fact, there are reasonable suspicions that, if not actually set up by them, the contactee movement was embraced and fostered by the American intelligence community.

Absurd as this sounds there is a trail of evidence. This was a very paranoid era of the Cold War. The CIA was covertly involved in UFO study, because they feared that Communist sympathisers would stir up bogus UFO activity in the prelude to an invasion. A July 1952 wave of sightings over secret airspace in Washington DC was enough to convene a panel of top advisors to plan drastic moves that would defuse public interest. Schemes discussed included using cartoons to trivialise the UFO mystery and make aliens seem friendly and absurd.

Contactee tales fit surprisingly well into this plot. The timing was perfect and the stories gave a boost to the then secret CIA schemes. Indeed the released

George Adamski (left) with Long John Nebel [main picture]; a hoaxed photograph of a Venusian spacecraft taken by contactee George Adamski [inset].

records show the CIA commenting favourably without admitting a role in bringing the stories to life. It is certainly not beyond the bounds of possibility that they did. Contactees deterred a number of influential people, such as scientists and journalists, who in 1952 were starting to respond to UFOs.[16]

Some famous contactees set out on almost evangelical crusades. George Adamski went from running a fast-food stand to cult hero, meeting world leaders and the Pope, after claiming rides with blond-haired, blue-eyed Venusians in the Californian desert. In many subsequent space jaunts he visited the Moon and heard of alien plans to let Earth join the cosmic brotherhood.[17] Contactees became galactic ambassadors. One even stood for President!

1954: THE BIG WAVE

As if in response to the rank absurdity of the blossoming contactee tales, the first credible entity sightings soon followed. Over 60 cases are documented for the period between September and December 1954, two-thirds of them from France. They had many hints that a 'hidden memory', perhaps of an abduction, was involved. But nobody at the time was looking for such things.

A typical case took place on 30 September near Marcilly-sur-Vienne and involved a team of eight builders hard at work. One of these, Georges Gatay, felt compelled to walk away from the group and was overcome with a strange sensation. He saw an oval shape floating just above the ground and a humanlike man wearing a grey 'diver's helmet'. This being had a 'light projector' on his chest and held a 'rod'.

Gatay, who had fought with the French Resistance, was not easily scared, but tried to flee. He could not move. Then the figure simply vanished – or perhaps there was a 'memory lapse', following which the entity was gone. Gatay then saw the oval shape rising upwards, making a high-pitched whistle. At a certain height it too performed a magical vanishing act. Surrounded by a bluish haze or fog, it simply 'went away'. Now free to move, the builder rushed back to his colleagues. They had also been immobilised and claimed to have seen the strange object. In the weeks following the incident, Gatay could not eat, felt weak, had pounding headaches and found it impossible to sleep. Today abductees frequently refer to these *post-traumatic stress disorder* effects. The fact that witnesses to close encounters or abductions report PTSD helps to establish at least a subjective degree of reality.[18]

Other cases in the 1954 wave hid deeper stories. Britain's first major alien encounter took place at a farmhouse in Ranton, Staffordshire, when Jessie Roestenberg (then 29) and her children (aged 6 and 8) hid under a table on 21 October whilst a lens-shaped craft floated overhead. In a large cupola two human figures with long blond hair had stared down with wistful expressions.

Over 30 years later, I discovered untold aspects of the case when I traced Mrs Roestenberg. Like Eileen Arnold (see page 18) she felt 'primed' to have this experience through 'strange sensations' hours beforehand. During the encounter the 'Oz Factor' occurred, 'It felt like hours passed but it must have been seconds … time was suspended,' she said. She was also paralysed, 'It felt like I was in a vice.' The UFO 'vanished' – 'I turned to my children, looked back and it was just gone.' Her son saw its return through the window, but it became covered in a blue/violet haze of light and then disappeared. The similarities with the French case only three weeks before (which Jessie apparently had not heard about) are obvious.

Like Eileen Arnold, Jessie later had many 'psychic' experiences. 'Mental images' came from nowhere with alien messages. These said that aliens are friendly, just surveying us but being discrete so as not to frighten us into hostile acts. As for modern-day abduction tales, Jessie has no truck with them. Why? Because she *knows* the visitors are human and not the ugly, egg-headed 'grays'. She insisted 'I do not believe in little men – not after what I have seen.'[19]

Jessie Roestenberg on 22 October 1954, the day after she saw a UFO over her cottage at Ranton, Staffordshire.

1955: CONVERSATIONS

1955 was to bring a case where the witness hijacked the alien craft and the poor crew did not know what they had let themselves in for!

Josef Wanderka was an Austrian raised in Hungary who suffered badly during the Nazi invasion. Even after returning to his native Vienna he faced many traumas. In the summer of 1954 he had his first alien encounter, while riding his new moped on Roter Berg, a local hill. A cigar-shaped craft glided overhead and was watched by Wanderka and a group of Soviet soldiers who bragged that it was one of their secret weapons.

Then, in early September 1955, Josef was walking in woods near Arbesthal. It was mid-afternoon and he was surprised to come upon a large, grey, metal egg on the grass in a clearing. A ramp led to an open hatchway. Seizing the initiative Wanderka leapt onto his moped and accelerated to climb the ramp. When inside he switched off his engine and coasted to a halt. Several 'people' came to meet him. They were about 6 feet tall, with immaculate 'babyish' faces, blond hair, no evident sexual distinctions and were wearing grey coveralls. Indeed, these beings were most similar to those seen during the previous year by the Roestenbergs in England (see above) and are by far the most common type reported in Europe. The term 'Nordic' is used owing to their almost Scandinavian appearance, although witnesses often likened their complexion to that of an Oriental and in this case Wanderka reported that they 'bowed' in an Eastern fashion when he left them.

After he apologised for his intrusion the beings explained (in German with an English accent!) that they came from 'the topmost point of Cassiopia as seen from Earth'. Such daft astronomical origins became a regular feature of alien contacts. A truly extraordinary dialogue then proceeded, in which the beings seemed interested in his moped engine and he insisted on lecturing them about socio-economic politics! Wanderka claims to have brought the aliens to tears with his tales of Nazi oppression, death camps and the unequal distribution of wealth, but they rejected his pleas that they use their superior knowledge to set the Earth on the right track. Instead they advised that they would not interfere, but he could do so. Their plan that Josef become world 'leader' provoked disagreement from the witness when he informed the aliens of how previous megalomaniacs had fared.[20]

This bizarre case had an interesting parallel in England on 7 September 1957, when apparently the same aliens were seen again. A young man, James Cook, felt in an 'odd mood' and with a 'tingling' in his head responded to an urge to go to a hill outside Runcorn, Cheshire. He was rewarded by the appearance of a light that resolved into a strange craft, which floated just above the rain-soaked fields. He was told not to touch its metal surface but to 'jump' inside, take off his clothes, don a silvery translucent suit and was ferried to a larger craft. The small craft used an electromagnetic field, he was told, and was highly charged in wet weather. The big craft used an 'ion propulsion' mechanism that could not operate inside the atmosphere because it would damage our air. Such plausible eco-science was very advanced for 1957, but has been repeated during later abductions.

Several 'people' came to meet him. They were about 6 feet tall, with immaculate 'babyish' faces, blond hair, no evident sexual distinctions ...

The larger craft took Cook on a trip to a 'strange place called Zomdic'. The aliens were tall, humanlike with fair hair, babyish faces and no sexual features – just as Wanderka described. On Zomdic Cook was told to convey a message to the world to stop 'upsetting the balance' by our selfish acts. He told his captors that as an ordinary chap nobody was going to take any notice of him and they should help us out. The aliens declined saying they were 'concerned observers' but would not interfere and seemed upset at Cook's lack of will to change the world. On returning home, Cook was amazed to learn he had been missing two days.

No researchers saw the patterns between cases like this. But these two unrelated and unreported cases may be persuasive evidence that something more than mere imagination is at work.

1957: ONE MAN'S 'FANTASY'

What might seem like a young man's sexual fantasy occurred in October 1957. Of course, it cannot be divorced from the number of other types of abduction that contain similar elements. Sex and reproduction also played their part in fairy lore (the theme of 'fairy babies' being taken from humans being one) and the Anne Jefferies case (see page 13) shares some features 350 years before!

Antonio Villas Boas was a 23-year-old in a large family, farming land near Sao Francisco de Sales, Brazil. In mid-October 1957 there was great interest in space because the Soviet Union had stunned the Americans by launching Sputnik, the first orbital satellite. Villas Boas had seen a strange light over the farm around the time of the launch. A red light was seen again on the night of 15 October, but he still went night-ploughing. At around 1.00 am a strange egg-shaped craft landed. Villas Boas was some way from the farmhouse, but tried to escape on his tractor. Unfortunately, the engine failed and its lights went out. At this point, he was physically attacked by four beings, about 5 feet tall, who were wearing masks. They dragged him into the craft. Inside was a softly lit room. He was stripped, a blood sample was taken, he was rubbed clean and then some kind of 'gas' seeped into the room in a process that resembles 'disinfection'.

Next a female entity appeared. She was beautiful, humanlike and with very blonde, almost white, hair. She uttered weird noises, yelping like a dog. Intercourse followed (twice – the second time a semen sample was taken). Afterwards, with Villas Boas claiming to feel 'used', she rubbed her belly and pointed to the sky. Oddly he interpreted this to mean that she was going to come back, but it more likely infers 'I am going to have your baby in space.'

After a tour around the craft Villas Boas was led back outside. Over four hours had elapsed. Villas Boas was not – as has often been portrayed – some hick farmer. Indeed he later gained a doctorate and became a lawyer.

His first step afterwards was to contact a Rio magazine that had featured UFO stories. They chose not to publish anything, but invited him to be examined by a doctor. Dr Olavo Fontes was impressed by his test results. He found skin lesions and other effects that suggested mild radiation sickness. Villas Boas also had professed headaches, nausea and excess tiredness in the days following the encounter.[21]

Although this case was recorded in Brazil in early 1958, most UFOlogists wrote it off as fantasy. That did not change until the British journal *Flying Saucer Review* printed details in early 1965. This slow genesis is important as it guarantees the independence of two other cases that followed in its wake. Both of these were reported just after they happened and so their witnesses cannot have known about the Brazilian case. We can be certain that Villas Boas was under medical study by early 1958, so his case was not influenced by these events. As such we have three cases that establish the 'reproduction' pattern as central to the abduction plot.

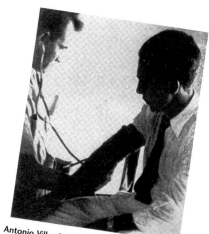

Antonio Villas Boas, UFO abductee, Brazil, 1957.

THE WEEK THE EARTH STOOD STILL

Balls of glowing light were reported swarming over Texas and New Mexico in early November 1957. They landed on roads, lured pursuing police patrols towards them and then zipped off. On one night alone they were claimed to have stalled a dozen car engines within a few square miles. There can be no question that a major event took place.

In the early hours of 3 November, Sputnik 2 – containing a dog – was preparing to take our world into the galactic club. At the same time security guards patrolling bunkers in New Mexico observed one of the dazzling egg shapes that had been stalling car engines during the past four hours. They had been guarding no ordinary bunkers. These held the test silos from 1945 that hosted explosions of the first atomic weapons.

Far away, in the Australian desert, it was late afternoon and about 15 RAF personnel were clearing away the equipment used to explode the final 'Antler' atom bomb at Maralinga. Suddenly, hovering over the precise spot where the 'Taranaki' blast occurred, another UFO appeared. Two RAF personnel have separately described this startling event to me, saying that the object was 'like a king on a throne' and 'sent the military into a frenzy'. It defied the intense security and then just stood on its edge and rocketed skyward before jets could arrive from Alice Springs. One of the witnesses, Derek Murray, then 22, now a Home Office technician, swears 'as a practising Christian' that this was not an illusion or a fairy tale.

The timing of these events is suspicious, as are the locations. Alien contact stories emphasise an alleged concern with how atomic weapons are 'upsetting the balance' of the universe. This joining of real events 10,000 miles apart at the very same time must suggest more than a myth at work.[22]

Balls of glowing light were reported swarming over Texas and New Mexico.

It is difficult not to see deep meaning here. Aliens warn humans about our atomic weapons and how we are upsetting the cosmic balance. Then, at the very moment that we prove our ability to export destructive technology into space, a mass demonstration of superiority occurs through multiple car-stops that cause no injury but make a point.

Alongside these events, simultaneously (allowing for time zones) but with no possible collusion, UFOs brush aside the strictest security imaginable and appear directly above the sites of the very first and the most recent atomic bomb blasts. This is an astonishing set of circumstances.

1958: BABY BOOM

Assuming one can ascribe any reality to the story of Antonio Villas Boas (see page 26), his 'space baby' would have been born in the summer of 1958. At about the same time a British housewife was having her own *very* close encounter – although this being Britain things were more discreet! The story was reported, briefly, at the time, but the full extent only emerged from a series of long unpublished interviews by Dr John Dale, a clinical psychologist.

Cynthia Appleton was a 27-year-old mother of two small daughters, married to a steel worker and living in an old house in Aston, Birmingham. On 16 November 1957 she experienced a strange 'time lapse' during which she lost all awareness of the passage of an hour (the 'Oz Factor' yet again). She had assumed that the exhaustion of motherhood had taken its toll. Later she was told instead that this was a 'failed attempt at contact'.

The failure was shortlived. Two days later Cynthia experienced the onset of an altered state of consciousness, often noted as a trigger to alien contact. Cynthia reported a dizzy, floating sensation, a pressure 'like a heavy atmosphere before a storm' and then a strange 'rosy hue' that seemed to colour the environment. Amidst this a tall figure appeared in her living room from nowhere, accompanied by a flash and faint smell that she later recognised as ozone and sulphur. The man had blond hair, fair skin, blue eyes – a Nordic although Cynthia termed him a 'Greek athlete'. He wore a one-piece suit and a bowl over his head.

Communication occurred without speaking. The being, she says, 'assumed control of me', explaining that no harm was intended, that they wanted to observe us peacefully, but could not make open contact 'until you stop having wars'. To meet 'them' we had to 'travel with a sideways attitude' – perhaps this meant through other spatial dimensions and not strictly sideways.

The entity drew his hands apart and a three-dimensional TV image (what we might today call a hologram, although these had yet to be invented in 1957) appeared in thin air. After a while the entity said he would return, giving a date in January for this rendezvous.

On 7 January 1958, he did, and this was the first of a long series of appointments. By now Cynthia posed questions – *why choose her and not a scientist at Harwell?* The alien answered, 'The human brain is like a radio set. Each mind is set to a certain frequency.' But, he added, they were in touch with scientists developing a 'ray' weapon. This would soon appear. Several months later the invention of the laser was announced.

Cynthia insisted that, whilst there was a TV-image quality to the alien appearances, they blocked

... a tall figure appeared in her living room from nowhere, accompanied by a flash and faint smell that she later recognised as ozone and sulphur.

out light and were real. A whistling noise accompanied them and the first arrival left a scorch on a discarded newspaper where it had appeared.

Later visits (the first on 7 February) saw the entity arrive at the front door, having been dropped off by a large car! The visitor had burnt his hand. Cynthia bathed this in boiling water, but to combat Earth bacteria the being used an object like a pencil into which a capsule was placed. She later found a piece of skin in the water. Dr Dale got a Manchester University biologist to study it with an electron microscope. This revealed that the skin – whilst pink and translucent – was not human, but resembled pig skin.

In many later monthly visits, Cynthia (and her children) were regaled with alien science – 'A flow of life fills all things', 'God lives at the heart of the atom', 'Life is the most important thing', 'Time is a cycle.' The visitor baffled Cynthia with a 'cancer cure'. This involved realigning the 'three particles in the nucleus pressed together by life energy'.

The remarkable conclusion came in summer 1958, when the alien told Cynthia she was pregnant. A doctor's appointment confirmed the shock news. At the time of the visit she can only have been a few days past conception. The alien reported that the child (a fair-haired boy) would be fathered by her husband 'but be of the race of Ghanasvarn' (Venus). This enigmatic statement made no sense to either parent. Today, in an age of IVF techniques and genetic manipulation, the way in which two humans might give birth to an 'alien baby' is less difficult to envisage. In saying goodbye, the visitor reported the birth date, physical characteristics and weight of the child – all fulfilled in summer 1959 to close approximations. This 'alien prophecy' had been placed on written record many months before the birth.[23]

1961: PROTOTYPE

By the start of the new decade, with the race to reach the moon now in full-swing and interest in all things alien rapidly gaining momentum, the public was ignorant of most of the sightings reported so far. One case was to gain wide attention and as a result become the prototype for many later abductions.

The witnesses were 39-year-old postal employee Barney Hill and his 41-year-old social worker wife Betty. A mixed-race couple, they were active in the local civil rights movement and the church in Portsmouth, New Hampshire, USA.[24] Returning home from a short holiday in Canada at 11.00 pm on 19/20 September 1961, they drove through the White Mountains and saw a strange light that seemed to be travelling with them. Near North Woodstock, Barney got out to investigate and took a gun with him as the area was wild. He also carried binoculars to observe the object. Walking forwards he could see a 'pancake' shape and several figures on a corridor. The thing came towards him.

By now Betty was shouting for him to come back and Barney jumped into the car insisting that 'they' were trying to capture him. The couple recalled

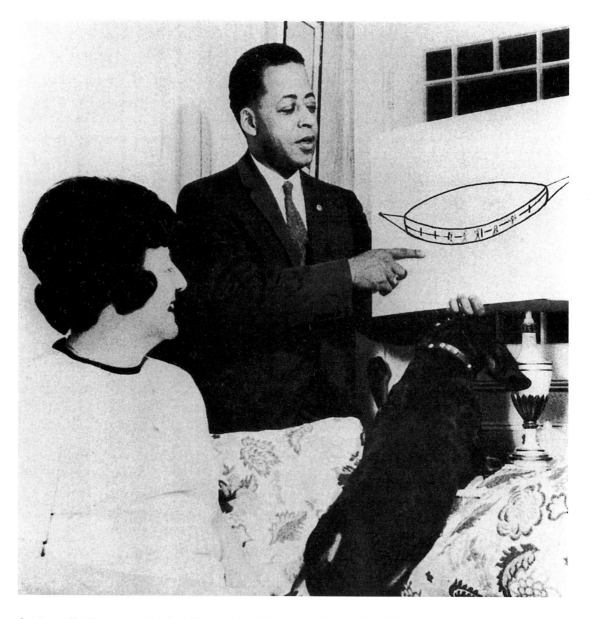

Betty and Barney Hill who believed they were abducted and taken aboard a UFO in September 1961.

driving off. Then, near Indian Head, a loud beeping shook the vehicle, their bodies began to tingle, there was a shift in their state of consciousness and things became 'dreamy'. The next event the Hills recall was of driving sometime later near Plymouth, hearing more beeps and eventually realising they were 35 miles further along the deserted mountain road.

Arriving home at around 5.00 am, they were immediately aware that the journey seemed to have taken an unexpectedly long time and both felt very odd. Barney stood by a mirror examining his genitals, which were sore. Betty had faint recall of a moon-shaped object sitting on the road.

On 26 September, Betty wrote to a man called Donald Keyhoe. She had found one of his books on UFOs in the library and discovered that this ex-marine ran a national group called NICAP. Her letter noted that she was considering finding a psychiatrist who performed hypnosis to try to plug memory gaps. While Barney sought to put it all out of mind, Betty was plagued with nightmares. These involved seeing men, just over 5 feet tall, with greyish skins, big noses and dark hair, but otherwise human. They wanted to conduct tests. These vivid dreams left her feeling disturbed long into the next day. A complex dream-plot unfolded in which Betty and Barney were taken into a landed 'craft', separated and then given various painful tests – including a needle placed into her abdomen. The strange 'men' explained this to her as a 'pregnancy test'. Slowly Betty began to suspect that these nightmares might be more than imagination.

On 21 October, Boston astronomer Walter Webb, on behalf of NICAP, spent 6 hours taking details at the Hill home. In his preliminary report a few days later, he dismissed Barney's now acute memory blockage as 'not of any great significance'. But he felt both were credible. The existence of a time lapse in the journey was formally calculated. There was a two-hour memory gap.

... men, just over 5 feet tall, with greyish skins, big noses and dark hair... wanted to conduct tests.

In March 1962 Barney developed warts on his groin that had to be surgically removed. A local doctor, Patrick Quirke, listened sympathetically to the Hills' story and was convinced they had had some kind of real experience. But he recommended against hypnosis. Another doctor said much the same. Eventually the Hills found Dr Benjamin Simon – a leading Boston psychiatrist. During six months in 1964 he regressed Barney, always out of earshot of Betty. She was only regressed after her husband responded positively to this treatment.

Simon was a total sceptic regarding UFOs and refused to read serious literature offered to him by Webb. He was sure the Hills were genuine, but felt they probably saw something like a secret aircraft – out of which Betty's dreams and Barney's paranoia developed into a full blown abduction 'fantasy'.

Under hypnosis the Hills' story was much as it had been consciously recalled from soon after the sighting, but detail was added. Barney recalled how sperm samples were taken and both told how the aliens were particularly intrigued by the physical differences between the couple. Benjamin Simon ultimately concluded that Barney had come to share in Betty's vivid dreams while she had adopted some of his paranoia, a state known as *folie à deux*. But something – probably mundane – was the trigger.

The case became public knowledge on 25 October 1965 via a small Boston newspaper. The Hills had spoken in public at a church meeting (the indirect source of this story). Eventually they (and their doctors) agreed to talk with respected local columnist John Fuller, who promised to influence public opinion by writing a book. This appeared in 1966 and single-handedly launched an era of alien abduction stories.[25]

Barney Hill died of a brain haemorrhage in 1969. Betty was adopted as a darling of the UFO circuit and saw many further lights in the sky (although no aliens). Interestingly Betty has never embraced the modern abduction trend, disputing the credibility of much of what she has heard, rejecting current hypnotic methods and claiming – like Jessie Roestenberg – that the 'real' aliens are not today's 'grays'.

1965: THE ALIEN PLAN

It is difficult to suggest any logic to what was supposedly happening. Were aliens simply observing, or taking biological samples, as at Valensole, France in July 1965?[26] Did they render witnesses unconscious, or seek to abduct them? Were they intent on some galactic code of honour or did they perform bizarre mating experiments? And who were the aliens anyway – little men like dwarfs, large, fair 'Greek athletes' or egg-headed 'grays'? Did they speak verbally or communicate by telepathy? Did they fly in ovals, saucers or rugby balls; use jets or magnetic fields, ion drives and other futuristic methods? And did they live on Mars, Venus, Cassiopia, Zomdic or in fairyland?

It is easy to see why such a confusing mix suggested little beyond human imagination at work – perhaps responding to topical events and updating a space-age myth. But hardly had the Hill (see pages 29–32) and the Villas Boas (see page 26) abductions become public knowledge, than things became a lot more confusing.

On 7 August 1965 three highly respected witnesses had an encounter in Venezuela. It was not reported to the media since the witnesses feared damage to their prestige. Two were rich businessmen involved in the gold and silver industry. The third was a top gynaecologist. All were interviewed separately by a longstanding South American UFOlogist, Horacio Ganteaume.

At 4.00 pm on a sunny day, the three men were at a friend's thoroughbred stables 40 miles south of Caracas. As they discussed business matters in this beauty spot, there was a brilliant flash of light in the sky. This resolved into a ball of yellow light that emitted a deep humming noise which drilled into their brains. One of the businessmen sought to flee in terror, but the doctor held him back sensing this was a unique opportunity. As the object reached some 5 feet above the ground, swinging like a pendulum, a beam shot out and struck the soil. Inside the beam two tall men with long blond or yellow hair and large penetrating eyes appeared. These classic Nordics approached the petrified witnesses and (by telepathy) advised calm.

In response to questions spoken by the doctor, the three men all heard the aliens explain their purpose. They were from 'Orion' on a 'peace mission' and were 'studying the psyches of humans to adapt them to our species'. Aside from Earth, six other inhabited planets had been visited. These included 'a small planet in the outer dipper'. This is typical pseudo-scientific claptrap, common to such alien contact tales.

In further debate the aliens told how their 'peace mission' involved the study of whether breeding with humans was possible 'to create a new species'. Other aliens, they stated, had different purposes. Those from Kristofix were collecting specimens for a kind of galactic zoo.

1967: 'SLEEP, SLEEP'

There had been half-a-dozen hypnosis attempts during the years following Dr Simon's pioneering experiments with the Hills (see page 31) before Hans Holzer regressed Shane Kurz (see below). Simon had carefully warned that he did not regard hypnosis as a 'royal road to the truth'. It would be easy to get carried away with its use in search of abductions. Of course, Simon never accepted that a real abduction had occurred and saw hypnosis as merely reinforcing Betty Hill's nightmares. But the new toy proved too tempting for many UFOlogists.

The beings from the 'dipper' were only 3 feet tall, less friendly and we should keep out of their way.

Much else was conveyed of a nature that none of the witnesses understood, even after asking for clarification. The gist of it was that there were three types of life. Humans were 'the beginning' (primitives?), these aliens were the 'morphous' but were 'at the beginning of the amorphous' and the advanced 'amorphous' were 'living by means of crisostelic ascending neural evolution'! Beyond the galaxy was a place described only as 'the life of contrasts'.

This reference to small, aggressive beings by the more peaceful Nordics fits remarkably well with the chain of evidence we see in retrospect; although such patterns were not yet evident to UFOlogists. The way in which a gynaecologist is told of the attempts to create some kind of genetic enhancement programme is also intriguing. The Cynthia Appleton case (see page 28), the as yet unpublished Hill abduction and the only recently revealed Villas Boas story strongly back this otherwise weird concept.[27]

Around the same time, a woman from Adelaide in Australia, reported to a psychologist how her experiences began through a series of vivid dreams. Eventually she recalls being in a strange room with small, thin creatures that had oversized, grey-coloured heads with large, dark eyes and little sign of a nose or mouth. One held a small child for her to touch, inferring this to be somehow connected to the abductee.[28]

Even more intriguing is the case of 19-year-old nursing aide Shane Kurz, studied in the early 1970s by Hans Holzer. It took place late on 2 May 1968 in Westmoreland, New York, after Shane had seen a cigar-shaped object. She went to bed and fell into a deep, trancelike sleep. At around 4.00 am her mother found her 'missing' and assumed she was in the bathroom, but when she checked again the girl was seen to be lying on top of her bed covered in mud. The front door was open and footprints showed that she had 'sleepwalked' outside.

Two days later Shane began to suffer powerful migraines and two red rings formed on her abdomen. Her menstrual cycle stopped until 1969 and was irregular until early 1973. She was studied by doctors and also by gynaecologists, who were baffled by her symptoms. Hypnosis revealed an 'extended memory' from years of recurring dreams. In these Shane had been awoken by a light in the bedroom, made to walk outside and then struck by a beam. Strange little creatures with off-white skins and large eyes took ova samples through a tube, then told her she was a 'good breed' and had been selected for an experiment to see if she could give them a baby ('we want to see if we can', one said). Reacting hysterically to this, she was told that she would 'forget' what happened next.[29]

The second abduction to be studied by hypnosis was officially sanctioned. This was in 1968 when scientists at the University of Colorado were probing Air Force files on behalf of the US government. Their 1,000-page report was used by the Pentagon to close official UFO study in 1969, despite failing to resolve one-third of the cases and often finding scientific interest.[30]

The only abduction examined by the University was the sighting by a 22-year-old police officer, Herb Schirmer, on 3 December 1967. He was patrolling near Ashland, Nebraska, investigating some cattle that were unduly upset, when his headlights lit up a 'truck' that turned out instead to be a strange craft. After this flew skyward, he returned to base and realised he was now unexpectedly late. He became agitated, felt nauseous, later suffered nightmares and kept hearing a buzzing noise that gave him headaches.

The Colorado team arranged for University of Wyoming psychologist, Dr Leo Sprinkle, to regress the police officer in February 1968. Schirmer then told of how the UFO landed and a strange form got out. These aliens – he reported – flew using 'magnetic force' and drew energy from water and power lines. After further hypnosis with a second doctor, he offered more detail. The entities were small, with pasty faces and cat-like eyes. They asked if he was 'the watchman' and took him into their craft to show him the different types of propulsion system used ('reversible electromagnetism' being one). They were interested in whether they could enhance humans by 'experimental breeding programmes'.[31]

This case did not persuade the Colorado scientists, despite the support of the Ashland police chief. The lack of physical evidence was one concern. But the case left a deep impression on Dr Sprinkle, who has since worked with hundreds of other abductees. It also severely traumatised Herb Schirmer, who quit the police and found it a struggle to fully regain his normal life in either a physical or mental sense.

CULTURAL TRACKING

By the late 1960s UFOlogists had a dilemma. Alien contacts and the slowly rising number of abduction claims often featured credible witnesses. Their stories were rarely identical but frequently shared chilling similarities.

Superficially the references to little things like advanced propulsion systems seem good evidence that real alien contacts were happening. But physical evidence that might prove this was almost non-existent. However, there had also been signs of 'cultural tracking' throughout the history of the UFO.

Some researchers began to suspect that the UFO was just a light phenomenon not an alien craft. Witnesses described more structure and shape simply because the human mind seeks order out of chaos and wishes to place meaning into random images.[32] As such what was just a 'light' might be perceived as an airship, when such a craft was at the limit of our technology, or as an alien spacecraft today. Would the same tracking of our own culture and technology be obvious within alien contacts? This is a key test of reality behind abductions, because if cultural tracking is rife and alien science mirrors our own then this infers that the stories must have an inner origin.

Almost predictably what we find is confusing. There is certainly cultural tracking but also plenty of intriguing signs of greatly advanced alien technology. Witnesses often speak of oozing light coming from no known source, or of doors that open in incredible ways without any sign of seams or hinges. Transportation by light beam, the ability to pass through solid objects, defiance of gravity and various other activities by aliens seem impossible to us, but may simply be greatly advanced science. On the other hand, most of these things occur in space-fiction tales, so can, of course, be readily imagined.

> *The human mind seeks order out of chaos and wishes to place meaning in random images.*

More difficult to explain is science that seemed absurd many years ago but is now beginning to make vague sense in the light of modern progress. Ova sampling by tubes, genetic engineering, laser beams and three-dimensional holographic images were all apparently described by witnesses 40 years ago, but in terms that involve quite liberal interpretation on our part. We might be in error. There were also nonsensical comments made to witnesses about ion drives, reversible magnetism or realigning atomic fields to cure cancer. These seem less absurd now than they once did.

If abductions were merely following the rules of cultural tracking then reading old accounts of alien abduction should be like viewing the first series of the hugely popular TV series *Star Trek* made in the mid-1960s. Clunking number-counters fill the bridge of the original Star Ship *Enterprise*, a craft from the supposed far future. We now have digital displays in our homes that are more advanced. Hand mikes and communicators that would fit into a 1960s broadcasting studio abound on this future craft but there are no microchips. It is obvious from today's perspective that science imagined in 1967 was just an artistic concept long since overtaken by real events. Yet most abductions involve technology that still seems 'beyond our ken' today. If it too was just imagined, would it not also appear antiquated?

But cultural tracking undoubtedly has a strong part in these reports. Researcher Peter Rogerson found an obscure 1967 novel in which aliens abduct two men and perform genetic experiments upon them. Although written at a time when almost no such cases were known, it featured many aspects that would recur in reputedly real episodes – such as the 'Oz Factor' and Bullard's 'doorway amnesia' finding.[33]

Several early cases spoke of the UFOs emitting a 'beeping' as described by the Hills (see page 29). But beeping sounds are not reported today. One case came just days after the movie of the Hill's story made its debut on American TV. When abductee Whitley Strieber received huge global publicity, describing his entities as unusually having a 'smell of cinnamon', a number of cases swiftly followed in which seemingly genuine witnesses reported this feature. In 1988 the TV series *The Colby's* showed aliens abducting one character. An apparently sincere woman in Lancashire reported being abducted by an alien with the name given to the butler in that soap. Her sighting occurred in her bedroom on the very night she watched the series!

As all this shows, cultural tracking clearly shapes the abduction evidence to some degree, but it does not *cause* these cases to happen.

1973: THE MAN WHO WAS NOT THERE

A major problem regarding abduction cases is evident. Most of them involve single witnesses, at night in isolated locations. This is not true of simple UFO sightings, many of which feature multiple witnesses. Along with the physical evidence and photographs, they often possess a reality not found with abductions. Statistics show that simple sightings have around 2.6 witnesses per case. Abductions have approximately 1.25 witnesses per case – less than half. They are subjective in the same sense that our dreams are single-witness events (dreams have a witness per case ratio of 1.0 because, of course, nobody else shares them).

There are, however, abduction cases that have included several independent observers. One invaluable case featured 27-year-old Maureen Puddy from Rye in Victoria, Australia. She had a series of encounters that began on 5 July 1972 when driving to see her son in hospital. A blue, egg-shaped object passed her car. Days later she heard a voice in her head calling her name and a second UFO sighting followed near Frankston on the Mooraduc Road as she drove home from the hospital. This time her car lost all power to its engine and lights and the 'Oz Factor' took hold, with 'all sound being drained out of the air'. A

vortex of pressure was pushing down from above, not unlike a tornado. Indeed the car was tugged off the road by this force. A voice seeming to come from the UFO and told her that she should 'Tell the media. Do not panic.' Then her car engine and lights began to function again.

UFO researchers Judith Magee and Paul Norman investigated this case and were impressed. But then they received an urgent call from Maureen on 22 February 1973. The alien voice had returned and asked her to meet on the road. On route to her rendezvous a humanlike figure with long, blond hair materialised inside Maureen's car and then vanished. Eventually the two UFOlogists arrived at the meeting point and got into the car. Maureen now claimed to see the same figure outside the car and entered a trancelike state, in which she talked to the aliens as if in a deep sleep. 'They' were there, she insisted sombrely.

Magee and Norman were amazed by this news. Maureen was a normal family woman with no medical or psychological problems. Yet as she was describing this experience unfolding, Judith Magee reported that she had felt an electric tingling sensation within the car.

The investigators regarded Maureen Puddy

HYPNOTIC FACT AND FANTASY

UFOlogists eagerly using hypnosis to find further cases assumed that they were coaxing memories of forgotten abductions from otherwise limited stories. But it is wrong to expect hypnosis to serve as a scalpel to dig out true recall from the deep recesses of the mind. Instead it can provoke fantasy or stimulate imagination, and so might critically change the nature of the reported event. In fact, UFOlogists could well have been creating a flood of previously unsuspected abductions from more trivial events that were never really alien kidnappings.

Stage hypnotists may appear to use the technique to 'force' helpless victims to grunt like pigs or stare in horror convinced they are stark naked, but in fact hypnosis merely lifts up the drawbridge and lets the content of your

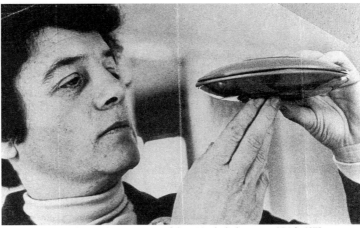

Maureen Puddy explaining the appearance of the UFO which she saw on 25 July 1972.

as a genuine witness. But now she was seeing an alien that was supposedly only feet away and yet – to their eyes – not really there. Norman got out and walked past the spot where the alien 'stood' (Maureen said it stepped out of the way!). She then began to describe a landed object into which she was being taken by the aliens. Suddenly, Maureen broke down and began to shake. This seemed to return her to normal awareness. The UFO and aliens were gone. It seemed as if she had sleepwalked right through an alien abduction.

Here we have two independent witnesses, persuaded of the credibility of the abductee and themselves believers in UFO reality, who *knew* that the UFO and abducting aliens were not physically present in any normal sense of that word.[36] In all the cases I have studied where an abductee has been witnessed during their encounter by independent observers, these observers report that the abductee went nowhere. In one case, in Flint, North Wales, a teenage girl was seen prone on her bed in what her mother described as a 'catatonic trance' from which she could not be woken. When she did come to, she described travelling with aliens in a UFO. Six similar cases are known where the witness was thought asleep, or drunk, but had not gone anywhere. There are certainly not six cases where aliens have been clearly seen by independent witnesses physically taking a victim away.

What does this mean? Do abductions only happen subjectively? Are no kidnaps really occurring?

subconscious mind emerge. It lowers inhibitions. You retain control and what pours forth might be imagination (used for creative fantasy) or recall of consciously forgotten facts. Experiments show that at best half the recalled information brought out by hypnosis is genuine. This was proven by, for example, taking a person back to their schooldays, getting them to recall under hypnosis the class layout and then checking this memory against school records. When their hypnotic memory was matched with the factual evidence, it was found that some things were simply imagined.[34]

Checking facts is possible with such experiments. But if someone is regressed to an alien abduction, how do we check that? It may be real, it may be imaginary, and experimental evidence suggests that at best it will be a mixture of both. This means that hypnosis is not a particularly good way to study abductions. Especially not when we have already seen that the border between reality and imagination is blurred and that clues such as the 'Oz Factor' suggest witnesses are in an altered state of consciousness. Modern experiments involving regression to the sighting of a (mundane) light in the sky have shown that when checkable data (such as the day of the week) is 'recalled' under hypnosis much of it proves wrong! This hardly bodes well for the more fantastic claims made in the same way.[35]

I was subjected to hypnosis experiments by clinical psychologist Dr John Dale. Under hypnosis images flooded out as if I was daydreaming, but there was no way at the time to determine whether their origin was from memory or fantasy. If you want to believe in aliens and are being guided through the hypnotic process with that prospect in mind, then it will be easy to opt for that interpretation. But many of the things I 'saw' concerned facts I could later check and I was able to prove that some of these things simply did not happen, although they came out under hypnosis with as much conviction as alien imagery often does. As such any testimony I may make under hypnosis must be highly doubtful. Hypnosis allows you to creatively imagine what might have occurred. At times it may let you see what *did* happen but have forgotten. But it is often impossible to make a choice.

It is wrong to expect hypnosis to serve as a scalpel to dig out true recall... Instead it can provoke fantasy...

1975: THE DAM BREAKS

By 1975 hypnosis was a regular tool and abductions were being found through it all too often.

In October 1973 two fishermen were dragged into a landed object at Pascagoula, Mississippi by entities with claws. When left alone in a police station (and secretly recorded), these men not only failed to show any sign that the story was untrue but one broke down and started praying into the empty room.[37]

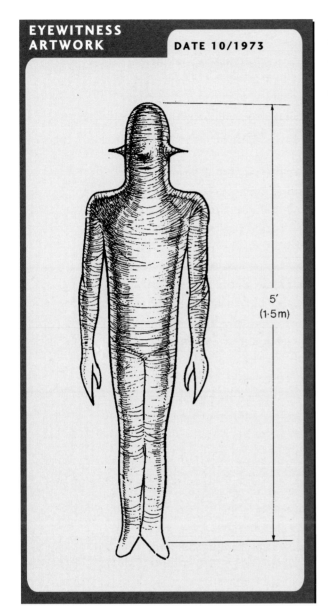

EYEWITNESS ARTWORK

DATE 10/1973

5'
(1·5m)

An artist's impression of a UFO entity seen at Pascagoula, Mississippi, October 1973.

Then on 27 October 1975 two men camping at a lake near Oxford, Maine encountered lights that emerged from a glowing fog with strong electrical effects. These stalled their car and swamped the radio. Eventually they were left wandering, disorientated and very tired with burning eyes and throats and suffering disturbance to their balance. Peculiar visual hallucinations of strange shapes crossing the sky persisted for some hours. Although not drug-induced, the similarity with such hallucinogenic behaviour is marked. Under hypnosis a meeting with 'grays' inside a UFO was subsequently 'recalled'.[38]

This case is a curious cross between the standard medical examinations by sample-taking aliens alongside an out-of-body adventure with psychic overtones. This curious blend of physical reality with visionary experiences is often found within the abduction, but is swamped by the emphasis given by UFOlogists to alleged physical reality. In Europe such 'fuzzy edges' to a case are embraced more readily.

As such, when abductions spread out of the USA to other parts of the world, it almost seemed as if there were two kinds of phenomenon. This is important because it shows how differing investigation methods have had a significant effect on the data being studied.

1977: GLOBAL CONQUEST

Britain was one of the first countries outside the USA to start seeking abductions. This came just before the Steven Spielberg movie *Close Encounters of the Third Kind* was to have such a global impact. The film covered abductions only in passing and did not include any on-board scenes or medical examinations.

In the movie the aliens are portrayed as being small in stature with large heads and eyes, similar but not much like the more horrific image of the 'grays' that was beginning to take shape. Spielberg had quite intentionally made a movie that 'deified' the alien contact. The question was would Spielberg's childlike aliens translate through cultural tracking into a new abduction mode that would follow his lead (see page 129).

The first British abduction was fascinating. An entire family, two adults and three young children, had seen a blue light on their way home from visiting relatives. Moments later, on a country lane near Aveley, Essex, they drove into a bank of green mist that caused the radio to spark. They seemed to swiftly come out on the other side, but on arriving home found that they were now inexplicably 90 minutes late.

This event occurred in October 1974 – a year to the day before the not dissimilar Oxford, Maine, case (see page 39). During the next three years the family went through tremendous changes. The husband became artistic and almost mystical (eventually 'dropping out'). They became vegetarian, ecologically minded and far more aware of the meaning of life than they ever had been. They also suffered sleeplessness and nightmares of seeing horrible alien faces. This drove them to a dental surgeon who used hypnosis in his studies of the paranormal. Two local UFO researchers, Andy Collins and Barry King, then took on the case and Collins himself hypnotised the adults (the children being purposefully excluded). I sat in on one of these sessions at the family home and my personal concerns about regression began. This was notable when the wife, Sue, started to answer a rhetorical question I innocently posed. She did so as if she *was* the alien replying to me! In this way Sue was acting like a medium conveying tales from the other side, with the exception that her contact was not a dead person in some afterlife but a Nordic alien on board his UFO.

Collins and King did an impressive and caring job documenting this case. The witnesses told under hypnosis of how the car was stopped in the mist and they were then 'beamed' into a UFO. They could see their own physical bodies back in the car, as their 'other selves' wandered about the UFO.

Two types of entity were on the craft, as is not uncommon. The smaller beings were furry-headed monsters, similar to ones in the then popular British TV series, *Dr Who*. These beings were an engineered lifeform that performed menial tasks. But the ones in charge were tall beings in silver suits, typical Nordics. There were medical tests, but nothing like the explicit sexual probes or painful implants in American tales.

Humans were a long-term experiment – almost the children of these godlike beings.

On board the UFO the couple were split up. Between them they described a guided tour and being fed much information by the aliens about their purpose on Earth. Humans were a long-term experiment – almost the children of these godlike beings. They watched over us, tried to encourage us but did not directly intervene. However, they warned of ecological and other disasters that the Earth might face by screening holographic images to the family and provoking strong emotional responses.

This case is fascinating, both for the familiar features that it includes and the aspects of American abduction lore that it does not. The 'grays', ova sampling, implanted probes and more terrifying aspects would reach the UK eventually, but are missing from what remains one of the most intensively investigated abductions there is.[39]

However, what do we really have when we strip down this famous case? Most people will perceive it as a friendly alien-human contact on board a spacecraft. In truth we can only be sure that there was a pretty mundane light seen in the sky, followed by a certainly curious, electrified green mist into which the car drove. Then there was some missing time. This was followed by years of stress and nightmares. The whole abduction sub-plot emerged across four years through dreams, interactive discussions between family members, doctors and UFOlogists and, of course, as a result of various hypnosis sessions. From what I saw of these I was persuaded of two things. John and Sue were totally sincere and reporting what they genuinely experienced. But they were describing images that were welling up inside their minds at the behest of the hypnotic state and urging of UFOlogists (myself included). I was not convinced that I was hearing about a real kidnap into a spaceship. Indeed, witnesses frequently react unconsciously as if they do not believe it either. If they *truly* did, then would they not demand round-the-clock police protection?

Something curious *did* happen and triggered a major life change for this family. But it had psychic elements. The second phase of this abduction memory is far more like an out-of-body trip than a ride in a spacecraft. In the late 1970s doctors and psychologists who knew nothing of UFOs were swamped by similar tales and even created a name for them – 'Near Death Experiences'. In NDEs people went 'out of the body', headed towards a glowing light, met strange beings and received mystical messages that changed their lifestyle. Nobody thought that they were abducted. To the enquiring doctors and people who experienced these visions (often at times of great stress – for example, after a car crash), they were hovering between life and death and glimpsing an ineffable reality beyond the mortal.[40] We might need to ask if this family from Essex experienced an alien abduction or an NDE.

1982: RESPONSIBILITIES

The lessons of the Aveley case were learned by some researchers. Were we explorers of a mystery that we were charting through witness tales or were we architects helping to build up its nature? Imagine that this Essex family had assumed the mist was fog, had recovered awareness with the car off the road in a ditch and had later explored their vague recall through a psychologist who knew about NDEs. He might have surmised that they were reporting visions of a near-death state following a car accident. Would the 'facts' then uncovered have involved aliens and spaceships or would John and Sue have been gently led into sending a 'postcard from heaven' describing what they saw?

We cannot know if the alien interpretation placed upon such recall is not itself determining the form of experience that then emerges through hypnosis. Having experienced hypnosis at work on both a UFO sighting and a reputed past life, I have seen just how difficult it is to figure out the reality of the result. The context and the theories that surround the experiment clearly influence the outcome.[41]

Unfortunately it is difficult to know how to test this premise. Once a witness is led into one interpretation of any imagery, they cannot be led into another. But it is possible that what seems to be evidence for real alien abductions is forged from initially genuine and puzzling experiences by the social conditioning, expectation and investigation methods imposed on the witnesses afterwards. Once such implications begin to dawn, the need to try to change our approach to this phenomenon seems obvious. That is why in Britain in 1982 the first 'Code of Practice' was established. It had fierce opposition from UFOlogists, who termed it meddlesome and unnecessary. But what the Code set out to do was ensure that UFOlogists saw their primary responsibility was to the witness. Abductions in particular were such alluring cases, attracting media attention and book deals, that there was a danger these priorities would be forgotten. I think the Code helped to steer a path away from that 'pothole', even though the chasm opened wide elsewhere. Sadly few organisations – even in the UK – were to take this matter seriously enough to adopt the Code in practice.

One vital thing the Code did was regulate the use of regression hypnosis. There was already a trend whereby UFOlogists were not willing to pay psychologists expensive fees. Instead they were 'learning' hypnosis by observation and doing it themselves. This speeded up cases and allowed more to be probed. The Code stepped in to insist that hypnosis be properly supervised.

Then came a case in the East Midlands. A man who professed long-term alien contact said that his encounters began as a child, when he was swallowed up by a light that fell from the sky. His story resembled someone seeing a lightning strike too close, but, of course, UFOlogists considered other options. He was regressed using hypnosis and the trauma of the recall induced an epileptic seizure. Thankfully the man recovered without harm, but the incident alarmed my team at the British UFO Research Association (BUFORA) enough to recognise that a voluntary code governing hypnosis was not enough.

1983: TWO-WAY STREET

The 1980s rapidly grew into the decade of the abduction. With the explosion of media attention, alien abduction stories were brought to the attention of millions. In the USA (which by 1983 had still provided more than 90 per cent of all abductions) the media boom came first – through cable channels, TV shows like *Unsolved Mysteries* and eventually mini-series and movies that took

Budd Hopkins at the Fortean Times UnConvention, London, 1997.

real-life abduction tales and turned them into horror 'faction'.

The first UFO author to make the big time as a result of this was Budd Hopkins. In 1981 he wrote a modest book called *Missing Time*.[42] Published by a small art company (Hopkins is a noted New York artist) it had limited impact on the media. But its collection of American cases had the support of psychologist Dr Aphrodite Clamar and left a smouldering 'fire' that would gradually take hold.

Hopkins had a modest set of cases that showed there was a pattern to the US data. Seemingly unrelated witnesses were describing closely similar incidents and reacting in such a way that Dr Clamar was certain *they* believed what had happened. Nor did they seem psychologically unstable. Most featured the 'gray' type of alien, which was becoming common in the USA (but not elsewhere). Hopkins was the first to document the medical examinations and probes used to take samples from witnesses.

I first met Hopkins at a conference in Nebraska in 1983. Budd – who is an unassuming and genuine man – gathered a handful of researchers and told us quietly about the 'big case' that would ultimately lead to his media stardom. It involved a whole family from Indiana, who had experienced a wide range of visits by the 'grays'. There was also a sexual element to the case. Hopkins soon had enough evidence to conclude that aliens were interbreeding with humans and some women were recalling being shown the resultant hybrid baby during a subsequent abduction.

In 1985 I wrote a book with Peter Warrington, based on an article we published in *New Scientist*.[43] This was a rather restrained piece about how science could benefit by studying UFO reports, especially atmospheric physicists who might study energy phenomena. *Science and the UFOs* expanded on this article, at the request of an Oxford science publisher – who had never seen serious writing that argued *for* UFO reality *without* endorsing aliens. We included the Code of Practice and early work by Budd Hopkins.[44] This book had few readers, but one was a man who was sent it as a Christmas gift.

That man was a New York horror novelist, Whitley Strieber. He had penned many successful tales that had become movies and was commanding million-dollar advances. He had had a series of odd experiences, seeing fleeting images and having powerful dreams. When he read our book, Strieber says he reacted in unexpected terror – treating it like a 'coiled snake'. He now began to suspect that his dreams might mask an alien abduction, something he had not

considered. Living by chance near Hopkins, Strieber met him, hypnosis followed and a terrifying abduction account emerged.

In the UK a few abductions were now surfacing. I was closely involved in researching some, such as that of police officer Alan Godfrey, who saw a swirling light at Todmorden in West Yorkshire in November 1980.[45] Only upon reconstruction did a possible 15-minute time lapse appear, leading to hypnosis sessions the following summer. In these sessions Godfrey described being hit by a beam of light and awakening inside a room where little robot-like creatures 'the size of a 5-year-old lad' were probing him (but not sexually). Clues that hint beyond objective reality here include the sound made by the robots – 'bid-de-bid-de-bid-de' – similar to that of a character in the then popular TV show *Buck Rogers in the 25th Century*. No 'grays' appear in any of the UK cases from that first batch, indeed Alan Godfrey's abductor was a tall, bearded man who said he was called Yosef. Alan, a credible man, told me candidly that he had read UFO literature in the months between his sighting and the hypnosis work and could not say with certainty whether the images he described were true memories. They might be fantasies. This honest appraisal is very important and it is not by any means unique. UFOlogists often have more confidence in the reality of an abduction than witnesses.

Alan Godfrey with his sketch of the alien craft and entity which abducted him at Todmorden, West Yorkshire in November 1980 (photographed 1982).

He now began to suspect that his dreams might mask an alien abduction ... hypnosis followed and a terrifying abduction account emerged.

1987: THE TURNING POINT

Whitley Strieber.

The spring of 1987 was the point of no return for abduction research. Whitley Strieber had rapidly told his amazing story.[46] Because a vast sum had been paid to him, his publishers ran a huge publicity campaign. He toured the world and large posters were placed on billboards and bus shelters, carrying an image of the 'gray' that also dominated the cover of his book – which was a massive success. The abduction phenomenon in all its detail was portrayed in newspapers, magazines and on countless TV shows. In the USA in particular Strieber struck a chord. In Washington in June 1987, I was approached by many people who had read his book and who seemed desperate for hypnosis. The sincerity of these people was rarely in doubt, but sincerity is not the same as proof of physical reality.

Budd Hopkins published his second book soon after Strieber's media blitz.[47] His account of the Indiana abduction (see page 43) and the hybrid baby theme gave the 'new angle' needed by the media to keep the 'pot' boiling. The Indiana case was turned into a TV mini-series. Hopkins, now able to devote most of his time to what was almost a crusade, uncovered tales of alien scientists treating us like laboratory rats. But Strieber was searching for what almost amounted to a spiritual dimension. This aura of mystery (clearly visible in the abduction data) is well expressed by his superb prose and was maintained in the 1989 movie, *Communion*.

There was simply no way back now. Almost everybody knew the form of an abduction – the standard American 'gray' performing medical experiments with sexual connotations. What few could know, was that this format was simply one nation's variation on a theme. Had the media blitz started in Britain, it would have been a different story. Certainly there would have been similarities (e.g. the bright light provoking time loss), but there would be little trace of 'grays' or alien genetic experiments. Instead friendly, near-human aliens and an emphasis on psychic themes and mystic assistance might have been perceived as the basis of the abduction tale. But the die was cast. The nasty 'grays' had landed.

The so called 'new UFOlogy', or 'psycho-social' theories, argued against literal alien kidnaps and for links between social and cultural trends. A war of attrition was underway, with both sides overemphasising the failings of the other. The huge triumph of the American model, through the media circus that had begun in 1987, meant that this war was over before it started.

Yet good things were being done beyond the USA. In Australia, for example, Keith Basterfield was working with psychologist Dr Robert Bartholomew to seek out the relevance of important new research by mental health specialists. In the UK, BUFORA had launched, through investigator Ken Phillips, a programme of psychological profiles of witnesses, that ascertained much beyond the details of the abduction. It gathered data about a subject's dreamlife and long-term psychic experiences, and assorted physiological and psychological clues that were emerging – from preponderance of migraine and epilepsy amongst witnesses to more subtle things such as the unusually high level of early-life recall.

UFOlogy had polarised into two camps – one a belief system (alien contact) desperately seeking hard evidence; the other a collection of evidence and clues desperately seeking a workable belief system.

PAUSE FOR REFLECTION

In 1987 there were a number of long debates at the BUFORA investigation department as to what to do about this crisis. We realised that in the mass of abductees flocking to us (and to other less vigilant groups) there were bound to be some genuine, suffering people. But there was also the serious risk of leading people into false beliefs about non-existent – yet highly terrifying – alien kidnaps. Such things could scar a person psychologically. Indeed stories were soon filtering in about suicides, and one woman in the USA murdered her children to prevent them from being abducted. This was long before the 'Heaven's Gate' cult, where mass suicides occurred in order for the victims to be rescued by aliens!

When news filtered in from the USA that the latest trend was for children as young as five to be identified as possible abductees and regressed (even by non-medically qualified people), we knew something must be done. At our next meeting a complete ban on the use of regression hypnosis was introduced in BUFORA. This was a risk. But we honestly believed that hypnotic regression had been proven unreliable – and dangerous. In 1988 I did a poll of 15 British abductees who had been regressed. A third of them said they regretted being hypnotised and four others that they felt it had left them more confused than beforehand. Sadly our signal to the UFO community went unheeded. Regression goes on everywhere.

Witnesses with conscious recall still came forward and we encouraged them to share their dreams and waking images, however relevant. Some of the cases from the 1990s that came this way are very interesting. But we stopped getting more than a trickle of full-blown abductions or stories with medical and sexual probes. Yet such incidents were soaring in numbers in the USA where hypnosis was rife. Indeed several other countries now obtained some cases thanks to the rising use of hypnosis. Even in the UK many groups beyond

UFOlogy had polarised into two camps – one a belief system seeking hard evidence; the other a collection of evidence seeking a belief system.

BUFORA still used regression and with the increasing popularity of the UFO field, through tabloid stories and TV shows, dozens of abductees appeared.

It was soon clear that a major sea-change dominated these new cases. The post-1987 abductions had almost no reference to Nordics or the other friendly, mystic aliens that had been so common before. Instead, over 80 per cent of the new British cases (compared with under 15 per cent beforehand) were now of the very American 'grays' involved in terrifying breeding experiments. So dramatic was this switch, it is impossible not to believe it is connected with the media blitz.

The same picture emerges elsewhere. This surely is proof that – at least with the hypnotically revealed 'memories' of an abduction – there *is* marked response to changes in the collective cultural mood.

Budd Hopkins responded as always with passion. He suggested that British researchers might not have probed far enough in the past and the nice aliens could have been what he called a screen memory, hiding the more horrific nature of the 'gray' abductors. Now the barriers were broken down, British witnesses were able to recall their true captors better. But if this were correct, why are seemingly traumatic memories blocked from a witness at all and yet so easily released by hypnosis? Does a witness *want* to remember the terrible nightmare? Can the 'grays' cross the universe and use science far beyond our knowledge, yet be unable to block hypnosis?

It is hard to accept that *true* memories of a terrible nature are being unleashed into the mind by hypnotic regression. And, of course, if they *are* then what right do the UFOlogists have to inflict such torture upon adults (let alone children)? A UFOlogist will wring out facts, give lectures, write a book and move on to the next case. The witness is left to face a lifetime of torment.

1989: OBSERVED ABDUCTIONS

Despite the widening gulf between those who argued that abductions were real and those arguing they were images of some visionary phenomenon, both sides came to agree on one important fact. And it challenged a basic premise of the sceptics, whose last line of defence, if a case could not be explained in some other way, was often that the witness made it up for reasons of fame, fortune or sheer bloodymindedness.[48]

Of course, there are hoaxes – including made-up tales of alien contact. But these are rare. Researchers agree that under 0.5 per cent of reported sightings are faked. Support for that opinion has come in a whole series of psychological tests. Regardless of whether studies of abductees are made by sceptics or believers they endorse the general credibility of the witness. The vast majority of abductees are sincerely reporting what they believe.

Dr Elizabeth Slater, a vocational psychologist who had had no experience of abductees, agreed to meet nine ordinary people (five men and four women) and conduct a massive battery of standard psychological tests on each. She regularly vetted people for sensitive jobs and so did not suspect the true reason that she was seeing this group. They included businessmen, secretaries, salesmen and a sports coach.

Slater's report on the group found interesting patterns. Although the American UFO community usually stresses her conclusion that the nine were generally of above-average intelligence and psychologically stable, rather more interesting was another finding. Slater saw a pattern of a 'rich inner life'. Indeed she noted that their unusual ability to perceive vivid and realistic images was such that it 'can operate favourably in terms of creativity and disadvantageously to the extent that it can be overwhelming'. This is exactly what concurrent BUFORA anamnesis work was revealing about close-encounter witnesses. Abductees are gifted at visual creativity. They can often create poetry, artwork and see stories unfold in their heads. Many have eidetic memories. Children's author Enid Blyton was like this. She reported that she used to relax into an altered state and daydream. She then saw her characters act out whole plots in front of her and all she had to do was type them up later. Today some would no doubt be investigating her contact with an alien called Noddy!

When Dr Slater was told that the nine people in her study were, in fact, abductees, she was stunned. None had received publicity. She checked her results. None of the nine showed signs of psychopathology, fugue states or multiple personality. The sole pattern traced was the vital clue that the American UFOlogists forget. Abductees clearly have an enhanced mental-imaging capacity.

If one were to draw up a balance sheet of evidence regarding the abduction phenomenon, it would seem very disturbing. For it offers no clear track towards an answer. There were now thousands of people worldwide (but the vast majority in the USA) who seemed to think they had been abducted by aliens, experimented upon and even used to breed hybrid babies. All psychological studies supported their sincerity and apparently normal mental health. The cases were very similar to one another, often interacting in a complex web of detail. Certainly it was neither foolish nor indefensible to argue, as most American researchers did, that this evidence inferred that real aliens were coming here.

Yet nobody had returned from an abduction with any non-terrestrial object, not even a scraping of alien dust under their fingernails (not that such a quest for proof has ever been attempted). There were no photographs of aliens or the insides of spaceships or even landed craft in full glory. Aliens seem to be hopelessly incapable of blocking memory of an abduction, but brilliant at getting rid of hard evidence.

There were clues that pointed towards reality (the alien science offered to some witnesses) and others that suggested some kind of mind phenomenon (the prevalence of visually creative witnesses, for example). There were also those cases of 'observed abductions' where the witness believed that they had been inside a spaceship but had travelled nowhere, remaining in an altered state of consciousness. UFOlogy needed that elusive case where the abductee was *seen* to be physically taken away.

There had been 'near misses'. On 24 March 1974 a young man called Harald was taking the air at Lindholmen, Sweden. Suddenly a voice in his mind told him to walk across the road and a blinding flash of light appeared from above. He crashed to the ground unconscious and came to on his doorstep, with his wife expressing concern at his groggy state and a burn on his cheek. Harald went to the Danderyd Hospital and a few weeks later – after he had recovered from the physical trauma – Dr Ture Arvidsson regressed him. This revealed the story that as the light beam struck, he had begun to float upwards as if in an out-of-body state and had seen tall figures wearing hoods who had pressed something on his forehead and told him they would meet again. Harald was also left with numerous psychic experiences (e.g. dreams about the future that came true) and his body seemed hyper-charged with electricity for days after the encounter. When he went near electrical equipment, it stopped working properly. It was as if he had been struck down by a lightning bolt or some kind of energy beam. The investigation team then found a witness on a nearby road, who had passed the spot at the correct time. The witness had not seen Harald lifted into the sky by a UFO but had observed a light beam fall to the ground. So the UFO 'energy beam' was real; the aliens perhaps not. Was Harald 'taken away' or left prone on the ground, 'dreaming' of contact later elaborated upon by his regression hypnosis?

Here there *was* verification of the UFO that triggered the abduction, but no confirmation of the abduction itself. Exactly the same thing occurred in 1980 in the Alan Godfrey case (see page 44). Some other police officers on a surveillance operation atop a nearby hill saw a bright *light* in the sky at the appropriate time, but neither a strange flying craft nor PC Godfrey or his car being abducted skyward.

1992: UP THE POLL

The 'Manhattan Transfer' case (see page 50) first received an airing in the summer of 1992 at a momentous event. A millionaire UFO enthusiast, in conjunction with a team of American experts, persuaded the prestigious university, the Massachusetts Institute of Technology (MIT), to open its doors to the first ever symposium that debated abductions. This was not run by MIT or a public event. The media were excluded and tickets were not sold. It was limited to about 120 participants in a week-long venture and attendance was strictly by

MANHATTAN TRANSFER

This case provided a major breakthrough! At a fascinating lunch I had with Budd Hopkins in Boston in June 1992, Keith Basterfield and I were telling him about our deep concerns following cases such as Maureen Puddy (see pages 36–7) and Harald (see page 49). Surely, we said, these suggested that abductions did not involve literal kidnaps. But he had discovered the 'big one' (that five years later would form his third book).[49]

It had occurred in the middle of the night in November 1989 when a woman, Linda Napolitano, had been 'taken' from her high-rise apartment in Manhattan. She had been floated through the window by 'grays' and given a fairly standard abduction with medical probes while her family slept oblivious below. The big difference was that Linda and the aliens had been *seen* mid-kidnap by uninvolved passers-by.

Budd had been investigating Linda's case for more than a year, retrieving memories through hypnosis, when the amazing news had emerged. Two secret-service bodyguards had written to him advising that they had endured a terrible experience (one had reputedly suffered a nervous breakdown as a result). While driving a 'world leader' through the quiet streets, they had stopped outside a high-rise and seen a woman being floated into the air in the company of some little, grey men. They could tell Budd which apartment to check out, but they had been too scared to go themselves in case the woman had never been returned. Hopkins had told them not to worry, had given *them* the address and urged them to call on Linda. They had been amazed but relieved that the woman had been returned by the aliens.

Later other witnesses had come forward to Budd

– claiming to be on a bridge crossing the river with a good view down onto the same apartment block. Although they had said nothing for a couple of years, they now wanted to report that they too had seen a woman floated out of her window by aliens.

There are a few problems with this case. The security men had communicated semi-anonymously by letter and taped message, but Budd had been unable to meet them to verify their tale. The 'world leader' (reputedly former UN Secretary-General, Javier Perez de Cuellar) had denied any knowledge. The way in which the case had fallen into the lap of just one UFOlogist also worried some; although nobody disputes Hopkins's integrity or has reason to doubt Linda. An independent investigation by sceptical UFOlogists discovered that a newspaper loading-bay had been a hive of activity at the time and had a good view of the abduction site, but no workers had seen anything.

Hopkins argued this case well and defended the seeming integrity of the witnesses. But it fails to convince all UFOlogists that it is unimpeachable.

The flats from where Linda Napolitano was allegedly abducted in 1989 – the newspaper loading bay is on the right [top]; Linda with Budd Hopkins in 1991 [bottom].

invitation. Preference was given to those who were conducting original research or could offer new findings.

The team that co-ordinated the symposium included psychologists, physicists, UFOlogists and abductees. It set a series of questions, starting from such a simple premise as 'How do we uncover abductions?' and moving on through every facet of the experience. In conclusion, dozens of papers were presented and a huge database of knowledge was established, via a mammoth tome that surfaced two years later.[50]

The MIT event set new research in motion – notably definitive testing of the fantasy-prone personality theory (see page 152). Harvard psychiatrist, Dr John Mack, admitted he was hooked by the abduction mystery.

Aside from Mack and all the other key figures in American abduction research, the MIT event featured specialists in psychological research such as false memory syndrome and other potentially relevant work. However, only four or five researchers from beyond the USA were present. This did rather skew the findings towards the US model, much as the explosion of media interest had previously done.

In the run-up to the event, several of the participants, including Budd Hopkins and his fellow researcher, historian Dr David Jacobs, were involved in setting up a mammoth opinion poll conducted by the renowned Roper organisation. This asked questions of a sample of the US population and came to extrapolate conclusions about the real extent of abductions. As of 1992, about 60 cases were known in the UK and a US statistical study had uncovered about ten times as many. But how many undiscovered abductions were there?[51]

For the poll, 5,947 people were surveyed with 11 questions. Some questions were general. Others were 'trick' responses to weed-out those who sought to answer 'yes' to make themselves seem like abductees. Five questions supposedly offered major clues – anyone answering positively to most of these key questions would be a good candidate for hypnotic regression and might prove to be a closet abductee.

People were asked if they had puzzling scars on their body, whether they had seen unusual lights in their room, whether they had experienced missing time of more than an hour or had ever 'flown through the air' in some odd way and whether they had woken up paralysed in the night to see a strange presence in their room? Because some 2 per cent answered 'yes' to at least four of these questions, the well-publicised 'conclusion' of the survey was reached. This stated that there were potentially 4 million abductees in the USA and over 1 million of them in the UK.

Unfortunately there are serious problems with the questions asked and these amazing findings are dubious. Britain's best-known abductee (police officer Alan Godfrey – see page 44) would not even qualify since he had no scars, his time lapse was only 15 minutes long and his experience did not fit the majority of the other criteria. On the other hand, the question about paralysis and a sense of presence in the room is directly attributable to a well-known psychological phenomenon – the night terrors (see page 148–9). Moreover, many people dream that they are flying (at least a third of the population), but it would be unwise to regard *them* as abductees.

This poll was a brave effort, but flawed. Unfortunately, the media took it to heart and for a good while we heard stories about armies of secret abductees unaware that the 'grays' had got to them. This led to an insidious, creeping paranoia that began to filter down through society. With the hit TV series, *The*

1994: THE PERFECT CASE

What might prove the 'perfect' case came to light quietly. It occurred in Victoria, Australia, very near to the site of that other case – the Maureen Puddy episode (see pages 36–7) – that had done so much to call into question the objective reality of alien kidnaps.

According to 27-year-old Kelly Cahill, a married mother of three, she was driving with her husband in the foothills of the Dandenong Mountains near Melbourne in the early hours of 8 August 1993. Kelly had seen a ring of orange lights on the drive out to see a friend, but on the return journey – passing near Belgrave South – they drove towards an object hovering low over the mountain road ahead. It was orange, round in shape and had glassy patches on it. Behind these 'windows' or 'transparencies' Kelly said she could see 'people' but at that point the object simply disappeared. Moments later a brilliant light filled the road ahead and they drove straight at it. Then, again in an instant, it was gone.

Kelly recalls saying to her husband 'Weren't we just about to see a UFO?' and he suggested that they must have 'turned a corner or something'. Kelly felt unwell, could smell vomit and so settled back. But she was uneasy. On arrival home, she noticed a triangular cut or scar near her navel and from the time, now 2.30 am, that they seemed to have taken far too long for the journey. Her husband disagreed, saying they must have left for home later than assumed. But their friend confirmed the true

departure time, which implies that an hour or more of missing time was unaccounted for.

In the wake of the experience, traumas haunted the couple. Kelly's husband, Andrew, sought to deny any significance to the memory. Nevertheless, she knew something was awry, not only because of the physical effects but because her period came on immediately after the sighting, many days early. Within three weeks she was in hospital suffering from an infection of the womb. The doctors were mystified, feeling that the most likely cause was a terminated pregnancy. But tests proved that this was not the case.

On 1 October, while driving along the same road (an isolated spot between Belgrave and Fountain Gate), Kelly had a sudden flashback to seven weeks before and now remembered what had happened. They had rounded a corner and a huge craft with orange lights and blue flares had been beside the road. The couple had stopped and got out to see tall, dark figures with large, red eyes 'gliding' towards them. They had spoken telepathically, saying that they meant no harm, but Kelly recalled her husband screaming in fear and then being thrown onto her back with a 'kicking force'. The beings had said that they were 'peaceful' and would not hurt Kelly. She had felt sick and woken up back in the car. However, perhaps most intriguing was Kelly's new memory that another car had evidently stopped on the road near to the UFO. Some

X Files, picking up immediately after the Roper poll and pandering to these same ideals, the scene was set for the mid-1990s, when interest in all things alien would explode.

SEEKING PROOF

Today there is a campaign to bring common sense to what has become an obsessive quest for hidden abductions. Social security investigator Kevin McClure created the journal *Abduction Watch* with the aim of policing what he considers the excesses of the abduction community.

people had been standing outside that vehicle, surrounded by the same tall, dark-suited beings.

Between October 1993 and January 1994 Kelly had a series of vivid dreams. These involved a sense of paralysis, the feeling of being pulled out of the bed at home, desperately trying to wake her husband, and of seeing dark, cloaked figures. Even more interesting was Kelly's memory, through subsequent dreams, that she suddenly felt she had *killed* one of the aliens in her rage when her husband was led away. Another victim, a human woman, was even screaming 'murderer'. Later she was 'told' by the aliens that she had not murdered anyone. They had implanted this image as a means to control her anger.

On its own this case is fascinating, but what of the other vehicle that Kelly now remembered? She could describe it in detail. Investigator John Auchettl began to seek this crucial link and eventually found the missing car. In the second vehicle there were three occupants – a married couple and a woman friend travelling with them. Each had a vague conscious memory of the UFO events, but had no idea that Kelly Cahill had been there or had reported her sighting. As a result they had chosen not to go public.

Independent evidence was gathered from these witnesses. The husband had little recall, just like Andrew Cahill. Again it was the two women (Jane, the wife, and Glenda, who was a nurse) who, like Kelly, appear to have had the central role in the abduction. They told how they saw the UFO, felt ill, ran the car off the road in panic but then drove on until they came upon the landed UFO. Even under hypnosis, the husband, Bill, recalled only odd smells and sounds. The two women consciously described (and independently drew) the same tall beings that Kelly Cahill reported. They did not recall seeing the Cahill's car but remembered a medical examination inside the craft. Both women had vaginal swelling after the encounter and ring marks on their thighs.

Under hypnosis Jane and Glenda added further dramatic news. A third car – this time with a single male occupant – had also been stopped by the roadside. In 1997 this man was finally traced. While he has proved reluctant to talk, he has confirmed basic details of the UFO. Also the field by the road in which the UFO came down was studied. Unexpected magnetic deviations were recorded on a compass.[52]

It is unwise to base too many conclusions on one case, but this encounter *may* prove vital. Never before have three sets of independent witnesses claimed that they did not know one another but shared an abduction. This case is either a hoax (for which no evidence has been produced and most UFOlogists dispute) or it may be the incident that challenges all our ideas about alien contact.

Witness stories alone are not going to convince anybody that the aliens are here – such evidence is open to misinterpretation and distortion. The key might lie in the quest for physical proof. Some witnesses – rising in numbers since the start of the 1990s – claim that aliens have 'implanted' something during an encounter. If any alien artefacts can be found inside the body then this would go a long way towards establishing that proof.

The American team behind a *Nova* science documentary in 1996 reputedly offered UFOlogists the chance to have MRI (imaging scans) carried out on any witness who claimed to have an alien implant. These expensive tests are usually impossible to organise because medical science consider them a waste of money. However, they could resolve whether such 'implants' are real and whether abductions happen in reality. Sadly, *Nova* claimed that no UFOlogist was able to provide a suitable witness.[53]

To date, all searches for such physical evidence have revealed few implants. But some small items have been removed from abductees. These all proved to have an earthly composition and might have entered the body through normal means. One 'implant' sneezed out and studied by scientists proved to be a cotton-fibre ball!

A stunning new case from Sydney, Australia, was reported by Bill Chalker in May 1999. A builder, Peter Khoury, awoke from semi-sleep to undergo a sexual liaison with a tall, pale blonde entity with Oriental features. Moments later he found a white hair coiled around his penis causing great pain. UFOlogy funded expensive DNA testing with astounding results. The hair appeared to be of Scandinavian or Icelandic origin but its DNA profile proved to be Asiatic and from one of the rarest genetic profiles on Earth. Is this physical proof of hybrid human/aliens or that Nordic aliens are in fact of human origin?

There is no doubt that the abduction mystery is complex and confusing. It would appear to have an obvious choice of answers: either the witness is telling the truth or they are suffering from some kind of delusion. Unfortunately, neither of these options is easy to accept. Some evidence backs one side of the argument, but plenty can be found to mount a spirited counter-offensive.

We face a dilemma similar to physicists a century ago when trying to understand the nature of light. Some experiments seemed to show that light was made of solid 'particles' called photons – fired like bullets from a gun. But other tests revealed that light was an energy field. So which was it – the scientists asked – particles or energy waves? It proved to be a difficult problem to resolve, manifesting as either according to circumstance. Advances in our understanding of the world were necessary before we came to see that our answers seemed confusing because the questions being posed were wrong.

PART TWO

AN ALIEN WORLD

We will now take a global tour, stopping off to look at the evidence reported about aliens. I offer a snapshot of similarities and differences worldwide. Aside from reporting some of the intriguing cases that have been studied, I also provide a few basic facts and figures about each country. I offer some data on the history of reports and the main kinds of entities seen. Facts and figures about alien contacts allow comparisons and contrast.

In the chapters that follow you will see the evidence along with its strengths and weaknesses. Cultural tracking operates in an important way. If aliens are visiting the Earth, then the same aliens, doing the same things, ought to be witnessed globally. If not, then something is amiss with that popular interpretation.

If cases emerge from our consciousness, then one would expect that some national flavouring will occur. The more trace we find of this influence on the evidence, then the more likely it must be that our mind *is* somehow the medium through which these close encounters manifest. Alternatively, the more consistent that these cases appear, then the more we would have to consider that we *are* being visited from some place else.

AFRICA

Many traditional UFO sightings have been reported from the countries to the north, such as Libya and Egypt. However, there are almost no known abductions. What cases we do have come from the vast states to the south, notably **South Africa** and

If cases emerge from our consciousness, then one would expect that some national flavouring will occur.

Zimbabwe; although with a few from Tanzania and Mozambique. Much of the inland African regions are strongly populated by poor, tribal cultures that are only slowly adapting their lifestyle to the modern world. Whereas in the oil-rich regions of the north and the 'Westernised' south, there is considerable contact with European and American culture, as a result of business enterprise and tourism.

One interesting case was reported by Cynthia Hind, who has done much to document African UFO cases. This occurred in **Namibia** in 1970, near the Swakop River and the Rossin uranium mine. A group of villagers had gathered for a late-night feast, when the sky erupted into flame. This created an intense wave of heat that sent the gathering crowd into pandemonium, screaming and fearful of some great disaster. After about three minutes the phenomenon simply vanished. However, one witness, searching for a cause next day, found tiny footprints in the mud – indicative of a person smaller than a child.[54]

Another interesting case comes from Dar-es-Salaam in **Tanzania**. A girl, then aged 5, reported to me that she woke one night in 1950 while sleeping in her nursery with her brother. Mary described a 'strange vibrating noise' that

A LEGIONNAIRES DISEASE

Witness expectation seems relevant to a case in **Algeria**. It happened in March 1958 to a French sentry serving with the Foreign Legion at Bouahmama. He was obviously familiar with UFOs, having left France soon after the 1954 wave. But at about 12.30 am he claims that a loud whistling noise began. Looking upwards he saw the source as a lens shape that was hovering about 100 feet above ground. A greenish haze or mist surrounded the object and a vivid green beam projected towards the Earth.

Although the legionnaire was armed and there was a field telephone nearby, he said that he felt 'transfixed' by the sight and entered an altered, almost hypnotic state. The 'Oz Factor' gathered pace and he forgot all about the war. He added, 'It was like time running very slowly ... It was like being in another world.' Then the noise returned and the object accelerated away. At this, the witness felt a terrible sadness, as if he were saying goodbye to a dear friend. (In another

case, one woman described this typical emotion when the UFO departed as like post-natal depression.) Only gradually did the soldier in Algeria 'snap out' of his sadness. He was 'entranced' for 40 minutes.[55]

Today some enterprising UFOlogist would assume the legionnaire had been abducted, arrange hypnosis and seek to uncork from his mind what transpired during the 'missing time'. Nobody thought to do this in 1958 and we see here what an abduction might look like without the tacked-on memory of an alien kidnap. Certainly the witness continued to feel his conscious recall – of just standing there – was 'not quite right'. But he could not unravel what truly occurred. The hard-nosed military man was sent back to France and studied by army doctors in Paris. They used an EEG to probe the workings of his brain, seeking a mental illness or tumour that might have caused him to suffer 'hallucinations'. None were traced.

filled the air and a peculiar, itching sensation that made her skin tingle. She felt as if she was being watched. This combination of symptoms should be familiar.

Mary further told of how the 'Oz Factor' took hold. She lost all sense of time and felt 'weird' as a figure appeared at the foot of her bed. It had a pale grey/white face, was 3 feet tall with a domed head, pointed chin and large staring eyes – perhaps a 'gray'. But the case was described to me in 1987 *after* abductions became known and was from a woman mostly raised in the UK. She had always called this figure a 'ghost' and did not connect it with UFOs until she heard of abductions. After the encounter Mary was plagued with migraines.

SOUTH AFRICA

EARLY CASES

One of the first known reports comes from Greytown in September 1914 and was described by a farmer. He came upon a strange, landed machine as he crossed the veldt. The witness had

Abductions 10

Alien Contacts 30

Predominant Entity Type Humanoid, with Nordic features

never actually seen a plane, as they were still a rare sight in this region, but it became clear that this object was not one. Beside the craft were two 'men', collecting water samples from a river.[56]

Water also featured in a case at Paarl in the Drakensteen Mountains in 1951. A British engineer had (rather foolishly!) driven his car up a desolate mountain road after a homemade repair job and was approached by a short man who stepped out of the shadows stating firmly, 'We need water.' The entity looked human, although with a babyish face, and was dressed in a brown 'lab coat'. The engineer took the stranger to a mountain stream, filled up an oil can and drove him back to where a lens-shaped craft was lurking in the shadows. Invited inside, in a fashion typical of 'voluntary abductions' of the time, a second entity was seen prone on a bed and evidently injured. In exchange for his kindness the engineer was allowed to ask questions. The not exactly helpful replies indicated that the visitors came 'from there' (pointing skyward!) and flew by 'nullifying gravity by way of a fluid magnet'.

THEMES

The number of cases in which water plays a part in African sightings is significant, says active, African researcher, Cynthia Hind.[57] Is this cultural tracking in a land where drought is a way of life? In November 1991 a family at the village of Kommetjie were awoken at 2.00 am by a strange noise coming from the water-filter pump. Going to investigate, a blue, flickering ball of fire was seen in the garden. After some moments this just 'went out' and the noise stopped. But next day about 2,000 litres (around 10 per cent) of the water-pool had disappeared. There was no leak. Something had drained this away.

Other cases have similarities with data from the UK or USA, even to the extent of disc-shaped craft or Nordic humans. What is interesting is that native Africans report few 'alien' encounters. However, the files of Cynthia Hind show that they frequently report 'light phenomena' – such as the glowing wall of fire in Namibia (see page 56) – as true anywhere in the world (accounting for over 90 per cent of UFO sightings). Under 2 per cent involve aliens.

ABDUCTION PATTERNS

Cynthia Hind reported a trickle of American-style abductions from around 1987. Many early reports were of a 'psychic' nature. One woman in Johannesburg reported a white light that appeared within the wall of her house and a 'man' who emerged from a tunnel of light and attempted to take her away. She saw a white

NIGHT LIGHT

Debra works as a graphic designer in Johannesburg. Producing some urgent artwork for a TV commercial on 19 July 1988, she and her mother, Pat, worked flat out until 3.30 am when, exhausted, they decided to call it a night. Debra was driving her mother home and at around 3.40 am saw a bright light heading towards their car. For a moment she contemplated another vehicle heading for a collision, then the light swooped from above and submerged them in its glow. Pat recalls locking the car doors in case they were being attacked. Debra put her head in her arms and onto the steering wheel to brace for impact.

The 'Oz Factor' kicked in and memory became fuzzy. There was an image of a cloud of white mist and of being inside a room with a table or bed. Two entities, one male, one female, were standing there. These encouraged the women to lie down but Pat had difficulty as it was too far above the ground for her (small) height. So the male alien touched her and she 'floated' up. On the table a bar-like instrument 'took X-rays' and a 'knitting needle' was pushed into the body above the navel. Samples of blood and DNA

were extracted, they were told. While Debra remained subdued, Pat was more resistant.

The beings (with smooth, babyish faces) were too 'human' to be 'grays', but had a command structure akin to the then popular *Star Trek* on TV – designated by the colour of their collars. The woman was 'the commander'. Her voice was high-pitched and had a sing-song lilt; she named herself 'Meleelah'. It is worth noting how alien names seem earthly and can flow readily from our lips. Nobody ever seems to say – 'my name is Zzgyzpqtrxxcqy'. This is another way in which these abductions are described in subtle but far too Earth-centred ways.

The women 'awoke' in their car two hours later than it should have been. They did have a memory of the light 'engulfing' them, but the rest came back naturally (without hypnosis) in bits and pieces. Cynthia Hind reports that they responded differently. The mother recalls more, and was openly distrustful of the beings, but by the end of the experience found herself unaccountably swamped by a sense of 'love'. Indeed the two have disputed various aspects of their recall, as it came through 'flashbacks'.

'room', then lost consciousness and recovered back home not sure if she had been abducted or was hallucinating. This compares closely with an NDE.

Gradually more typical American-style cases appeared. In October 1987, Jean Lafitte from Roodepoort described a series of abductions that started in 1956. He reported being paralysed by a bright light, then finding himself inside a strange room with large-headed aliens. These entities had claimed to come from the 'Pleiades' and to be studying us. Another race – from Alpha Centuari – had also visited. To prove their good intent they had 'mopped up' radiation from the Chernobyl nuclear reactor fire.

> *The number of cases in which water plays a part in African sightings is significant.*

ZIMBABWE

EARLY CASES

At 2.30 am on 31 May 1974, Peter (23) and wife Frances (21) were driving across dry scrub from what was then Rhodesia to Durban in South Africa. Leaving Harare, they observed strange lights

Abductions 4
Alien Contacts 10
Predominant Entity Type Humanoid

between Umvuma and Beitbridge. As these paced the car, the 'Oz Factor' took hold. Everything went quiet and the outside scenery slid by as if 'not really there'. Peter added; 'It was like travelling in a dream. I lost trace of time. I felt as though in a coma.' Indeed he likened it to 'driver's hypnosis' – an altered state recognised by psychologists and commonly experienced by long-distance truck drivers.

Upon arrival at the South African border, Peter found that his trip meter (set at Fort Victoria) had recorded 200 miles less than the true distance and he had used almost no petrol. It was as if the UFO had transported the car. Frances was in an unusually deep sleep during this time and Peter was clearly the focus. He proved a classic abduction-prone personality. A gifted graphic artist, he had a lifelong record of telepathy, strange dreams, out-of-body visions and – aged 13 – had experienced another close encounter. He stated that the sensation during his contact was exactly like various 'out-of-body' experiences he could recall.

The conscious memory of Peter involved no aliens. Seven months later Dr Paul Obertik regressed him and a new story emerged. Frances had no deeper recall. But in his hallucination/memory Peter says an alien beamed into the back seat of the car and implanted images of a room to which humans were taken. Aliens of this type came from '12 planets of the Milky Way' but travelled back in *time* to reach Earth. Although humans see them as hairless, baby-faced entities they can appear in any form. Peter was told that if he wanted to see them as ducks, that's how they would manifest. These galactic time-travellers hoped to make Earth a better place, but would not interfere. They lived among us disguised as humans and influenced people as best they could.

Hypnosis threw up one intriguing point. Peter commented that the aliens were 'about 2,000 years ahead of Earth' (in terms of their technology and progress). But Dr Obertik misunderstood this answer and said, 'So it would take 2,000 years for us to get there?' Peter now supported this error and replied inappropriately, '2,000 light-years.' This clearly shows how hypnotic testimony *can* be influenced unintentionally.[58]

> *The galactic time-travellers hoped to make Earth a better place, but would not interfere.*

ANCESTRAL SPIRITS

One of the most significant African cases comes from a village by the La Rochelle estate on the border of Zimbabwe with Mozambique. On 15 August 1981, a group of native foresters heading home saw a ball of light drift across their path and climb a disused fire-lookout tower. Fearing 'spirits' were the cause, most fled, but the headman, Clifford Muchena, stood in defiance. Cynthia Hind was able to interview him. He was unaware of UFOs and aliens and interpreted what he saw in terms of ancestral spirits.

Clifford told how the lightball became a 'disc', that glowed fiercely as it floated around the estate. Fearing a blaze he raised the fire alarm but saw three, tall, humanlike beings silhouetted against the glow. He went towards them hoping they were estate workers who could assist in fighting the fire, but as he neared a 'bright flare of light' shot at his body and hit him in the eyes. As if struck by a rock, he was thrown backwards. This is much like the 'beam' often fired by aliens in early contact cases to render any would-be witness temporarily senseless.

Clifford related how he looked up from the ground, semi-conscious and paralysed. An unknown period of time passed before he could move and there was no sign of the ball of light or the men. The investigation of this case was made difficult by the fact that Clifford only spoke Mashona, a local, native dialect. It lacked any words for Western technology or that might match with abductions. There is no word for silver and this was the colour that the witness was trying to describe for the suits worn by the beings (he ultimately pointed to a coin to make his point).

With the help of estate workers who could speak English, Cynthia found a couple of others who saw both the light and the beings. The 'spirits' were carrying torches – and these 'torches' emitted the light that struck Clifford. Despite using powerful flashlights to try to duplicate the strength of this 'beam', the witnesses were adamant that the 'spirit' light was far brighter.

The likelihood of these witnesses being aware of alien contacts is remote. When asked about spacemen they thought the investigator was joking. When told that humans had walked on the moon they openly scoffed and said, 'Only God does that!'

These witnesses certainly had their own interpretation of weird events, but they saw things that can easily be labelled as an alien contact.

ASIA

Given this vast continent and the population of its major countries, Asia ought to be awash with abduction cases. It is not. Indeed there are many more in one, moderate-sized European nation and considerably more in places such as Brazil, the USA or the UK. Alien sightings are largely absent right across Asia. Understanding why is vital.

India is a huge anomaly. I have no record of any cases from here despite its population of 830 million (over three times that of the USA). Yet there are major cities and areas of dense population with people gaining high education (often coming to the UK or USA to attend university).

Indonesia has a few cases of little men, like the Bunian, but no network where stories are recorded and passed on to the Western UFO community. For instance, in June 1969 a 27-year-old man, Machpud, met a 'beautiful but strange woman' in Bandjar, Western Java. She led him to her 'house'. This had one big room that had a peculiar 'abundance of light'. The woman made it clear she wanted sex and the witness recalled losing consciousness and being found in a trance by a walker in the Gunung Babakar forest. Machpud was naked and his clothes were up a tree. There is little doubt how many words in this story could be substituted in our language by 'UFO', 'alien', 'taking a sperm sample' and so on.

Such examples show how cultures largely without UFO literature, tabloid media and other trappings that ram alien contact into our daily lives still seem to have recognisably similar experiences. Culture may indeed shape the details, the forms of language used, even the interpretation of what is happening to the victim, but at the heart there seems to be a stunningly consistent type of event.

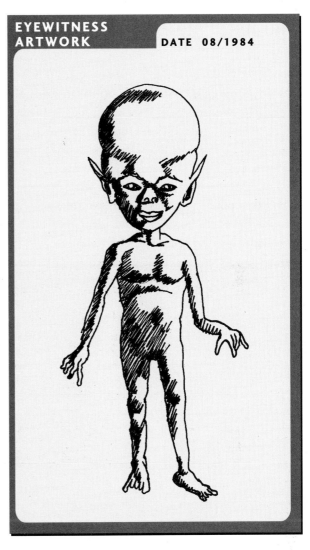

EYEWITNESS ARTWORK　　**DATE 08/1984**

An artist's impression of a typical Bunian entity, c.2.5 feet tall, seen in the Malaysian forest, August 1984.

The woman made it clear she wanted sex and the witness recalled losing consciousness...

CHINA

EARLY CASES

For many years little was known about UFO activity in the most populated nation on Earth. Things changed in 1978 when a reporter called Shi Bo introduced China to UFOs. Along with a researcher called Lin Wen Wei, he set out to

publish case files. More recently several translated books have appeared. Sightings have rapidly increased. By 1990 the tally was above 2,000.

The Chinese have always been good recorders of events and ancient scholars and astronomers reported sightings of what we would term UFOs 2,000 years ago. However, Wen Wei found a truly extraordinary case reported in the County Annals of Song-Zi Xian in 1880. This occurred on 8 May. Ju Tan, a local farmer, was walking home near a hill when he saw a glowing object in the bushes. He felt himself floating and was 'stupefied and numbed'. Then he became paralysed. There was a rushing/humming noise in the air and the farmer's next recall is of 'awakening' on a mountain quite lost. Eventually a forester told him that he was in Guizhou Province, 300 miles from home. More than two weeks had elapsed.

A fascinating case reported directly to me happened in November 1947 to a British woman. I am certain she is sincere. Dawn was crossing Nepal and Tibet to the west of the Chinese border, accompanied by her husband (a REME Colonel) and a Gurkha guard. They had stopped for supper in a desert plateau when their skins all began to tingle, they felt icy cold and an enormous pressure was pushing down from above with a vibrating noise that almost shook the convoy of trucks apart. The Colonel ran towards the source of the problems – a grey, floating mass that was spinning like a top and swooping at them. As if hit by a hammer blow, he fell to the ground, later recovering in a disorientated state. By now all sounds had disappeared. There was a jump in reality and at some point later (perhaps 5 minutes or an hour) Dawn recalled picking up her husband from the ground and looking to find the top-like object gone. The Gurkhas were so upset they refused to go on, despite being part-way through a long journey to see the Dalai Lama. That night all witnesses suffered nausea, pounding headaches and a rash on exposed parts of the body.[59]

THEMES

UFO cases in China have followed trends shown by evidence elsewhere. Over 90 per cent involve lights in the sky, some 2 per cent report electrical effects, including TV and radio interference, while 1.5 per cent feature an alien presence. There have been some well-documented sightings – for example on 11 June 1985, when a Chinese Airways Boeing 747 had an encounter above

Inner Mongolia during a flight from Peking to Paris. Seen at 32,000 feet, a 'yellow walnut' blocked their path and forced Captain Wang Shu-Ting to call for immediate assistance, requesting an emergency landing at the nearest airport.

ABDUCTION PATTERNS

An unexpectedly large number of aliens dominate Chinese sightings. Many of them simply feature beings met in the open without a UFO. They would, to most people, resemble ghosts or spirits. Such cases have also occurred outside China. At Risley, Cheshire, UK, in March 1978, a service engineer saw a strange 'man' with beams of light emerging from his eyes. This being crossed his path then walked through a security fence and disappeared. No UFO was seen but the engineer's van radio was destroyed during the sighting and analysis revealed that an enormous power discharge had struck the aerial and effectively blown its circuitry apart. The witness developed multiple cancers and died soon afterwards, still a young man.[60]

In China, on 29 July 1974, Ke Jingzhi was walking through vegetable crops in Genqing when a humanlike being appeared and began to glow. This glow increased until the figure disappeared. Others at the building workers' training complex nearby later saw the same ghostlike figure. Even more similar is a case collected by Win-Wei (writing as Paul Dong) from August 1971 at Chungking in Szechuan Province. A peasant, Zhang Rongchang, came across a man with a very large head, dressed in silver and glowing (or reflecting) light. He stood in a maize crop that Rongchang was guarding. Although Rongchang fled the scene with haste, his health deteriorated and he remained in a state of profound shock until he died five months later.[61]

That night all witnesses suffered nausea, pounding headaches and a rash on exposed parts of the body.

AUSTRALASIA

Although a 'new world', the countries of **Australia** and **New Zealand** have far more alien contacts than either Africa or Asia. Abductions were uncovered in the late 1980s – again following the American blitz. Before then encounters were aligned to the British/European model.

This pattern mirrors the cultural progress of Australia as it has gradually developed from a British colony to have stronger ties with Asia and the USA. That UFO data has experienced a similar transformation is interesting, although much the same could be said for Britain itself.

New Zealand has not moved so far away from its roots. Often the approach to alien encounters is more questioning than the overtly extraterrestrial viewpoint dominating the USA. The government has also openly admitted to studying sighting reports through Air Force channels. As in the UK there is little to suggest any meaningful outcome.

In Australia a Freedom of Information Act was passed in 1982. Learning from the media storm that provoked a frenzied hunt for Washington UFO files, the government in Canberra was sensible. It turned over an office to noted UFOlogist Bill Chalker, let him copy all the files and asked him to publish them for the UFO community. Chalker, an industrial chemist, did a fine job, studying the evidence in a very objective fashion.[62] He found what we might have expected – 1,258 sightings, with some by military personnel. Most were lights in the sky but there were cases of physical injury and electrical effects, a few that hinted at deeper, unprobed memories, but hardly any alien contacts.

The rational approach in Australia has seen researchers such as Keith Basterfield pioneer work into altered states and the fantasy-prone personality. But this should be seen alongside the media sensationalism and hype that, for example, accompanied the filming of strange lights over the Kaikoura area of New Zealand or an allegedly alien carjack at Mundrabilla on the Western Australia border. In some cases the hype was typical of how the British tabloids exploit the UFO mystery with alarming gusto.[63]

AUSTRALIA

EARLY CASES

Things began with the Parramatta case of 1868 (see page 15). In Africa, tribal culture had slowed witnesses from talking, creating the impression that only Western migrants had modern encounters. Native Australians (aborigines) have strong

Abductions 43
Alien Contacts 150
Predominant Entity Type Humanoid; 'grays' (post-1988)

traditions that we might term psychic – speaking of other realities (the 'dreamtime'), god-like beings from the skies and other paranormal phenomena. Centuries-old UFO reports, known as the Min Min Lights, are found across Queensland and Northern Territories.[64]

An intriguing case from 1951 involves members of the Unmatjera aborigines in the central region, who saw two silvery objects land. Small human entities with over-large heads got out of one craft and entered the other. Both crafts then departed skyward making a buzzing noise.

In 1955 a 10-year-old Adelaide girl (Janet) was experiencing severe nervous trauma. The psychiatrist treating her condition suggested hypnosis to try to alleviate the problem. He was stunned when she recited in this altered state how she had seen a UFO and three men had taken her into a strange room where she had been shown images of life on an advanced planet. Fantasy or not the story pre-dates nearly all known abduction cases; although it was not studied by UFOlogists until 1969.

Young girls were especially prone to this kind of thing as Bill Chalker found in another case, where a girl went missing in 1958 at Gippsland, Victoria. When found, she told how she had come upon a small human working on a strange craft and despite being signalled to step back could remember 'flying' in space and seeing her home from above.

THEMES

Australian cases feature the fairly typical spread of (mostly humanlike) aliens and a strong element of humming/buzzing noises, cloudy mists and 'Oz Factor' states.

A remarkable example, from a coastal area near Sydney in August 1965, involves a strange cloud of pink colour that floated towards the base of a cliff where a woman was standing. Out of this 'materialised' a white disc that emitted a low hum or buzz. Wisps of steam were coming from its side as if it were vaporous in nature. From this disc a ladder was lowered and a normal-looking man climbed onto it, shining an electric torch into the sea. Then a pink ball was ejected by the UFO into the sea – almost like a distress flare – and the craft sped off across the sea with the man still sat on the ladder.

Until the 1990s, hypnosis was hardly employed by Australian UFOlogists. Indeed in a 1994 study Keith Basterfield noted that only three witnesses had required this method to gain recall of their experience. Whether this major difference with the USA (and even the UK) produced a special flavour to the data needs thought. Certainly it has not prevented many consciously recalled tales of aliens. But there are instances where hypnosis may have brought out a story more involved than that which was remembered.

A case in point occurred near Mayanup, Western Australia on 30 October 1967. Mr Harris, a 30-year-old wool-classer had just paid-off his shearing crew and was driving to another ranch late at night, when his car lost all power. An oval object was above the road and a blue beam coming from this covered the car. The 'Oz Factor' quickly followed – with all sounds vanishing and a curious detached sensation. Then, without obvious transition, Harris was driving into Boyup Brook with all his electrical circuits and engine now working perfectly. His watch was several minutes slow of real time. Days of intense headaches followed – an unfamiliar symptom of an abduction in 1967. This led Harris to Perth psychiatrist Dr Paul Zeck. Our knowledge of this case comes from an in-depth medical 'case study', seeking a neurological cause. The

... a pink ball was ejected by the UFO into the sea ... and the craft sped off ...

'Oz Factor' and lights were assumed to be hallucinations caused by this condition. But there was no trace of a tumour or indeed of the primary suspect cause, temporal lobe epilepsy.[65]

ABDUCTION PATTERNS

Keith Basterfield has done an excellent job of documenting the shifting trends of abduction cases. Some figures he cites such as those of 1994, are illuminating. Since then cases have continued.[66]

He found 83 encounters in which there was evidence of missing time. These are all potentially abductions and many feature 'Oz Factor' symptoms. Basterfield had confidence to suggest that 39 of these were probably abductions and many of these 39 were confirmed by alleged recall. Yet in these cases there were only 46 witnesses. This gives an average number of witnesses per case of 1.18. This finding is consistent worldwide and is substantially lower

TRACK RECORD

When she was 6, Carol, from Largs Bay, South Australia, began to have odd experiences after she had seen a strange object in the sky. By the time she was 27 in 1990, she had undergone almost every kind of strange phenomenon one can imagine, including poltergeist attacks in the home, seeing the future in dreams, sharing thoughts with others, floating out of the body and having lucid dreams in which she could control what happened. She also suffered from sleep paralysis (see pages 148–50).

In 1989 hypnosis was used to regress her to a recall of an abduction from 1972. In this new memory she described a small being outside her bedroom window. It was a 'gray', with a large head, pointed chin, huge eyes, a slight, off-white body and little trace of a nose or mouth. Carol 'floated' into the air and then recalled being in a room with some beings now leaning over her. In her mind a voice was telling her, 'It won't be long. Won't hurt.'

A second abduction allegedly occurred while staying in a cabin with a woman friend. A bright light appeared, but when the other woman was regressed along with Carol, she only described the strange light – not any aliens or abduction. Carol recalled another kidnap.

Much of the detail about this case came through hypnosis that was actually being conducted for reasons unconnected with UFOs. Carol was undergoing deep therapy to investigate whether or not she had been a victim of child sexual abuse. The culprits were, of course, suspected to be humans and not the alien intruders that the hypnotic memory suggested to some people.

This case throws up many fascinating questions and is by no means unique. Witnesses commonly seem to grow with a wide range of 'altered states' and bizarre experiences. They have a very rich inner life that allows them to see many things they find difficult to interpret. Today some are of an alien contact.

> *... abductions are predominantly experienced by young people. Only two witnesses in the abduction set referred to were over 40.*

than in simple UFO sightings where the witness per case ratio is 2.6.

Another interesting trend identified in Australia is that abductions are predominantly experienced by young people. Only two witnesses in the abduction set referred to above were aged over 40. In my study from the UK, more than 65 per cent of witnesses are aged 21 to 30. You will have noticed in the case histories given in this book how such ages are frequently mentioned. This is a global pattern.

Basterfield also discovered that 97 per cent of all abductions occurred in two environments. These were in the bedroom (61 per cent) and in a rural location (36 per cent). The latter were often in a car on a lonely road. Over 70 per cent of abductions – again worldwide – occur between 9.00 pm and 6.00 am. These are therefore principally single-witness events that happen in locations favouring sensory deprivation. Basterfield suspects that this data offers an important clue. Given the 'Oz Factor' state, which appears to be a kind of artificially induced deprivation of all outside stimuli, then it is easy to question physical reality.

As for the entities seen, my calculations, based on data from both Keith Basterfield and Bill Chalker, are worth noting. Pre-publication of the Whitley Strieber case in 1987 (see page 45) and its huge publicity, the results were as follows: 47 per cent were normal humanoids, 27 per cent were tall humanoids (many of these two types had Nordic features), 18 per cent were small humanoids and 8 per cent were others (e.g. robots, monsters). There were no identifiable cases involving 'grays'. In cases reported after 1987, 20 per cent were normal humanoids, 20 per cent were tall humanoids, 20 per cent were small humanoids, 6 per cent were oddities and a remarkable 34 per cent were now 'grays'.

Abductions are far more common post-1988 and most involve the 'grays'. We cannot prove that had there been more pre-1988 abductions that these would not also have featured the 'grays'; although evidence does not support this view. All we can say is that there was a massive change in the type of alien contact experienced alongside the American publicity blitz for 'grays'.

Basterfield also found that certain types of people are prone to abductions. The results of his 1992 study closely match findings in both the USA and the UK: 70 per cent of abductees are female; many display excellent memories, including eidetic imagery (memories visualised as clearly as a photograph) and easy recall of very early life; and they report unusually vivid dreamlives and the capacity to become totally absorbed within.

UP THE CREEK

Typical of a modern Australian case is that reported to Keith Basterfield by a couple called Julian and Lydia. Hypnosis was conducted in 1992, but they had scattered conscious recall before then.

The events had begun when Julian lived in Tennant Creek, Northern Territory. He had often felt he was being 'watched'. This returned one day in July 1989 as he, his wife and two children drove home to Adelaide from their country property. The uneasy sensation persisted as they drove through a fierce storm. Once back in Adelaide they went to bed, as the storm still raged. Julian then heard a metallic noise outside and a low humming, but assumed it was a train on nearby tracks.

Lydia had heard the noise too but was more worried. She thought it was a thief. Then she saw a figure in the bedroom doorway. It was small with a fragile body and oversized head. Its colour was grey and its eyes black and like teardrops. There was no body hair and just a slit for a mouth. This was a 'gray'.

Sensing a kind of telepathic message that the being wanted to 'look at our bodies', she said aloud, 'Julian, don't worry. Everything will be all right. Just do as they say and there will be no problems.' He thought she was mumbling in her sleep.

Next morning the couple awoke 'feeling strange'. Julian was 'giddy' and disorientated as one might be after a long plane ride. He knew he had not slept well and checked his body for physical effects but found none. Nor could he recall what had happened. Lydia says she went through the next few hours 'as if I were in a trance'. As they talked over these odd feelings, Lydia said she had a vague recall of something disrupting the night and 'activity' in the hall and the children's bedrooms. She also had a memory of lying flat on a table and being looked at.

Hypnosis revealed a coherent story. In this Julian was floated into the air – or out of the body – accompanied by the high-pitched metallic noise. A tall humanlike figure (*not* a 'gray') was seen holding his young son and Julian fought to resist. He then found himself paralysed, flat on his back in a darkened room with three 'grays' surrounding him staring intently. The next thing he remembered was floating back onto the bed and then waking in the morning. Lydia's recall was less dramatic than this, with only bits and pieces of an 'experiment' conducted on her body. The children were not regressed.

In the years after this experience the couple became interested in peace, pollution and the state of the planet and also developed what they regarded as the ability to perform 'psychic healing'. They have a much more psychic and positive outlook on life than before their 'alien kidnap'.

NEW ZEALAND

EARLY CASES

There was a wave of 'airship' sightings in New Zealand in 1909, similar to those occurring in Europe at this time. In one case, during August, a farmer at Kaikoura claimed to have seen a grey torpedolike object that had three 'men' inside.

Abductions 3

Alien Contacts 12

Predominant Entity Type Humanoid (small), with 'gray'-like features

They had appeared normal and one had even shouted down to the witness in an unfamiliar foreign language.

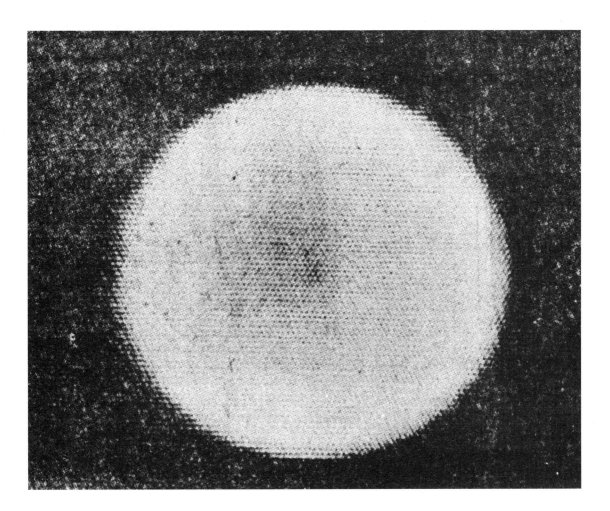

A UFO filmed by a TV crew in Kaikoura and Clarence area of South Island, New Zealand.

In 1974 Bruce Harding, a local UFO investigator reported a much odder case from the Sign of the Takahe region of Port Hills near Christchurch. This had occurred in August 1944 (or 1945). The witness, Mrs Church, an operating theatre sister had come upon an upturned saucer-shape made from tiles with entities only 3 or 4 feet tall. She described them as having large heads, out of proportion with their body. These 'gray'-like beings had seemed to be watching a city fair. Then a mass of cloud had covered the object and it had risen up and vanished into the mist, making a whirring noise. Mrs Church had felt a sense of loss as the beings disappeared.

Although far fewer cases are known from New Zealand than from Australia, an interesting one involves a native Maori. This occurred on 22 February 1969 at Awanui and shows a good example of cultural differences. The witness discovered a white glow coming from some bushes and went to investigate. Here stood several, tall entities with pale skins, thin faces and long, blond hair. They are apparent to us as Nordics, but to the poor Maori they were terrifying. Retreating to a safe distance, he then gave these 'visitors' a sight they were unlikely to forget – a special version of his tribal greeting. This consists of dancing around making 'gestures' and then urinating in a circle. The ritual is meant to ward off evil spirits, which is what he believed these 'aliens' to be.

The best-known case from New Zealand occurred on 31 December 1978, when a TV crew encountered strange lights above Kaikoura. This occurred as they filmed a reconstruction of an earlier mid-air encounter by the same cargo airline that was now carrying them. The footage they took of the dancing lights attracted global headlines and was variously explained as stars, moonlight shining off cabbage patches and a Japanese squid-fishing fleet! It was probably none of these, but may well have some simple explanation. The most alien thing about this case was the way the world media went to town, kicking the facts and the story around as if at a football match.

THE GUYS OF GISBORNE

The Waimata Valley in New Zealand experienced a wave of close encounters in 1977/78. On 11 March 1978 three young women – in response to these events – went UFO hunting near the town of Gisborne. Although they saw little and thought they had endured a sleepless night, their log recorded a two-hour gap when nobody could recall what had happened.

As they walked to their car in the morning air, they felt as if something was nearby, watching them, and their disappointment at not seeing any UFOs was tinged with confusion. All that they could recall were some 'hooligans' and how they had hidden from them in fear. One woman had felt herself floating upwards.

After the events were reported, an enterprising UFOlogist (who had seen hypnosis tried out on stage and 'picked up' how to do it) persuaded one witness to be regressed. In this state she saw herself 'sucked up' by a lightbeam along with another of the women and 'waking' in a strange room where she and her colleague were laid out on flat beds. A humanlike man was in the room and 'talked' to them, before they were 'sent back' and woke up on the hillside. The third woman had slept through it all.

In 1989 the woman who had been hypnotised contacted Keith Basterfield. He arranged an investigation, including a controlled hypnosis session conducted by a clinical psychologist. This was revealing. It found that the witness had the now familiar track record of most psychic experiences. The hypnosis also revealed that the kidnapping entities had long, thin faces with large black eyes – they were 'grays'.

As for the 'on-board' experience, the terror of this was described in the new session. With expletives deleted the witness reported: 'This guy says he knows me. I don't know him… Oh man, that's sick… Leave her alone… sticking things into her… you can't do things like that. This is my sister-in-law… guinea pigs…' I have myself sat in on several harrowing, regression hypnosis sessions where witnesses relive a trauma of this sort. Whether real or imagined the shock to the system is obvious.

Of course, in the Gisborne case one might be tempted to wonder whether the 'screen memory' (as Budd Hopkins would call it) was of 'hooligans' attacking them. Did this 'hide' alien activity or did recall of the alien abduction act as a mental shield against a vicious assault by all too human aggressors?

ABDUCTION PATTERNS

Karen Hardman told me of how she woke as if from a trance in Gisborne on the night of 31 August 1969 and found that she was staring through her bedroom window. Outside a saucerlike object was hovering above some trees. She was only eight at the time and recalled waking her brother (one year younger) to see the glowing craft as it 'faded away'. This was all that they could remember, although next morning both described it to their parents, who took the sensible step of separating the children and asking them to draw what they had seen. The pictures were so similar that the possibility of a nightmare was rejected.

On 13 July 1959 Eileen Moreland was gathering her cattle for milking in the pre-dawn darkness near Blenheim when she found her paddock bathed in a green glow. Approaching to investigate, she saw a mist or fog through which two 'green eyes' were shining. These lights were surrounded by an orange band. Fleeing for cover she watched a cylindrical object descend into her field, making a loud humming noise. In a dome on top two little men were clearly visible. They were under 5 feet tall, wore skin-tight suits and were gazing at something. Then, with a terrible screeching sound, the object climbed upwards and vanished into the cloud. It left behind a wave of hot air that was tangy like ozone and had a smell that was 'peppery'.

Mr Moreland was an officer at the nearby New Zealand Air Force Base. He ensured that the matter was quickly investigated and found that radiation levels at the site were unusually high. Tests also saw Mrs Moreland subjected to various audio tones. These established that the humming noise had a frequency of 15,000 Hz and the terrible screech was as high as 150,000 Hz. There were also some significant after-effects. The grass in the area grew very green and at a prodigious rate, whereas some nearby fruit trees quickly died and had to be uprooted.

The grass in the area grew very green and at a prodigious rate, whereas some nearby fruit trees quickly died...

Mrs Moreland also developed physical symptoms, which included brown areas of skin pigmentation on her face that persisted for several months – even several years in one place. Her hands also became swollen and her wedding ring was so tight it had to be cut off to revive the blood circulation. All of these events appear to be connected with whatever energy was being generated by the UFO.[68]

EUROPE

Of all the continental zones under investigation, Europe is the most diverse. In terms of area Europe is relatively compact, but it comprises dozens of nations – from the tiniest on Earth to several of the world's superpowers. It is impossible to do justice to the full extent of the alien contact here. All I can do is to hopefully provide some insight into the similarities and the differences that abound.

UFOs are seen everywhere. Some countries, notably **France,** were pioneers both in terms of having encounters and leading serious investigation. Others now have thriving UFO communities, notably much of **Scandinavia, Italy** and **Spain.** The former **Soviet Union** countries collated reports secretly from the 1950s, but waged a battle with the public to try to deny the problem while covertly setting up scientific and military commissions to assess it. However, in a more liberal climate the true extent of the UFO mystery across Eastern Europe is now in evidence. Nations such as **Hungary, Lithuania** and **Estonia** have embraced the subject with enthusiasm. Western books have been translated and conferences are staged.

FRANCE
EARLY CASES

France had what might have been the first abduction, just after the First World War in Marseilles (see page 16). Later there were other intriguing episodes. At Le Verger in the summer of 1944, teenager Madeleine Arnoux was picking berries

Abductions 6
Alien Contacts 100
Predominant Entity Type Little man in diving suit (not a 'gray')

when a dull grey machine, the size of a car, was spotted. Nearby were several 'little men' dressed in brown coveralls. Madeleine was rendered motionless by a ray as she tried to collect her bicycle and she then lost all sense of time. This left a tingling sensation that lasted several minutes, during which the little men returned to their craft. It flew away skywards with a blast of air.[69]

This became the typical method by which French witnesses were rendered senseless. Even today witnesses sometimes describe the tingling sensation – as if encountering an electric field – when in close proximity to a landed UFO.

Energy also features in an impressive case that occurred late on the night of 29 August 1975. A businessman and former gendarme called Cyrus, aged 48, was driving his Peugeot 404 near the village of Longages. Observing a dark oval in a field next to the road, he was astonished to see this become lit by a

One notable feature of French cases is that while the number of alien encounters rank it in the top six nations of the world, the number of abductions is low.

phosphorescent glow. The thing then swooped towards him on a collision course, causing him to throw his hands around his head and lose control of the car. This crashed into a ditch, thankfully without causing major injury.

With the object hovering overhead and pouring out light as bright as the sun, the witness became dazed and confused until another man stopped and opened his car door. He had been driving along the road in the opposite direction and had seen the UFO too. The Peugeot seemed about to explode. The UFO dulled to a red colour and disappeared upwards at speed. Several local residents reported to police seeing a bright light that night.

Cyrus was left unable to speak for a time, his eyes were sore and he lost his normal ability to sleep, doing so at unexpected moments during the day suggesting a disorder known as narcolepsy (see page 150). His watch was not working. It is not difficult to imagine that had Cyrus been hypnotically regressed we might now have here a deeper tale of alien abduction.[70]

ABDUCTION PATTERNS

One notable feature of French cases is that while the number of alien encounters rank it in the top six nations of the world, the number of abductions is proportionately low. However, we cannot be sure that the relatively limited use of regression hypnosis is not a factor in this. French UFOlogy places emphasis on psychological theories.

There are certainly quite a few cases where the possibility of deeper memories might exist or where the witness has hinted at, but not openly discussed, a more intimate alien contact. The extraordinary case of a leading scientist, known as Dr X, is an illustration of this. It took place at 3.55 am on 2 November 1968 in a house overlooking a valley near Provence. Dr X was woken by his 18-month-old child crying. Outside a storm was brewing and a bright glow filled the valley. Investigating from a side terrace, the scientist saw two lens-shaped objects sucking electricity from clouds. This bizarre experience left a series of legacies, ranging from out-of-body experiences and strange dreams to an instant cure of a serious axe wound on Dr X's leg. Most strange was a red, triangular blotch that baffled a consultant dermatologist. Days after the sighting this appeared on the abdomen of *both* Dr X and his baby (also exposed to the UFO). This faded but recurred several times during following years.[71]

A survey of 96 entity reports found that 40 per cent featured little men, over 50 per cent normal or tall humanoids and under 2 per cent anything like a 'gray'.

GERMANY

Surprisingly I could not trace a single obvious abduction from one of the world's leading nations. Even alien contacts are few. But there are interesting cases. Gordon Creighton reports the oldest, from 25 May 1948. It occurred after Hans

Abductions None known
Alien Contacts 10
Predominant Entity Type Mostly humanoid, but very mixed

Klotzbach jumped from a moving freight train upon which he was seeking to enter Luxembourg illegally. Falling down an embankment near the border at Wasserbillig, he injured his legs badly and collapsed from extensive blood loss. He awoke in a strange room bathed in blue light and a voice told him that alien visitors had found him close to death by the tracks. They had rescued him, taken him to their craft and were now warning him of dangers the Earth would face. After losing consciousness again, Hans came to inside a small wood 5 miles across the border and 'free' in Luxembourg. Four days had passed and whilst his trousers were covered in blood, his injuries had disappeared.[72]

During the 1950s the ongoing Euro wave mostly passed this nation by. But on 30 June 1952 at Hasselbach, two witnesses saw 'men' in one-piece, metal suits near a landed UFO, seemingly taking soil samples. One entity wore a lamp. Less typical of then European cases was the report at Brovst on 12 September 1953 when two beings of human form, but with rough skin not unlike fish scales, were witnessed.

More recent potential abductions are uncommon. In early April 1980 a 27-year-old woman, Patricia Dziomba, claimed an attack by a UFO near the border with Alsace in France. She had been driving in the Bas Rhin area when a white sphere of light swooped at her car and gave chase, even when she turned around and fled. As she rounded a bend, the engine and lights failed and the car coasted to a halt with the thing directly ahead. Patricia leapt from the car and ran screaming to a nearby house, whose occupant came out to see the light fast disappearing. The man took Patricia to the police who discovered that the staff at the Mulhouse-Basel airport control tower had seen the sphere of light as well. They could not identify it as any known aircraft.[73]

ITALY

EARLY CASES

Italy presents a far greater range of alien contact stories and has more abduction claims than France. Hypnosis has been conducted in several instances. This country produced the Villa Santina case (see page 21) in August 1947, possibly the

Abductions 14
Alien Contacts 76
Predominant Entity Type Humanoid (often tall), including Nordics

EYEWITNESS ARTWORK

DATE 08/1947

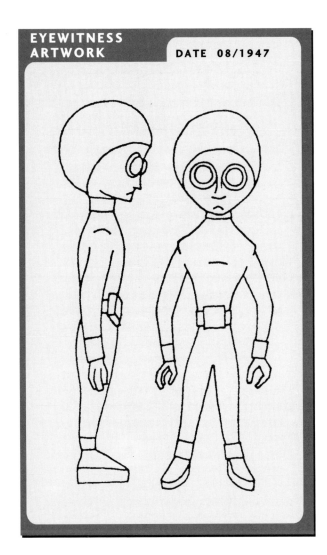

Drawings of two entities seen by Professor R. L. Johannis at Raveo near Villa Santina, Italy, August 1947.

earliest example of today's 'grays'. But that entity type was not common afterwards. Many Italian reports feature tall beings.

Entities over 8 feet in height made an appearance at Veghenza on 14 August 1951, when a farmer found several inspecting a cemetery near to a landed 'pie dish'. They had white faces and large, blue eyes. A 'tube' that emitted a light beam was fired at the witness, but this failed to do anything and the creatures fled up a ladder into the craft – which promptly soared into the air making a noise like a vacuum cleaner.

The 1954 wave of sightings brought several cases like those in France. For example, on 21 October (the same day as Britain's first Nordics were seen at Ranton) a being in a diving suit emerged from a landed UFO at Melito. A green beam was used to paralyse the witness, but as the entity came closer a barking dog caught its attention and it hastened back to the UFO.

THEMES

During early encounters it was common for a witness simply to be knocked out. But whenever a conversation of sorts ensued (usually by telepathy), then this tended to focus on the dangers of nuclear war. This was at the forefront of human concern at the time with the threat of global destruction imminent. That tends to suggest an element of cultural tracking with the alien contacts mirroring true life public thinking. Today there is much of both a technological and scientific experimental nature in abduction cases – which seems to match the way the modern world focuses on topics such as genetic engineering, disease control and cloning.

There was a curious set of cases during the 1970s when aliens offered dire warnings for the Earth. They had now moved on from the nuclear holocaust theme to concerns about ecological or climatic disasters. A few words of specific advice then about the unseen hole in the ozone layer or dangers from abuse of CFC gases might have been more helpful than vague platitudes about 'distant planets', but we never got them. Perhaps this glaring omission is strong evidence that no real aliens are out there and 'contacts' only reflect the level of

A WITNESSED ENCOUNTER

At 6.30 am on 1 November 1954, a Catholic feast day, Rosa Lotti Dainelli, a poor farmer's wife and mother of four children from outside the small village of Cennina (near Florence) was carrying her shoes and stockings (so as not to get them dirty) across the muddy fields to church. She was clutching a bunch of carnations to lay on the altar. As she walked through some thickets towards the village she came upon a landed object like a spindle, no larger than an upturned car. There was a glass window or door in the middle, behind which were visible two old-fashioned seats. As Rosa stared at the craft, two beings 'almost like men but the size of children' stepped from behind and grabbed at her. These entities would be at home in a folk tale. They wore skull caps and old-fashioned cloaks. Although they looked like grinning humans, Rosa added 'It would have taken two of those things to make a man.' They spoke in a lilting tongue reminiscent of Chinese and waved their hands, without menace, as if trying to be understood.

The beings tugged at Rosa, taking her bunch of flowers and yanking away one stocking despite her resistance. Seeing her protests, one entity gestured to hand a few flowers back before studying them with curiosity and throwing the bunch into the craft through the open door/window. Then one entity pulled out a small, square object

from the craft and turning again to Rosa, tried to point this straight at her. But the woman had seized the moment to make a run for it.

Rosa noted that in the presence of the 'men' she had felt oddly calm and at first unable to move, but the spell broke as she forced herself to run and once further away the more 'natural fear' overwhelmed her. This suggests that the 'Oz Factor' state may be strongest in the immediate vicinity of the object but dissipates rapidly with distance.

On reaching the village Rosa reported the matter to the police. But oddly her memory was already less clear, as if parts were missing. Several villagers went back to the spot after the commotion. A large 'crater' was found in the soil where the object had sat. Many local people were already there because a farmer had gone there when alerted by his two sons. They had been near the thickets tending to some pigs and saw Rosa and the strange men in confrontation. They rushed home to warn their father and by the time senior police arrived from the nearest main town, sightseers had destroyed any hope of 'forensic' evidence being gathered. Later enquiries revealed that at least half a dozen local people – farmers, villagers, people driving on nearby roads – had seen the spindlelike object streaking skywards that morning.[74]

awareness we possess at the time. Visiting aliens, studying our world with advanced science, would surely know of things yet to be revealed.

A typical case came in July 1968 when Walter Rizzi was driving in the Grodner Pass of the Dolomites. He had stopped for a break during his long journey and was suddenly 'woken' by a burning odour. Leaping from the car, he found that a disc-like craft had landed nearby and some beings had got out. These were like a

... he found that a disc-like craft had landed nearby and some beings had got out ... They had grey skins and hairless, rounded heads ...

mix between the then well-established Nordics and the coming dominant race of 'grays'. They were only slightly smaller than average human height, had grey skins and hairless, rounded heads, but their features were more that of Nordics with, for example slanted, cat-like eyes.

During a protracted contact, Rizzi was told that they came from a 'far galaxy' using two types of propulsion – one for use in space and a 'magnetic drive' for use within our atmosphere (reported here yet again). They stayed on Earth only for short periods because our world made them 'age' quickly. They were 'not allowed' to interfere, but were happy to warn that our planet was dangerously unstable. Soon there would be a massive shift of the magnetic poles and this would bring about sudden climate changes of a horrific nature. Most life would be destroyed and any left confined to a narrow, habitable belt.

ABDUCTION PATTERNS

An ambiguous incident happened on 4 July 1978 on the slopes of the volcano, Mount Etna. The witnesses had an impressive pedigree, being two Air Force sergeants, a Naval officer and his girlfriend. They were on holiday in the area when they saw a red triangle high in the sky and were so intrigued that they set off to investigate.

A bright light appeared to detach itself from the thing and land behind Mount Sona. So the four drove after it. Rounding a bend they were now confronted by a dazzling light that blocked their path and forced them to stop. Getting out they were trapped between the light and a steep cliff wall leading to the sea. Down below in the darkness was a domed object and a group of strange beings, two of which were scrambling up the slope heading for the cornered witnesses. These beings were Nordics, tall, with beautiful features and blond hair, but dressed in black suits. The witnesses had no obvious escape route and could not get back to their car because a strange tingling had filled the air and they were temporarily paralysed. The beings were smiling as they approached the witnesses and then nodded towards the landed craft as if indicating that this was where they were about to take their captives.

The next thing recalled by these four people was that the UFO began to glow brightly. Then a car approached on the mountain road. Instantly the craft 'switched off' and the witnesses felt the hold on them being released. The strange sensation disappeared and they ran back to their car and drove away at speed. For some time afterwards the witnesses felt as if all energy had been drained from them and they slept for many hours.[75]

SCANDINAVIA

This region covers **Denmark**, **Finland**, **Norway** and **Sweden**.

EARLY CASES

The Scandinavian group – SUFOI – relates a fascinating case from July/August 1940 in Central Jutland. A youth reported meeting three moderately sized, human entities dressed in shiny one-piece suits. As he walked through some fields

Abductions 9
Alien Contacts 37
Predominant Entity Type Mainly humanoid (small), but varied

towards them, they turned away and the witness gave pursuit. He saw them approach a dome-shaped craft the size of a plane, but without visible doors or windows. When just a few feet from it, the beings simply disappeared. The craft then rose vertically and shot away.

Another early case came at the end of the 1954 wave, on 23 November, when two 'little men' who were otherwise human in appearance were witnessed inside a strange craft at Torpo, Norway. The three women who watched this scene from only feet away saw the entities react in terror at being spotted, moving what seemed like levers in a hasty attempt to escape. Unfortunately, the

CRASH COURSE FOR UFONAUTS

Torpo (see above) is not the only case to suggest less than competent skills on behalf of alien pilots visiting Scandinavia. Swedish UFO researcher Anders Liljegren investigated another intriguing report of events at Mariannelund just before 7.00 pm on 29 September 1959. Gideon Johansson had rushed outside after a power cut in his home. There he found a bright light falling swiftly towards his house. This resolved into a dome-shaped craft with a large window in front, which in a less than controlled descent swerved just in time to miss his house but smashed through a tree in the garden.

Inside the craft could be seen two small beings with large eyes, beautifully expressive in nature. They had domed heads, slit mouths and pointed chins. The craft began to drift away and then – with a huge flash of light – disappeared completely. A rush of air was sucked in to the space vacated. Power workers

later discovered a glasslike powder scattered over the cables. They were never able to explain the power failure. The maple tree struck by the UFO died a few months later. Mr Johansson suffered a period of acute tiredness, nausea, headaches and inflammation to the glands. His testicles became swollen, much to his embarrassment. This may suggest a radiating energy field that was somehow connected with the UFO.

Other people in the area described seeing the light and Mr Johansson's young son also witnessed the entities from the garden. This case is widely considered one of the most impressive in Scandinavia because of the physical evidence, and the strongly attested character of the principle witness, who readily agreed to being studied by psychologist Ewert Martensson. 'He has definitely seen something' was Martensson's unabashed appraisal of the man after these sessions.[76]

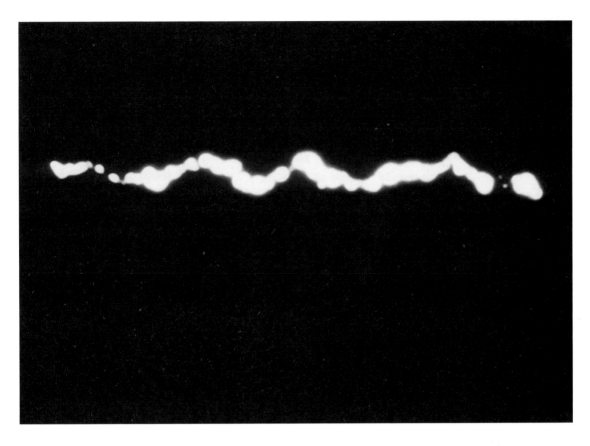

Strange lights photographed by Project Hessdalen, Norway.

navigational skills of this alien crew were not what they might have been and the UFO struck power lines, sending a shower of sparks to the ground. This did not impede its progress, however, and an escape was made.

THEMES

The Scandinavian nations have some of the most objective and enlightened UFO research communities in the world. Along with Italy, they are the only other countries to adopt a code of practice like that in Britain (see page 42) and to legislate against the use of hypnosis. There have, of course, been a few private cases where hypnosis was applied. But generally the numbers of traditional abductions are limited to the few that have emerged through conscious recall. Debate rages as to whether this is artificially suppressing knowledge of hundreds of abductions that can only be found through hypnosis or preventing a flood of spurious fantasies that in other places artificially increase the apparent number of cases.

The remote valleys around Hessdalen in Norway, not far from Trondheim, are the scene of many light-in-the-sky type sightings that have been subjected to intensive study. Special cameras, spectrographs and radar have tracked waves of activity and produced much good evidence for the reality of what appears to be a form of plasma energy floating above the mountains.[77]

Sweden has its own hot spot – the Dalecarlia region. Some of the reports from here have noted associated effects usually found as a prelude to abductions. On 17 April 1987 at Soderbarke two families were in a house affording a fine cliffside view over the South Barken waters. One of the young daughters, playing with some dolls, began to scream hysterically that a flying saucer was heading for the house. The four adults and two older children all looked out to see a strange object floating over the water towards them.

Witnesses said they felt in a very strange state for some time afterwards, feeling what they can only term near-religious 'ecstasy'.

HAPPY NEW YEAR

On 31 December 1987 the Dalecarlia area in Sweden produced one of its best cases. Mrs Bensson, a retired nurse in the small town of Sater, noticed at about 2.00 am that her cat and dog were both restless. They wanted to leave the house, but on going outside returned immediately. Finally leaving them outside, Mrs Bensson went to check through the window and saw in horror that her dog was shaking in terror, looking at an ice-blue globe of light over some nearby trees.

Seeking to rescue the animal, Mrs Bensson saw that the object was only a few feet off the ground and at least as large as a car. It was surrounded by a greyish, orange mist and from its base a series of 'lightning bolts' was striking the soil. This occurred intermittently every few seconds. As she stood there, Mrs Bensson felt a strange sensation wash over her body. Her skin was tingling and prickling with what felt like static. Her head was pounding and her jaw ached badly. She tried to call out to her husband, but could not move. Such was the change in her state of consciousness that the woman said it felt like her mind was being 'sucked out' and that at any moment she would die.

Back in the house Mr Bensson had been alerted to his wife's antics with the pets and was also listening to a faint humming or buzzing noise, the origin of which he could not fathom. After pondering this for a time, noticing that his wife was missing, he decided to get dressed and go to investigate.

Outside, by the door, Mrs Bensson was still transfixed. Before her husband arrived, she felt a sharp 'pin-prick' in the top of her spine or base of her neck and noticed that the globe had disappeared. Mr Bensson found her immobile in a deeply catatonic state with the dog and cat nearby, also just stood there unmoving. The smell of sulphur filled the air. After getting his wife settled into bed, Mr Bensson returned outside with the dog to investigate. Nothing was visible but the air was tangy with the taste of ozone.

Next day Mrs Bensson awoke with a severe migraine. It persisted for five days making her feel very unwell. The jumper that she had worn had a 2-inch burn down the back where the acrylic fibres had melted. The story was reported to the police and investigated by Brigit Salgstron of UFO Sweden. The National Defence Institute agreed to test the jumper and concluded that a severe electrical discharge had melted the fibres and bonded them together. Police found several other witnesses in this rural area who attested to seeing a vivid blue light streak into the sky around 3.30 am.

A NORDIC SAGA

Investigator Anders Liljegren says this case is more like a traditional saga or myth than an extraterrestrial contact. Two men, farmer Esko Viljo and forester Aarno Heinonen, were skiing down slopes in a forest near the village of Imjarvi, Finland, at dusk on 7 January 1970. It was −17°C with a star-filled sky. They paused for a rest but heard a buzzing noise and spotted a light heading into the clearing. As it descended to treetop height the buzzing increased markedly. Now they could see a grey/red mist surrounding the ball of light.

This motif of a cloud or mist enveloping a UFO is strong in Scandinavia, but here things progressed much further. The mist spread through the area and the men saw a disc-like craft with a beam of light projecting from it. A figure was standing *inside* the beam. There was now total silence with the mist covering the whole area, making it eventually impossible for the two men to see one another. Electric sparks were being thrown from the object onto the ground. Then the beam retracted upwards, there was a huge silent explosion of light and the mist was simply 'blown apart'. The forest was left empty.

The two men were stunned by this event, but Heinonen was also feeling numb. He had been closest to the object with one side facing the glow. This side of his body was now tingling. As he took a step forward he collapsed. His legs were paralysed. Leaving their expensive skis in the woods where they fell, Viljo had to help his friend back to the village. By the time they got there both men were ill and had less than perfect memories of what had just happened. At first they recalled only the mist and light, then Heinonen said he had seen a 'distorted image' of Viljo through the lightbeam. Then they both realised it had been a strange, troll-like being, only 3 feet tall with waxy features, green clothes and gauntlets.

Viljo suffered mild effects akin to sunburn. His skin turned red and his face swelled up leaving sore eyes. The farmer received medical treatment, as did Heinonen who was more badly effected. His paralysis persisted for days, he suffered migraines, nausea, pains in his neck and passed discoloured urine. Even months later he was still under medical care suffering from urinary infections. The psychological damage, including concentration problems, affected him so badly he did not work for years.

Several doctors attested to the physical effects on both men, noting the possibility of radiation sickness. But no evidence was specifically found and soil samples taken from the area had no abnormal readings. Moreover, Heinonen went on to claim countless bizarre experiences, such as meeting a female Nordic who explained that three types of beings were visiting Earth. He claimed he had seen a 'whirlwind' and found himself in a strange room, before losing consciousness and waking on a mountain. The aliens had told him that a device had been planted inside his head to ease contact. As a side effect it had given him 'psychic powers'. He is not the only witness who has travelled down such a slippery slope of credibility after his initial encounter.[79]

One man admitted he leapt behind the sofa in panic. He described what all the others also said they felt — strange tingling sensations, a dreamy state of consciousness and an awareness that normal surroundings had disappeared and a 'weird world' had taken over.

The UFO itself was a large oval, glowing orange at the base and with central windows. A swirling mist or fog engulfed it. The thing swung and vibrated like a pendulum as it moved. Then, as if suddenly swallowed up by a large, black hole, it simply disappeared. Witnesses said they felt in a very strange state of consciousness for some time afterwards, feeling what they can only term near- religious 'ecstasy'.

ABDUCTION PATTERNS

The earliest consciously recalled abduction dates from 1963. Olaf Neilsen was walking in some woods near Halmstd, Sweden, when he was struck by a swirling sensation that made him dizzy. He floated upwards and could see a hovering object. His next memory is of being inside a room on a couchlike bed with an entity of human size and appearance nearby. This Nordic apologised for the need to abduct the man, then showed him an 'underground base' where they were building a 'magnetic shield' to protect themselves from small, ugly beings from Orion that were also coming to Earth.[78]

This obscure case is impressive for many reasons. It was documented before the first abductions (of Villas Boas and the Hills – see pages 26 and 29). It also contains many features now standard in abductions – even the recognition by the entities that another, less friendly, species was also visiting Earth.

These events were consciously recalled by the witness, as was the story of Aino Ivanoff, a young woman driving near Pudsjarvi, Finland in the early hours of 2 April 1980. A strange mist surrounded her vehicle and she 'came to' inside a room, being examined on a bed by several small entities. They talked to her by telepathy, saying that war was evil and she should join a peace group. Then they added that they could not have children and she was helping them in that regard. Budd Hopkins's first American cases of this type had yet to appear in 1980. This case was not responsible for their appearance since it was unreported in the USA. This is yet another link in the chain suggesting that more than a myth is behind these abductions.

FORMER SOVIET UNION COUNTRIES

Once the largest landmasses on Earth, this area is now divided into many individual states – some large (such as **Russia**), others small (such as **Estonia**). Since the fall of Communism it has become clear that all have had alien encounters, knowledge of which was formerly repressed.

EARLY CASES

Writing for the first Russian UFO research journal, *Aura Z*, Yury Roszius reported an event of 15 August 1663, uncovered from the St Petersburg Archaeographic Commission. The location was the Robozero Lake near the town of Belozersk. A huge ball of fire with 'beams' from the front was seen, surrounded by blue smoke. It approached with a loud noise and

Abductions 8

Alien Contacts 40

Predominant Entity Type Humanoid, with several robots

then hovered above the lake. Moving slowly across the waters, it periodically faded out and then reappeared. Many villagers, attending church, came to watch in terror and some brave peasants went after it in a boat but were driven back by an intense heat. Such was the brilliance that the beams illuminated the water right through to the lake bed and shoals of fish were seen 'fleeing' the thing. When the object disappeared, a brown film floated on the surface of the water, but this was very light and was blown away by the breeze. The authenticity of this event is not in dispute and has been traced back to contemporary testimony of one of the villagers, Lev Fyodorov.[80]

Other early encounters include the famous event in the Tunguska River area of Siberia on 30 June 1908, when something exploded in mid-air and devastated hundreds of square miles of tundra.[81] On the night of 27/28 April 1961 a similar incident occurred at Lake Onega after farmers saw an object veer across the sky, venting a green mist, near Irkutsk. At the lake itself divers found sand that had been melted to glass and a huge hole dug into the ground, indicating how the object had 'bounced' back into the air. As at Tunguska, there was no evidence that this object was a meteorite. Was this a secret Soviet disaster after an aborted attempt to reach outer space – or another UFO event?[82]

THEMES

Some UFO sightings from the former Soviet Union seem tied in with covert space operations. Military launches from the site at Plesetsk were routinely the cause of UFO scares during the 1960s. The Kremlin seem to have actively encouraged these misperceptions in order to prevent awareness of their activities.

An even more frightening event came in May 1983 when a UFO crossed secret airspace near Gorki, was tracked by radar and warned to leave the area, but did not do so. It was not intercepted. Some months later a similar event occurred over Sakhalin Island, again crossing military airspace. The same procedure was followed, but this time a Soviet fighter did shoot the 'UFO' out of the darkness. Sadly it was not a UFO at all but a Korean Airlines Boeing 747, full of civilians, that had strayed off-course. The tragedy brought short-lived condemnation from the world. Was that because the UFO connotations of this case were known to intelligence agencies, if not to the grieving relatives or the world at large?

In June 1908 something exploded over the Siberian tundra devastating miles of forest and 'frying' animals in a nuclear-like blast. Nobody knows what caused this, but some theories suggest it was an alien spacecraft, although it was most probably a comet.

ABDUCTION PATTERNS

Alien contacts in the former Soviet Union are far less common than the wealth of UFO activity would suggest. Most post-date 1984 when cosmonaut Pavel Popovich set up a commission to collect cases.

One very early alien contact, reported later, occurred in 1950 at Liiduvere, Estonia. A young girl described going to a wood after feeling an impulse to do so. Upon arrival she saw a silver egg-shape on the ground and four 'men' walking about. They were tall, essentially human with 'red' faces and communicated by telepathy, although she could not recall what they said. Upon seeing their eyes at close quarters, the girl turned and fled, looking back to find the 'egg' rising silently into the air.

Another encounter involved two youths at a physical training camp near Kaarna Lake in the summer of 1968. The details they provided, long before Western UFO literature was published in the USSR, seem impressive. They reported that the night became strangely silent and a sense of 'anticipation' and a tingling paralysis struck them. In the sky was a brightly lit, oval object that landed and was surrounded by orange beams of light. Emitting a buzzing noise the object disappeared, but a humanlike entity was seen standing where it had been. This was about 5 feet tall but vanished instantly as the witnesses went towards it. In the ground next morning, a strange, circular mark was found, as if grass had been burnt away.[83]

The first apparent abduction was reported in

The Kremlin seem to have actively encouraged misperceptions in order to prevent awareness of their activities.

May 1978 by a military officer called Anatoly. He was walking on the shores of Pyrogovskoye Lake when two beings appeared and communicated through telepathy. They were humanlike but wore suits, seemingly made of cellophane. The officer tried to persuade them to help rid the world of capitalism but they ended by trading philosophy!

The beings advised that they came from another galaxy and gave Anatoly something to sip. It was a salty, soft drink. Anatoly asked them why in their highly advanced civilisation they did not drink alcohol. They responded 'Perhaps if we did, we would not *be* such an advanced civilisation.' (The first known 'ET' joke, perhaps – and from Russia of all places!) The drink seems to have made Anatoly lose consciousness and he came to wandering by the lake, feeling as if he were still 'living inside a dream'. Despite pressure from his wife to keep silent, Anatoly reported his abduction and was predictably accused by the army of attempting to evade court martial. He escaped punishment only after thorough testing by psychologists, hypnotic regression and lie detector tests satisfied the military authorities.

UNITED KINGDOM

The UK has produced more abductions and alien contacts than most nations. The reason for this needs thought. Almost certainly it has something to do with the strong bond formed with the USA. It may be linked to the massive media exposure for all things alien. But the large size of the UFO enthusiast community is also relevant.

Abductions 87

Alien Contacts 237

Predominant Entity Type Humanoid (tall and Nordic); 'grays' (post-1987)

Britain had a wave of airship sightings a century ago, was the scene of the first known government investigation into UFOs (launched by Winston Churchill in 1912) and only missed being the country that published the first UFO book by a few weeks. This tradition has kept public awareness high.

One of the leading exponents of the alien and conspiracy theory, Tim Good (whose books attract huge advances), is British. Yet paradoxically, the UK UFO community has been reluctant to embrace the extraterrestial hypothesis (ETH). Comparing leading American and British groups shows dramatic differences. The UK fights to resolve cases almost to the point of being termed sceptical by the media (who, naturally, prefer exotic solutions). Britain has pioneered research into such topics as UAP, earthlights, plasma vortices, electromagnetic pollution as radical alternative solutions. The UK has fought shy of – even written laws to prevent – the excesses of hypnotic regression, although many of the smaller groups do still use it.

This has all affected the essence of the alien contact evidence, but has not made it disappear.

EARLY CASES

The first alien contacts of the twentieth century were very different from medical probes by aggressive 'grays'. A typical case occurred at Bournebrook in the West Midlands in 1901, when a large 'hut' with little men wearing tin helmets landed in a field and took off with a glow of electricity beneath it.

Possibly the first report of a standard entity was at Meriden, Warwickshire. Cathie Connelly described walking in fields one day in 1940, when she saw a metal dome on the ground emitting a powerful blue light. Around this were several tall Nordics with tanned skins. They appeared to be working on the craft. Passing by thinking they were 'foreigners' mending an aircraft, she looked back to see it had all vanished. Cathie later had many psychic experiences and claimed to have received messages from these aliens.[84]

A case akin to those in Scandinavia was investigated by John Llewellyn. This occurred in January 1959 near Stratford-upon-Avon. Leonard Hewins saw a red ball of fire descend to the ground, which was then surrounded by a blue hazy mist. Within this curtain of smoke three tall humanlike entities were seen and appeared to ascend into the ball. After a few moments the object turned a bright red and climbed skyward, making a sound like rushing wind and showering sparks down onto the ground.

THEMES

In autumn 1967 in Sussex, a bizarre case was reported by 'Edwin', a retired audiologist who lived in a remote house at Sedlescombe. Philip Taylor of the Royal Greenwich Observatory investigated. Edwin claimed numerous visits from thin humanoids wearing black, one-piece 'diving suits'. These beings were slightly smaller than normal. Their faces were 'grey like parchment', they had no body hair and their skin felt like 'withered leaves'. Edwin let them take plants from his garden and enter his house several times.

During his nine encounters, the aliens spoke to one another using whistling and twittering sounds, but

A memo from the British Prime Minister, Winston Churchill, demanding an enquiry into UFOs following the June 1952 invasion over Washington, DC.

Edwin ... was astonished to see that their craft did not 'take off' into the air but literally vanished ...

AN ATTACK IN EAST ANGLIA

Rendlesham Forest between Ipswich and Felixstowe in Suffolk is the location of Britain's most famous alien contact. This complex case from December 1980, involves numerous civilian and military witnesses, radar tracks, physical traces and a live tape recording made by a USAF patrol. According to some witnesses, small silver-clad entities were floating out of the UFO and passing through military trucks like ghosts.[85] But the same area produced a less well-known though still intriguing case on 21 September 1965. It was investigated by medical doctor, Bernard Finch, who was able to access hospital records.

At 10.30 pm 25-year-old Geoff Maskey was driving a car in which his friends Michael Johnson and Mavis Forsyth were passengers. They were parked in a lane after an evening out, when Johnson suddenly leapt from the car and headed into the bushes. Minutes later the other two occupants heard a high pitched humming/whistling noise and the whole lane lit up with an orange glow coming from a large oval mass. Desperate to find their friend they reversed the car at speed and suddenly he staggered from the undergrowth clutching his neck, then crashed to the ground unconscious. Maskey drove him straight to the local hospital, where he regained consciousness a little later, rambling incoherently about a noise, a light and how something was trying to 'get him'.

Doctors found that the man's neck was burnt and he was in severe shock. Transferred to a bigger hospital in Ipswich, after 24 hours he seemingly recovered. All

he could recall was that he had felt an 'urge' to leave the car and when in the bushes a huge object had swooped at him. A shadow 'man' had been behind the orange glow.[86] During that same week, ten other alien encounters were reported, including one at Derby while Michael Johnson was in hospital. It was reported immediately by the *Evening Telegraph*. Two men walking down a footpath had heard a whining noise and then seen a round object 'rush down' on them. Behind a green glow in the object a shadowy figure could be seen.[87]

Dr Finch had already been pursuing an incident that had happened one week earlier at 1.00 am on 14 September, just 20 miles away from Felixstowe at Mersea Island. Here engineer Paul Green, returning by motor-cycle from a visit to see his fiancée, had reported hearing a high-pitched humming that had grown to an intense buzzing noise as a blue light approached across the coastal marshes near Langenhoe. The motorcycle engine had spluttered, then stopped and the lights had failed. Clambering off his bike, Green had stared at the blue light – now seen to be inside a dome on top of a flat disc. His skin was tingling, as though from an electric shock, he felt paralysed and his head was hurting as if a tight band were clasped around it. With a massive effort he had grabbed the bike and stumbled down the road, relieved when the engine had restarted. Next day his clothes and hair had been so full of static that they crackled each time he had touched them.[88]

never to Edwin. Edwin drew a map of the solar system and asked them to point to their home. They marked a spot well beyond Pluto. But this was the only attempt at communication, although they did indicate an interest in taking Edwin's pet dog with them. After much effort Edwin persuaded them to take a china ornament instead! In return he was given what appeared to be several uncut diamonds. Edwin defied an odd ban on watching the entities leave and was astonished to see that their cone-shaped craft did not 'take off' into the air but literally vanished on the spot.

Taylor was able to verify every aspect of Edwin's story that it was possible to check. The witness still had the 'diamonds' but noted that they were not what they seemed to be. A London merchant confirmed that they were 'probably quartz' and had a specific gravity of 2.64. This gift was also sent to the Institute of Geological Studies. The 'diamonds' were indeed proved worthless – being *terrestrial* pieces of glassy quartz.

ABDUCTION PATTERNS

In my UK database traditional abductions are outnumbered by bedroom visitor cases that have no sign of a UFO, but are psychic-orientated tales. Other forms of contact that might, for instance, be termed as near-death visions occur too. They appear to form a continuum.

However, American-style abductions, such as those at Aveley in 1974 (see page 40) and at Todmorden in 1980 (see page 44) *have* occurred in Britain. About 25 are on file, ranging up to an incident in Telford in 1981, in which three women were abducted together from their car and later separately hypnotised (see page 97).[89]

Most cases of this sort involve hypnotic regression and depend upon single witnesses. About 70 per cent of the UK witnesses are female, whereas in routine UFO sightings about 70 per cent are male. Abductions are significantly different in other respects too. There are often two types of entity together. One is a humanoid, sometimes akin to the Nordics and at times described as female with long, white hair. The other is small, sometimes robotic. Although most recent cases *do* now feature 'grays', before 1987 very few were reported.

An exception was the October 1984 sighting by Roy, a design engineer from Altrincham in Cheshire and a typical visually gifted man with a history of poltergeist and strange experiences. He saw a small, thin entity with a white-skinned face wearing a tight, black diver's suit. He described the face as long and pointed at the chin. Indeed, not having heard of 'grays', Roy amusingly noted that it resembled entertainer Bruce Forsyth! The entity appeared twice. The first occasion was in his bedroom as Roy awoke at dawn. It was inspecting Roy's alarm clock and vanished on seeing him. The second time was in Roy's office, when a 'flashback' image imposed itself onto Roy's mind and effectively took over reality for a while.

Invaluable clues were offered by both episodes. Both had occurred during altered states of consciousness (in the office Roy had been idling on 'automatic pilot'). The bedroom entity had just vanished, but Roy noted that no air had rushed in to plug the gap as it ought to do if the figure had occupied

American-style abductions have occurred in Britain. About 25 are on file ...

real space. This inferred that it had been an hallucination. But to see the figure in his bedroom, Roy had had to 'screw up' his eyes to bring it into focus. Was this – he mused – because he had not been wearing his spectacles? If so, how can an hallucination be affected by poor eyesight? Could it have been a perception *inside* the brain?

TAKING A LEEK

Impressive cases continue, but many witnesses fear public ridicule. Bill, a successful businessman, encountered a golden light at 1.30 am on 16 June 1991 near Leek in Staffordshire. This stalled his car and he was 'swooped upon' by the UFO, triggering migraine-like head pains. Bill recovered consciousness an hour later, with half his clothing missing and his trousers emitting powerful sparks of electrostatic charge when he brushed himself down.

BABY BLUES

The ultimate in abduction stories is the kind that was reported by Corinne, a woman in her early 30s from Birmingham. Her experiences began in the 1970s, when she was just a child and display a vast array of paranormal phenomena. Her parents can also recall a couple of significant incidents where they found their daughter in what appears to be a catatonic trance. She was so 'deeply asleep', that she could not be woken and they thought she had died.

At just 18 months of age, Corinne terrified the family by screaming that a 'little man' had floated outside her window at night. In subsequent dreams (or sightings) she saw more. He was child-sized with a white face and coal black eyes. Then, as she grew older, Corinne 'knew' that there was some sort of rapport with this being, 'he knew me but I did not know how'. By her teenage years her 'dreams' of the aliens were so vivid that she had developed a way to handle them. Once when several of the beings had floated into her bedroom, Corinne grabbed a can of hairspray from the bedside table and used it as a weapon to send them packing! When she was 18, the experiences became different. Now she had

horrible dreams in which 'they' made her give birth to a super-intelligent baby. This baby had wrinkled skin, thin hair and ugly features. They explained that it was a 'hybrid' of human and alien DNA and she had to look after it. Corinne denied any reality for these later experiences, insisting they were merely 'Frankenstein' nightmares. But she was more open to the actual reality of the aliens themselves.

Corinne is not the only British woman to describe things like this to me. Although sworn to secrecy by most witnesses, I can report that in five cases I have come across similar stories of alien-human hybrid babies. Indeed, in four cases women have reported suffering a spontaneous abortion or what appeared to be some form of phantom pregnancy in the weeks following their abduction. It is hard to regard this as merely a coincidence because none of these women were seeking publicity and all were frankly petrified of their families finding out, in case they were accused of improper sexual liaisons that they swear did not take place. The pregnancies were not the result of relations with a boyfriend – at least not any they could remember!

NORTH AMERICA

North America, and in particular the USA, has fathered, mothered, reared and fostered the alien abduction mystery. This is not merely because there are more cases there than anywhere else. America has been the leader in science and technology during the twentieth century, as is manifest in its space-research programme. Most searches for radio signals from space (so far fruitless) have originated in the USA. The mass media and movie industry, which has taken aliens to its heart, is rooted in the USA.

Unfortunately, this has all achieved something insidious. America is xenophobic. Its UFO knowledge of alien contact beyond its shores is minimal. Elsewhere, such as in Europe, that is less true.

Although there is no question that the story of alien contact is global, the many differences that are significant have been smoothed away by the American style of alien. American books, movies, TV programmes and cases have been promoted so extensively that they are accepted as the norm. The inevitable outcome has been that in 1999 there is far *less* variety in cases than in 1989, and certainly less than was visible in 1979. The American prototypical story – of 'grays' abducting humans to perform medical examinations – has taken over the world. This kind of tale was once far less important (even in the USA). The emphasis placed upon it by UFOlogists and the media has changed all that.

CANADA

EARLY CASES

Canada shares much culture with the USA and yet also with Europe (notably France and Britain). Do alien contacts follow any national pattern?

One interesting event happened near Nipawin in Saskatchewan one night in summer 1933. In response to a series of sightings of orange lights, two men and a woman drove out to a local marshland to investigate. This frontier settlement comprised of farmers trying to breathe life into the rough soil. The lights had been dismissed as a natural phenomenon – gaseous vapours associated with the marsh – but as the three witnesses closed in by pick-up truck, they saw a landed, disc-shaped craft with a ladder.

Standing nearby were several men, apparently small humanoids. They wore silver, one-piece suits with ski caps and were engaged in what looked like

Abductions 27

Alien Contacts 58

Predominant Entity Type Humanoid (often small); 'grays' now common repair work. The area surrounding the UFO was 'deathly silent'. Realising that they could not reach the craft, the witnesses tried to find a way around the marsh but by the time they did so, were low on fuel and had to return. Two nights later with proper equipment, including a camera, they went back. The UFO had gone. There were, however, marks on the ground, including foot-prints.[90]

THEMES

On 17 November 1967 at Calgary, Alberta, David Seewalt lost 40 minutes during a walk home from visiting a friend. His sister recalled him rushing in and hiding under the bed, screaming that a flying saucer had chased him. A missing shoe later turned up on the road. Investigator W.K. Allan confirmed within a couple of days that David was in an emotional state.

Entities with skin like a crocodile took his clothes off. The witness was too terrified to continue with the regression.

Five months later David woke from a vivid nightmare with his memory about the missing 40 minutes returned. A dental surgeon used hypnosis to 'flesh out' the details – this being Canada's first case to use such a method. In his new recall, David told of hearing a high-pitched humming noise, then being lifted up by an orange beam and placed on a table in a room filled

SEND IN THE CLONES

One of Canada's most bizarre cases is the saga of a Vancouver woman, Alvina Scott. This case has been probed extensively by Lorne Goldfader of UFORIC.[92] Alvina first encountered aliens called 'Hoova' in July 1985. This was while she was living near a hydroelectric plant. They allegedly floated her through a bedroom window to a room where they removed ova samples ('to examine them'). At the same time they performed surgery (dressed in what appeared to be 'doctors' clothes') and placed an implant into her kidney to ease pain. Her GP, who was considering an operation to remove the organ, was reputedly astonished to find from an ultra-sound a now healthy kidney. Sadly the implant 'flushed out through the urinary tract' before she got to hospital. Around this time Alvina

also suffered a mysterious miscarriage.

The Hoova at first appeared human, but Alvina went on to experience a long series of abductions by them and discovered that they were in fact 'grays', with the large heads and huge wrap-around eyes. The human form was an 'hypnotic projection they used to put an abductee more at ease'. Most of her recall was conscious, although some hypnosis was used to clarify this.

Hoova 'cloned' soulless bodies (kept in large vats) so that when their original's organs wore out they could replace them from their waiting clone! This was part of a genetic project that mixed human and alien DNA. Indeed in 1987 Alvina claimed that a Nordic appeared in her bedroom – this being an alien 'grown in four days' using human genes.

with computers. Entities with skin like a crocodile took his clothes off. The witness was too terrified to continue with the regression.

However, David *was* regressed later, as an experiment by the psychology department of the University of Calgary. In that session he recalled in detail emergency surgery received for appendicitis while at primary school. Years later, under hypnosis and in a UFO context, had he thus remembered (or imagined) the time when he truly was under deep anaesthetic, including the way that his body was cut open and how one orderly had 'wrinkled skin'? Was this the trigger for his later abduction fantasy?[91]

Note just how many alleged abduction memories retrieved by hypnosis relate to witnesses encountering entities in masks or gowns, standing by a table in a brightly lit room using medical probes. One has to wonder if subconscious recall of real life surgery might have triggered many other cases.

USA

EARLY CASES

There were a number of dubious 'spaceman' stories during the airship waves of 1896 and 1897, including claims that the body of a dead UFO pilot was buried in a graveyard at Aurora, Texas. These were often inventions of the media.

Abductions 1,272
Alien Contacts Over 3,000
Predominant Entity Type Humanoid (small); 'grays' (post-1970)

Researcher Ted Bloecher's alien sightings catalogue, *Humcat*, records many interesting early reports. One of the first, dated spring 1910, tells of a sighting at Baltimore, Maryland. Lawrence Crone was playing on a baseball diamond when a dark cigar-like craft drifted over. Through windows some strange little men were seen 'staring' at him. Gradually the cases blend into a pattern of fly-by missions where entities stayed behind windows in craft or were disturbed on the ground and fled. There is no sign of an abduction theme.

On 19 August 1949 (in one of the earliest cases that was provably recorded on the day of occurrence) two prospectors in Death Valley, California, claimed they saw a disc-like craft crash-land. Two dwarflike entities, who were otherwise normal in appearance, leapt out. The prospectors gave chase but lost the aliens amidst desert sand dunes. When they returned to the scene the UFO had vanished.[93]

The first sign of a typical 'gray' dates to October 1944, but was only reported in a letter to Dr J Allen Hynek sent 36 years *after* these entities had begun to dominate UFO lore. However, the witness claims it was a family secret for many years and was told, by his parents, not to discuss the events.

Allegedly the family, who lived at Rochester, Pennsylvania, were awoken by a loud humming in the early hours. The father went to investigate and dis-

Perhaps the best-known US case involved pictures of the wreckage of a crashed UFO found at Roswell, New Mexico, July 1947, which the USAF said was debris from a weather balloon [opposite]. Many still believe today that this was part of a government cover up.

covered a bright glow and several beings about 4½ feet tall. One was dressed in a strange robe, the others wore 'metal suits'. All had a large head and a mouth that was just a slit. The beings ordered the witness to follow them out towards their craft.

Another case involving 'grays' and recorded when it happened occurred on 3 July 1955. Mrs Symmonds was driving from Ohio to Florida for the

BEHIND THE FACADE

Modern American UFO research struggles to take account of the psychic dimensions of the witness. Yet before alien genetic experiments came to the fore, the USA led the way in this field.

One case came on 25 November 1964 at New Berlin, in rural New York. The witnesses were the then 20-year-old wife of a chemical engineer and her mother-in-law. At about 12.45 am Mary went to look out at the surrounding hills as it was a beautiful night with a moon and many stars. After watching a meteor she then saw something much brighter glide across the landscape and land on the hills.

Her mother-in-law, who had got up to go to the toilet, was called out and for the next *four hours* they watched in fascination through binoculars as a dozen men conducted repairs on this craft. They were 7-feet-tall humanoids. Next day, Mary led her sceptical husband into the open fields of hay and alfalfa and easily found the landing site. Heavy indentations in a triangular formation were visible.

The witnesses made no attempt to go public with the story, but such a long sighting suggests an explanation (helicopters fixing power lines spring to my mind immediately). Psychiatrist Dr Berthold Schwarz subjected the witnesses to a barrage of psychological probes and hypnotic regression. The process revealed no hidden features to the case, such as an abduction. This 'failure' occurs in only a few cases.

However, what did emerge from this study was that Mary had a lifelong history of paranormal phenomena. This included telepathy and precognition. She had also experienced sleepwalking effects. Most intriguing was an incident five years before the sighting. This was recorded by Schwarz in 1973, thus predating the now famous 1975 book by psychiatrist Ray Moody often said to have introduced the world to the near-death experience – the NDE.[95]

Mary had had her own NDE after suffering a severe asthma attack on 25 December 1959. In bed with her inhaler, fighting for breath, she had suddenly found herself 'out of the body'. Then free and without pain, Mary had seen the ceiling 'vanish' and she had floated towards a bright light. Here she had met many people wearing robes. One was her dead grandfather, who had given her the choice to go into the light and 'die' or return to her body and use her life to 'do a job'. She went back.[96]

This is by no means the only time that an NDE and alien contact are tied together by a single witness. In one 1964 British case a man in a dentist's chair at Middlesbrough reacted badly to the anaesthetic and saw himself float through the ceiling into a strange room where he also met robed figures. He assumed them to be aliens in a UFO, not dead relatives at the gates of heaven. He had to fight back to his body resisting attempts by 'little creatures' to possess him. The dentist said that he briefly stopped breathing.

holidays. Passing Stockton, Georgia she encountered four entities beside the road. She described them as smaller than normal people but with 'large, bulging eyes … no visible mouth, a long pointed nose and a chin that came to a sharp point. Its long thin arms ended in claw-like appendages.' But there was no UFO, nor contact. One entity merely held what appeared to be a stick as the witness drove by.[94]

THEMES

Things changed from 1965 via publication of the Hill abduction (see page 29) and studies into cases such as those of Herb Schirmer in 1967 (see page 34) and Pascagoula in 1973 (see page 38). But these events had no sudden impact. Not until there was a widespread quest for hidden abductions, triggered by the use of regression hypnosis, did the pattern of today emerge and the New Berlin type of case (see opposite) fade. This process of transformation is significant. One might argue that 'grays' were subconscious fantasies unleashed onto the world by over-exuberant investigators. Do they mask the more gentle form of ongoing contact, still found in parts of the world where such a passion to unearth horrific kidnaps has yet to take hold?

One might argue that 'grays' were subconscious fantasies unleashed onto the world by over-exuberant investigators.

When contact occurred in the USA *before* the 'grays' appeared, it was of the more civilised European type and not the 'grab 'em and prod 'em' style now common. For example, in a letter to the group MUFON (Mutual UFO Network), dated March 1976, Mary Kleros reported how she was driving near Norwalk, Connecticut in summer 1973. Her radio began to fill with static and she suddenly 'found herself' inside a strange room with a tall, blond-haired Nordic type of being. He communicated by telepathy telling her 'welcome my friend' and promising future meetings. She was shown scenes of 'space' and warned that severe flooding would occur locally (as it later did) and that the friendly helpful visitors were from 'the galaxy Guentatori-Elfi'.

ABDUCTION TRENDS

On 26 November 1972 a 28-year-old woman named Judy was driving home at 8.00 pm near Zamora, California. She recalled crossing Cache Creek Bridge then nothing until reaching home at midnight to find her parents frantic. Hypnosis in 1976 by Dr William McCall revealed a detailed story. The car was surrounded by a dark void and Judy 'floated' out, regaining awareness in a brightly lit 'room' circled by stars. The entities that were nearby had eyes like insects and pale, translucent skin. But there was also a normal human woman acting to calm the witness. A traumatic physical examination followed, that involved a urinary catheter being inserted. She also suffered acute pains in her head, struggled to breathe and at one point was unable to see for a time. She kept asking about her sisters who had been in the car but was unsure what happened to them. Then she found herself 'falling' into the car seat and driving the 10 miles home to be greeted by her worried family. The idea of advanced aliens using a catheter seems absurd. Is this another hint that hypnotic recall brings out memories of real-life surgical trauma disguised as an abduction?[97]

Of key significance are abductions that involved multiple witnesses. On 6 January 1976 three women were driving by car from Liberty near Stanford, Kentucky. They were each regressed by Dr Leo Sprinkle. Their recall of what happened during the missing time after seeing a strange light was not identical. Forty-four-year-old Louise Smith had little memory, except of being held in

EYEWITNESS ARTWORK   **DATE 06/01/1976**

Elaine's drawing of examination by aliens (top left); Louise Smith, Elaine Thomas and Mona Stafford who believed they were abducted in Kentucky on 6 January 1976 (above); Mona's drawing of the UFO which abducted them (right).

a sort of limbo. Her 48-year-old friend, Elaine Thomas, spoke only of seeing strange little beings who appeared merely to be observing. But the youngest occupant of the car, 35-year-old Mona Stafford, found herself being medically probed whilst strapped onto a bed. The entities twisted her feet, hurt her eyes and she felt her 'insides' being blown up as if by a tube.

An extraordinary sequel to this case occurred on 16 July 1981, 3,000 miles away near Telford, England. Again three women in a car saw a UFO, suffered missing time and later, under hypnosis, relived different memories of the event. Valerie Walters, like Louise Smith, was held in a void by Nordics who took interest in her clothing. Rosemary Hawkins, emulating Elaine Thomas, was observed by little entities. But, in a re-run of Mona Stafford's abduction, Viv Hayward was medically probed by 'grays' and suffered frightening internal sensations as her body was investigated. The links between these two cases are chilling.

Another impressive multiple witness case from the USA involved four men in their 20s, two of whom were identical twins. They were on a camping trip down the Allagash River of Maine when they had a close encounter. This occurred while the men were night fishing by canoe on 26 August 1976.

Chuck Rak called to the others (Charlie Foltz and the Weiner twins, Jack and Jim) after a strange sensation of being watched. This was quickly followed by the sight of an oval object rising from some trees behind them. A rippling set of colour changes like 'paths of energy' were seen on the body of the object and it was said to resemble hot sauce coming to the boil in a pan. After shining a flashlight towards the object it reacted by heading straight for the canoe. A searchlight emerged and crossed the water. Despite frantic paddling to try to reach their camp the beam engulfed the boat and reality changed.

Charlie had no more memory until wading to shore, with the object departing an unknown time later. Chuck recalled the others leaping out as he stood in the boat staring in awe at the UFO. The twins describe a discontinuity between being caught by the light then standing on the shore looking straight up at the hovering object as it sped away. Only when they reached their campsite did the witnesses realise the big problem. The previously well-lit fire was reduced to a pile of glowing embers.

After the experience all the men, but in particular Jim Weiner, had experiences of a 'psychic' nature. These included apparitions in the bedroom, floating feelings and, in Jim's case, a sensation of something happening to his genitals. These were only connected with the UFO episode around 1986 by a doctor treating Jim after a head injury and what appeared to be resultant epilepsy.

Between 1989 and 1991 under the careful supervision of experienced UFOlogist Ray Fowler, all four men were regressed. Each described mutually consistent stories of being floated into the UFO and examined on a table by small creatures with over-sized heads, pointed chins and huge, dark eyes. They took samples of skin, body fluids and sperm using telepathy to keep the men calm. Then the stunned witnesses were 'tested' by walking through a 'portal' before being floated back down into their canoe.[98]

The epidemic of abductions shows no sign of abating in the USA. MUFON investigator Beverly Trout reports a series of events that came to her. They began on 7 August 1997 at Sioux City, Iowa, Frank, 22, was driving 11-year-old Justin to stay with his grand-mother, 50-year-old Brenda. During the drive through the wooded, ravined canyon of Stone Park they had a terrifying experience. This involved being chased by a triangular object and the car being hit by a strange creature with huge eyes.

Upon arrival both Frank and Justin were terrified. Brenda was worried because the 15-minute drive had taken over an hour! She stood on the doorstep

> *Each described ... being floated into the UFO and examined ... by small creatures with over-sized heads, pointed chins and huge, dark eyes.*

ROCKY MOUNTAIN HIGH

Dr Richard Sigismonde lives in Boulder, Colorado, perched on the edge of the mountains amid stunningly clear air outside Denver. As a social psychologist he had become involved in UFOs by default, when between 1967 and 1969 his university was given a government grant to study the mystery and – it would seem – dispose of the problem. In 1983 I stayed (with Allen Hynek) at Sigismonde's beautiful home during a long, cross-country drive. The doctor had a fascinating abduction enquiry to report.

On 19 November 1980, Michael and his wife Mary were driving just before midnight to the town of Longmont. Suddenly a blue beam of light appeared and there was a whistling, whooshing noise like displaced air. It approached the car, the headlights began to fade and the radio emitted static. Then the car began to float off the road into the sky. Just as quickly, the experience ended and the couple were driving onward, with the UFO now gone. Looking at their watches it was 12.55 am – an hour later!

After reporting the matter to Dr Sigismonde there was silence for some months. The psychologist wished to arrange separate hypnotic regressions for both witnesses, but, as he was later to learn, Mary became seriously ill in the wake of the encounter. A red patch had formed on her abdomen within hours and it was then discovered that she was pregnant. The pregnancy was revealed when she was rushed to hospital suffering from what was assumed to be pneumonia brought on by some kind of infection. She was so ill that for a few days her life was threatened. However, she pulled through and, even more remarkably, the child survived – although born premature the following spring.

When this trauma ended Michael agreed to be regressed, but Mary had linked the two events in her mind and preferred to put *both* behind her. Under hypnosis, Michael recalled how the car was surrounded by a glowing mist and a strong smell 'like arcing electricity'. The UFO projected a 'ladder' and at the end

... they had a terrifying experience. This involved being chased by a triangular object and the car being hit by a strange creature ...

berating them about their claims, saying that there was no UFO. But they pointed towards an orange object in the sky, out of which 'little globes' were emerging. This soon vanished but all three witnesses set off in their car trying to find it again.

That night Justin woke from a nightmare. He saw hands touching him and felt himself paralysed as he was put onto a 'couch' and then a needle appeared. Checks into the boy's past revealed that he had often had visionary encounters with strange beings that he called 'angels' but did not consider friendly. These had entered his bedroom. Other 'paranormal' episodes had even led to his parents arranging for a psychiatric counselling session. But nothing had been found 'wrong' prior to the UFO sighting.

As I write no hypnosis has been conducted and this case remains in the sort of limbo that thousands of other 'possible abductions' face. As Beverly Trout reports 'we, as investigators, are left with more questions than answers'.[99]

was a small humanoid that beckoned the couple aboard. It had a 'long head, bald with grey skin'. The chin was pointed. As a gifted artist (as are so many abductees) Michael was able to sketch the entity. Finding himself naked, he was then placed on a long table inside a strange room and examined. He felt burning sensations in his legs and as if his mind was emptied, scanned, then replaced with 'something' new.

The UFOs being associated with wind-like noises and lifting cars off roads, as in this case, has often been reported. The electrical distortions and smells induced into the atmosphere as if the air was being short-circuited or charged up in some way are also common. Descriptions of clouds or mists that envelop cars and trigger the close encounter are far more frequent than one would realise, since most of the literature focuses not on floating clouds but alleged starships. Hoaxers would follow the media line, but most authentic cases report a less-known, more ill-defined reality.

Following his return to the car after the abduction Michael stopped at a garage. But that night he felt very odd, wandering around totally disorientated. It was as if he were 'not all there'. The attendant at the filling station, seeing his lack of balance, eyed him with scorn, sensing that he might be drunk. But Michael just had no body co-ordination and was behaving like one does after coming round from an anaesthetic. Indeed he walked straight into the door jamb in his futile efforts to negotiate the filling station exit, causing him considerable embarrassment. Such feelings and behaviour are common after an abduction.

Indeed, in August 1992, one family who lost time and suffered the 'Oz Factor' on their Saturday morning shopping trip faced a terrifying consequence. After their encounter with a strange mist their body co-ordination was so poor that they could not grip the car door handles. They felt so odd that for a time they actually considered the possibility that they had died and were no longer part of the real world.

SOUTH AMERICA

South America is rather an enigma. Some countries, such as **Uruguay**, have yet to produce abductions. Others, particularly **Argentina** and **Brazil**, have so many that only the USA can boast more. **Venezuela** had many encounters with 'hairy dwarfs' – akin to goblins or trolls – but little recently.

Mexico is an interesting study, because it became obsessed with UFOs in the 1990s and often features regularly on TV shows about the paranormal. But this attention is almost exclusively concerned with strange lights, odd craft and dubious photography, not abductions.

There is also a strong culture of mystical races from the past, with the Inca and Aztec civilisations building renowned structures. The belief that this part of the world played host to alien voyagers centuries ago remains strong. The 'cloud people' built cities in the mountains amidst the Amazon. They had an advanced civilisation and were tall, fair haired and magical – like many modern day aliens!

Unfortunately, the media of South America can spin tall tales so well the borderline between reality and fiction is often blurred. A story is reported because it is good, regardless of verification as true. One South American claim, for example was that an alien ray had turned a witness's son into a green lump that was mistaken for an olive and drunk with a martini by the investigating police officer! Amusing certainly, but don't bet your mortgage on it.

ARGENTINA
EARLY CASES

The first case, certainly reported at the time, occurred on 18 March 1950 at Lago Argentino. Rancher Wilfredo Arevalo claimed to have seen a disc land with a second object hovering above. Rushing to investigate, he found the landed object

Abductions 117

Alien Contacts Over 1,000

Predominant Entity Type Humanoid (tall), with Nordic features

covered in a bluish/green glow that smelled like benzene. Through a transparent section were four tall men dressed in cellophane. They were feverishly working on instruments. On seeing Arevalo's presence, a blue 'spotlight' was shone and flames emerged from the rear of the craft. Then – accompanied by its hovering cousin – the UFO shot away leaving a trail of gas. Next day Arevalo went to the spot with ranch-hands and found a burnt circle of grass, prompting a report to an air force base.[100]

One of the most active hot spots for UFO activity in the country is around Salto. A classic case here, on 18 February 1977, involved rancher Angel

Tonna, his family and their farm-hands who were herding cattle at 4.00 am when the generator failed and the barn lights went out. Going to investigate with an ex-police-dog, Topo, a Saturn-shaped, orange mass was seen near the barn. The cows were going crazy and the rotating object was emitting near tornado-force winds, ripping branches off nearby trees.

Topo bravely flew at the invader but when 15 feet away began to howl and crashed to the ground. What looked like 'lightning bolts' were earthing themselves beneath the thing and a wave of heat struck Tonna as he went to the aid of his dog. Waves of heat were accompanied by electrical tingles. Tonna was left with a severe skin rash. Even less fortunate was Topo. After refusing to eat for three days, the dog was found dead at the site of the incident, where a scorched circle was left in the grass. An autopsy by the local vet found that Topo had been 'cooked' inside as if by a microwave. Blood vessels had ruptured.

THEMES

Argentina has produced many alleged 'teleportations', where after encountering glowing clouds drivers claim to be suddenly transported – Star Trek-fashion – to some distant spot. In one case a journey to Mexico City was claimed – a huge distance impossible to drive by normal means in the time available. The stunned car occupants presented themselves at the Argentine consulate desperate to get home![101]

In December 1963 at Resistencia, the three-man footplate crew of a freight train arriving from Presidencia La Plaza met a being that was 7 feet tall. It stood on the line ahead, looking human with long, blond hair. Unable to avert imminent tragedy, the men looked on in horror, but then the being floated upwards as their thundering locomotive was seconds from a collision. As if 'picked up by a whirl-wind' the figure climbed into the sky. A few hundred yards away in the nearby town, Justo Masin and his son were eating in their garden when, as they told police, a strange, tall man with blond hair floated over their heads.

In a more famous case, at Trancas on 21 October 1963, the alien trainspotters laid siege to a trackside farmhouse, emerging from floating tubes and discs and hovering about the lines as if daring trains to flatten them. Searchlight beams were projected from the alien craft onto the house.[102]

ABDUCTION TRENDS

Possibly the first abduction involved building worker Gilberto Ciccioli from Buenos Aires. At 3.15 am on 4 October 1972 he was awoken by what he assumed was his dog returning to the house. But as he reached the door a blinding light struck from above. Ciccioli was immediately unconscious and awoke in a room he calls 'the laboratory'. There was no way to tell how he got there or whether he was in some craft or in a room on Earth. With Ciccioli were several tall beings with thin features.

The entities performed medical experiments on Ciccioli-taking a sample of blood with a 'pencil' from one of his fingers but without causing any pain. They also collected the expected sperm samples. Then his memory faded again until he regained his senses, on the floor inside his house. It was 3.55 am some 40 minutes having passed. After this experience Ciccioli noticed that his dog did eventually return but was far less keen to go out than before. He, himself, developed an acute intuition, accompanied by a curious itchy sensation on his neck. He also found himself fascinated by subjects such as philosophy and physics despite having had no educational background or prior interest in such fields.[103]

EYEWITNESS ARTWORK   DATE 05/01/1975

Another abduction soon after the Ciccioli affair came on 5 January 1975. Railway worker, Carlos Diaz was returning home after a moonlighting job as a waiter to help raise his young son. At 4.00 am, walking the streets of Bahia Blanca, he was struck by a bluish light. Immediately he felt a floating sensation. His next memory was of being inside a strange room, feeling dizzy and sick. A tall entity appeared dressed in a one-piece suit with a balaclava. It seems identical to the beings that abducted a whole family at Aveley, Essex, ten weeks earlier (see page 40), although that case was then unknown even in the UK. A medical examination of Diaz followed, with a suction tube being used to extract tufts of hair. At one point Diaz touched the entity and said that it had a texture rather like rubber. After a second 'blackout', he found himself awaking by a roadside. His watch had stopped at 3.50 am but he soon established that it was now four hours later. A passing motorist saw his dazed condition and, thinking he had been hit by a car, took him to a nearby hotel. It was only then that Diaz realised he was not in Bahia Blanca but in Retiro – 300 miles away!

An artist's impression of the abduction described by Carlos Alberto Diaz (see inset) which took place at Bahia Blanca, Argentina on 5 January 1975.

Back at home his wife was already frantic with worry and relieved when the police phoned to reveal that her husband was safe. The authorities sought some evidence of foul play, such as kidnapping and robbery, but failed. Diaz was tested by psychiatrists at the local hospital whilst his wife made the eight-hour train journey to be by his bedside. The doctors could only confirm that hair was missing at the roots. Police found another piece of supporting evidence. Just before he was attacked Diaz had bought a newspaper that had been printed in Bahia Blanca that night. He still had it, but at 8.00 am this could not yet have been bought in Retiro as the supplies took some hours to reach that town.[104]

BRAZIL

EARLY CASES

Brazil has produced an assortment of modern horror tales. They include the gruesome death of a hunter at Aracariguama in 1946, supposedly struck by a beam of light that made his flesh 'peel away'. Witnesses say he 'liquified' to a gooey mess and had to be taken to hospital in a handcart.

Some of these tales are sure to be media fabrications. They are certainly unique to this part of the world. But in 1988 scientist Jacques Vallee reinvestigated some reports from north-east Brazil, trekking for days to the remote Amazon village of Parnarama where many witnesses had been 'attacked' by blinding lights and made ill, suffering burns and convulsions. Several, he discovered, had died from the resultant shock. So there *has* been some verification of these extreme events.[105]

In March 1954 Rubem Hellwig learnt from the aliens why they were so interested in Brazil. Near Santa Maria, he stopped his car when a giant 'melon' landed. Nearby were two, tall, slim entities who were collecting grass samples. These beings spoke in a curious language but as they did so he 'understood' their words inside his head. They were seeking ammonia, he gathered. The UFO departed with blue and yellow flames, but returned next day at which time he was able to study the entities better. They had cat-like eyes and long, black hair. These aliens claimed to be scientists who were attracted by the natural wealth of minerals in the continent. They commended Hellwig for not running away as most witnesses did!

November/December 1954 – immediately after the very first major wave in Europe – brought a massive number of alien sightings to Brazil. A typical case was that of a farmer at Linha Bela Vista who heard a noise 'like a sewing machine' as he tended his maize crop on 9 December. His farm animals went crazy and then a hat-shaped craft surrounded in a hazy mist appeared above the ground. Three entities got out – Nordics in every detail – and one picked up a hoe, dropped by the astonished farmer, looked at it, smiled and handed it back to him. Then, taking some crop samples, the UFO shot away.[106]

ABDUCTION TRENDS

Once South America began to establish a pattern of abductions in the early 1970s, Brazil soon adopted the theme. A typical early case occurred on 3 March 1978. Eighteen-year-old Jose Alvaro was walking through the late-night streets of Fragata Pelotas to check that a property had been locked because the owner was away. Suddenly a blue beam of light appeared in the sky and within moments he lost consciousness.

Alvaro awoke 'in a daze' with mysterious images running through his head. There were pictures of war and a voice telling him inexplicably that 'the task' was now accomplished. Thinking he was dreaming, he slapped himself to make sure he was awake. He was amazed to discover that it was 4.00 am. Alvaro was soon under the care of psychologist Dr Palmor Carapecos and was one of the first South American abductees to be subjected to hypnosis. In these sessions, he recalled suddenly finding himself in a strange room with a tall, silver-haired entity who was female. She told Alvaro that they were to 'breed'

SEEKING CONTACT

The major Brazilian wave of 1957 was important as it brought the first reported modern abduction – that of Antonio Villas Boas and his alluring female captor (see page 26). But this case – in October – came after a series of events.

One impressive report in July was by Professor Joao de Freitas Guimaraes, a lawyer and member of the Catholic Faculty at Santos. He was sitting by the beach at Sao Sebastiao when a hat-shaped craft landed nearby and two tall Nordics got out. Despite trying his best to give a friendly greeting (using Portuguese, Spanish, Italian, French and English!) the entities made no response. But he felt a telepathic impression that they wanted him to 'come aboard'. He followed them into the device, noting that they leapt very easily inside. Once there he was taken for a flight into orbit and learned that they were intent on warning us to beware of the dangers of eliminating our own species.[107]

However, more violent attacks were also recorded. On 22 May 1973 Onilson Patero, a sales rep, was driving home at 3.00 am on the road from Itajobi to Catanduva amidst pouring rain. Suddenly a mass of static filled the radio eventually blotting it out. The car engine failed and a blinding light appeared above. Patero coasted to the roadside,

His farm animals went crazy and then a hat-shaped craft surrounded in a hazy mist appeared above the ground.

shielding his eyes from the blue glow. Almost falling out of the car, he was now surrounded by a spotlight beam projecting from an oval object. A suffocating pressure surrounded him but Patero could not escape. Looking at the car, he could see that the glow made the vehicle body transparent by some extraordinary means. Then he fell to the ground unconscious.

Patero was found face down in the mud by two passersby, who assumed his car had crashed and he was dead. Only when the highway patrol arrived, was it realised that the man was alive. He screamed that 'they' were after him. Assuming he was insane, he was sent to a local hospital where after several hours of tests by a psychiatrist he was allowed home. During the next few days, Patero suffered severe physical trauma, including bruises and spots that appeared on his skin and a dramatic darkening of his hair. Dr Elias Chediak at the Padre Albino hospital verified the strange burns saying they were 'caused by some strange rays'. Later police confirmed that they had other local reports of the glowing UFO but with two beings seen inside. On 26 April 1974 Patero disappeared on another short ride home. He was found by a farmer six days later, sat on a hill dazed and confused. This was near Colatina – 600 miles from home.[108]

and then there would be another 'task' to perform. This was all that the witness could recall.

However, UFO investigators searched for other witnesses. They found two stonemasons – the only occupants living in the fairly desolate area where Alvaro woke up. They recalled seeing this light 'flash' by and an hour or two later noting a young man slumped against a wall at the spot where Alvaro recovered. This was clearly at some point during the period when he believes he was inside a UFO.

Possibly more peculiar is the story told to these investigators by Mrs Alvaro, before the results of the hypnosis sessions were known. She told of a dream just after the encounter in which she heard a voice telling her that her son was about to become a father, but the child would be born on another world!

This thread of alien genetic experiments to create hybrid babies began of course with the Villas Boas case (see page 26). It crops up in various other reports. At Ponta Negra on 15 October 1979 an elderly, female concert pianist and a 25-year-old student to whom she had given a lift were abducted whilst driving in a remote area. Under hypnosis the 'grays' appeared. The woman was told that she was not suitable for their purposes, seemingly because she was too old. Her lift was another matter. He was used 'for research' and the entities proceeded to take sperm samples. In all other cases of such alien rejection the witness has been older than 40.

Perhaps the most interesting recent case happened on 31 July 1988 at Itacuruca, when a man was awoken by dogs barking at 4.00 am. A strange, glowing object like a wasp's nest and surrounded by mist drifted over. The man went on to have other encounters that culminated on 2 September when some lights 'like glow worms' appeared in woods near his house and he felt an impulse to follow them. Once away from safety, he discovered that the lights were on 'wands' held by several little men. They had thin bodies, dark eyes and short, blond hair. One of these beings led him to a 'cave' which contained a large space. Once inside he was made to lie on a stone 'bed' and was probed by these wands. The beings spoke, in Portuguese, appearing to know about the witness – including his name. They 'healed' a wound on his leg where he had fallen onto a nail.

After this experience the witness felt strange for some days, reportedly as if he were floating out of his body. He also was adamant that the place to which he was abducted was a cave and not a UFO and, in fact, he had picked up a rock from the ground inside this cavern.

For many the temptation to call this cave a spaceship would have been considerable. Indeed one might well have expected that to occur in this case more than ever, because the witness was Ludovico Granchi – son of Irene Granchi, one of the leading UFOlogists in Brazil.[109]

MEXICO

EARLY CASES

Today Mexico seems obsessed with UFOs. Since a major sighting during a 1991 eclipse, when dozens of people in Mexico City filmed a floating light, the media has chased the subject with a vengeance.

Abductions Possibly 1

Alien Contacts 45

Predominant Entity Type Humanoid (both small and tall)

Many of the sightings involve Venus and weather balloons prominent in the darkened sky, but it is worth noting that Mexico's current fascination with photographs depicting UFOs has a precedent since this nation produced the first known UFO on film. Taken on 12 August 1883 by astronomer Jose Bonilla through his telescope at Zacatecas, a spindly craft appears to cross the sun.

The relative dearth in contact stories is all the more interesting given that Mexico is by no means a UFO-free zone. It also borders to the north with the most abduction-saturated nation on Earth, the USA.

The first known alien sighting was on 18 August 1953 in the Ciudad Valley. Taxi driver Salvador Villanueva found that his vehicle suddenly stopped and he tried to try to fix the fault. He then noticed some legs beside the cab and, suspecting he was being hailed for a ride, scrambled out from underneath to apologise. Here he was confronted by two, small men with helmets 'like American football players'.

Despite their small stature, Villanueva thought he was dealing with airmen. But their accent was unfamiliar and they had difficulty with the language. None the less they talked of his car and accepted his invitation to shelter inside from the rain. Then they dropped the 'bombshell'. 'We are not of this planet,' he was told. Eventually they took him to see their craft – like soup plates on top of each other, with one plate reversed. He noted that as he struggled through the muddy fields they had a useful device. A light on their belts glowed and caused the mud to be repelled, so that it never touched their legs.

When the beings entered the craft they invited him to join them, but he declined stepping back and watched the object rise with a faint burn. After a few feet it began to wobble as it climbed 'like a falling leaf in reverse' and then flew away with just a faint swishing sound.[110]

This case shares features of early contacts during which a pleasant invitation to 'step aboard' is offered. Such reports form a bridge between the jolly contactee tales, in which witnesses met a congenial galactic federation, and the far less civilised encounters of today where alien needs come first and the witness is no guest but a victim. Indeed, in many respects these differences also mirror the considerable change in Western society that has occurred during the same 40-year period. An age of innocence when violent assaults seemed rare has been replaced by one where threat is a way of life or definitely within our collective consciousness.

PART THREE
ALIEN PORTRAITS

Over 6,000 alien-contact stories have been reported from around the world and there are certainly many more that have not been properly documented. But what sort of entities are seen during these encounters and to what extent is each different type described? The portraits that follow describe six of the main groups of alien that have been witnessed around the world over the past 50 years, along with some facts and figures. In conclusion I also report on the question of photographic and physical evidence for these various groups of beings, limited though it is.

While there have been many more than six different types of entity on record, most of the rest are just isolated examples or share many attributes with these major groupings. The ones included in this picture gallery feature between them in a massive 97 per cent of all the reported encounters.

Other entity types include robots, which rarely feature alone but are described as accompanying other beings in about 5 per cent of cases, and reptile-skinned creatures. Encounters with these have risen from under 1 per cent in reports before 1970 to 4 per cent in 1990s' cases. Almost all of these oddities have occurred in the USA and most postdate the popular TV series *V*, which featured invading reptilian aliens. Insect beings have been recorded in 1.5 per cent of cases and again these are almost exclusive to the USA. However, winged entities akin to 'Mothman' (in Virginia) or more angelic entities (in the UK) do occur from time to time, but are commonly not reported in the presence of a UFO and so are not included here.[111] This needs to be borne in mind.

The information given includes the relative percentage of all reports for each type of entity. This is listed according to decade so that you can chart the variation in the level of its appearance across time.

ENTITY TYPE:

LITTLE PEOPLE

Habitat:
Seen all over the world, they were particularly common in pre-twentieth-century reports and interpreted as fairies, sprites and elves. Modern sightings are rare, but they have been seen in Western Europe in the 1990s, commonly as bedroom visitors. Indo-China still produces examples of sightings in the outside world.

Description:
Commonly 2 – 4 feet tall, but some have been reported as small as 1 – 2 feet. Usually human in appearance, they wear bright clothes or uniforms.

Activities:
Inquisitive, they appear in bedrooms, inspecting people and objects such as clocks and watches. They have an unusual fascination with time and are known to play tricks on people.

Typical Case:
On 3 September 1976 in the mining town of Fencehouses, Durham, two women came upon a strange object sat on a mound of earth that was in a building site. The women were a 63-year-old grandmother and her granddaughter, aged 18. They were subsequently so shocked by the experience that they shunned all attempts to be interviewed in detail. The object resembled a small, glass dome on ski runners. Its surface was semi-transparent and smoky. Beside it were two tiny entities looking like dolls. They were human with long, white hair, plastic or pale faces and staring eyes. The two women felt drawn towards them and the object, and entered a 'cocoon' of energy that caused the air to tingle. Inside this all ambient sound disappeared and time lost all meaning. The women recalled walking away from the site with the object gone, but a watch worn by one of them was now inexplicably ten minutes slow. This case is very much like a twentieth-century fairy encounter, but with many modern UFO attributes.

Physical Evidence:
Rarely available. There are occasional references in 'fairy' cases to food being offered. They often show an interest in Earth crops and are more common in rural areas than in towns. Dubious photographs are very rare, including the widely accepted 'Cottingley Fairy' hoax by two teenage girls and a 'little man' photo from the mid-western USA (taken by a youth) which was later discovered to be a doll filmed next to a sewage pipe, lit-up by flashlight!

Number of Cases:
1950s – 35 per cent
1960s – 33 per cent
1970s – 30 per cent
1980s – 12 per cent
1990s – 4 per cent

ENTITY TYPE

GOBLINS & DWARFS

Habitat:
Reported worldwide, they were more common in the 1950s and 1960s. Regional variations are strong, e.g. hairy, aggressive dwarfs in South America; trolls in Northern Europe. Monstrous goblins feature in rare cases.

Description:
Typically about 3 – 4 feet tall, their features are basically human but with 'harsher' elements, including pointed ears, coloured skin and at times swarthy, matted hair. Sharp teeth are occasionally reported.

Activities:
Found close to homes on the edges of habitation and sometimes emerging from woods; they gesture and move about a good deal. Can be construed as aggressive, but mostly defensive. Often not seen near UFOs.

Typical Case:
On 22 August 1955 the Sutton family, at Hopkinsville, Kentucky, were laid siege in their house when goblin creatures with elephant-like ears appeared. Odd lights had landed by their well and the beings scuttled around the yard, leaping up and down but descending onto all fours as they ran. For several hours they climbed trees and walls and prevented the family from escaping. One entity was shot at point-blank range. The shotgun felled the creature, but it got up and

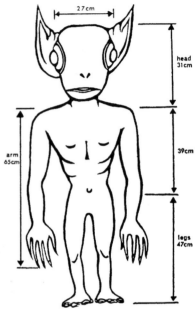

Drawing of goblin-like entity from UFO seen at Hopkinsville, Kentucky on 21/22 August 1955.

ran away. In a break in the action, the Suttons made a dash for their car and fled to the police, who later confirmed the Suttons' obvious terror. No sign of the creatures was found when police arrived back at the homestead.

Physical Evidence:
The best evidence for this type of entity is the single photograph taken by an ex-police officer on Ilkley Moor, Yorkshire on 1 December 1987. The witness claimed (in a letter written to me that day) that he had been taking photographs at dawn of surrounding villages when he saw the greenish/grey creature beckoning. It fled into a UFO behind a rock. One photograph of the

creature was taken, but none of the UFO. Although fuzzy, this clearly shows what the witness claims he saw. Tests on the picture by Kodak and other analysis seem to prove that this is a genuine image of a figure just over 3 feet tall. The tests could not establish whether this was a model, a child in a suit or an alien, but the witness stands by his story years later and has never sought to make any capital from his amazing photograph. As with many of the sightings of this entity type, the report location is noted for historical associations with monster and creature incidents.[112]

Number of Cases:

1950s – 4 per cent
1960s – 4 per cent
1970s – 3 per cent
1980s – 2 per cent
1990s – 1 per cent

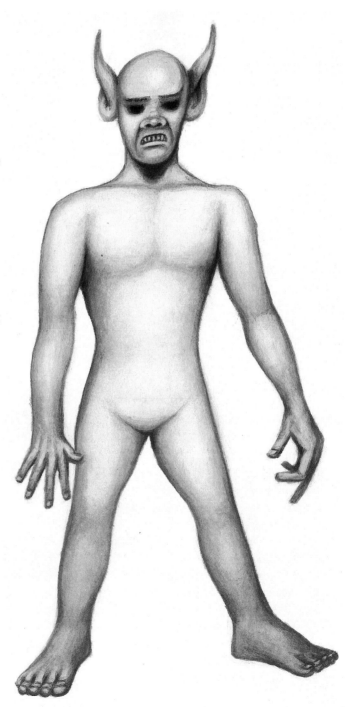

ENTITY TYPE

'GRAYS'

Habitat:

Originally reported in small numbers in the USA and Europe they became dominant in the USA from the early 1970s. Since the 1980s sightings have escalated rapidly throughout the world. They are now by far the most common entity.

Description:

About 4 feet tall, occasionally a little smaller or taller, with a disproportionately large head, they sometimes have a pointed chin and spindly body. Eyes are very large and often dark. Little sign of mouth or nose is present. Skin colour is white, grey or like parchment. Body hair is absent. Lack of sexual body characteristics is often alluded to.

Activities:

Of all the entity types by far, they are most likely to be involved in abducting humans (75 per cent of all cases involve them). They perform medical tests on witnesses in a cold, emotionless way, seemingly oblivious to any pain caused. They are rarely seen without a classic UFO nearby, but frequently abduct from bedrooms at night.

Typical Case:

Under hypnosis 29 years later, Jennie from Nebraska, USA, recalled that on 7 October 1955 when a teenager, she was visited by a being called 'the explorer'. This entity floated outside her bedroom and hypnotically lured her into a UFO shaped like two pie-dishes. She passed through the walls and windows as if they were not there and was medically probed on a long bed, blood samples being taken through tubes as the entity smiled, although Jennie told him it was hurting. The being was described as 'tinier than 4 feet, but bigger than 3 . . . I don't think he has hair. The head is shaped like an egg . . . The face is waxy – real pale, pinkish, grayish . . . The nose is just a tiny bump . . . The mouth is a slit. The eyes are like long slits with nobody home.'

Physical Evidence:

No photographs exist, despite the frequency of 'gray' involvement in sightings. In 1997 a video said to show one under study by the US government at a secret Nevada base (Area 51) was sent to a TV producer. It was shot in near-dark conditions ('to protect the alien's eyes'). Just the head is visible, jerking like a puppet. Many suspect that this is precisely what the film depicts. 'Grays' are the most likely beings to place implants – small objects allegedly put inside witnesses. Several of these have been surgically removed, as tiny, dark masses that resemble fibrous growths. None retrieved are of proven extra-bodily, let alone extraterrestrial origin.

Number of Cases:

1950s – 2 per cent
1960s – 3 per cent
1970s – 7 per cent
1980s – 31 per cent
1990s – 61 per cent

ENTITY TYPE

HUMANOIDS

Habitat:
Essentially humanlike entities, they are found in most parts of the world, but are especially common in Europe. They have a tendency to appear inside houses without arriving in UFOs. Numbers are decreasing.

Description:
Commonly said to so closely resemble human beings, they could be passed unnoticed in the street. Blond hair, blue eyes or an oriental appearance are often reported. Tanned skins are common. Height is typically within the normal human range. Males are most common, but female humanoids are seen far more often than the females of other entity types.

Activities:
Often seen to be involved in abductions but taking a back seat to the 'grays'. The latter do the medical probes, but the human entities are usually considered in charge. They show more concern for the witness and have been known to display films and other images, as if seeking a witness response. They communicate by telepathy and seek to put the witness at ease. Often, they express ecological concerns.

Typical Case:
A teenage girl from Bolton, Lancashire, lost a period of time as she walked home from the bus stop in January 1976. A large, oval craft had hovered above, pressing down on her with a force field. Under hypnosis she described having been taken into a room and studied by a humanlike figure, apparently

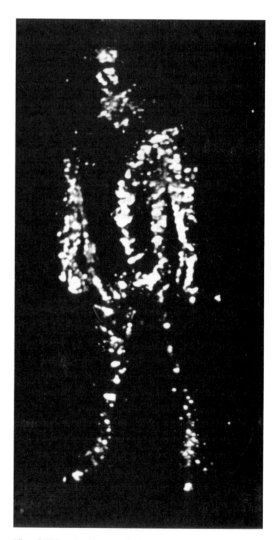

Alleged UFO entity photographed by police chief Jeff Greenhaw, Falkville, Alabama on 17 October 1973.

female, who had nice features and long blond or even white hair. The entity had been keen to pass on information to the witness of a psychic nature about the future of the world, as if preparing us for a coming disaster.[113]

Physical Evidence:
The only known photograph was taken by police chief Jeff Greenhaw at Falkville, Alabama in October 1973. This was during a wave of sightings. After an anonymous call that a UFO was in the sky, Greenhaw drove to the spot, saw no UFO, nor the caller, but did find a humanlike figure in a silvery suit. He chased it and took several pictures before it vanished into the dark. There are reasons to suspect the officer was hoaxed by persons unknown, who were seeking to discredit him and using the recent UFO wave as a basis.

Number of Cases:
1950s – 27 per cent
1960s – 26 per cent
1970s – 23 per cent
1980s – 18 per cent
1990s – 15 per cent

ENTITY TYPE

NORDICS

Habitat:

They have been seen in North and South America and in other continents, but are most common in Europe. They were the dominant entity type until the 1960s and were still common until 1987, when the 'grays' took over. They are now very rare.

Description:

Similar to the humanoids, they are often very tall (6 – 7 feet and even taller beings have been reported). Blond hair, blue eyes, staring hypnotic beauty and features related to Scandinavian (hence the name) and also Greek gods have been noted.

Activities:

Although some have engaged in abduction and medical probes, this is not common. More often they appear to want contact and com-municate (by telepathy) in a friendly, civilised and helpful manner – seeming to want to put the witness at ease. Often, they possess psychic abilities (such as materialising and dematerialising or floating). Witnesses claim to have been given help to see the future and to be engaged in a lifelong series of meetings with them. They have been known to tell of the 'grays' presence on Earth and talk dis-paragingly about these entities.

Typical Case:

In February 1976 an ambulance driver in Leeds, West Yorkshire, was lying on his bed after a tiring day when he saw a tall figure of Nordic appearance materialise in his room. The being conveyed images into his mind and indicated that his mechanical knowledge was required. The witness then 'floated' into the air with the being and found himself in a strange room surrounded by similar creatures who communi-cated a series of religious images to him about the beginning and the end of time. He then found himself back on his bed, unable to move until the entities had gone.

Physical Evidence:

No photographs of Nordics are known, save possibly the image of Semjase, a female, blond-haired entity said to make visits to Swiss contactee Billy Meier. Meier's other photographs (of spaceships and even dinosaurs taken during a time-travel experience) have been hotly disputed by many researchers, but he has won over some noted acolytes.[114] During Nordic encounters gifts are often less concrete (a legacy of psychic powers, healing abilities etc.) or bizarre (bits of glass, odd seeds and rocks).

Number of Cases:

1950s – 21 per cent
1960s – 20 per cent
1970s – 19 per cent
1980s – 17 per cent
1990s – 5 per cent

ENTITY TYPE

PROJECTIONS

Habitat:
Seen all over the world, they are often involved in bedroom visitations (without a UFO) or during car rides, when the UFO is seen to be a large, orange or green light.

Description:
Often 'unformed', they appear as shadows, or outlines within glowing masses. When seen in detail, they can be large humanoids with monstrous features. They have many attributes of a hologram – being barely mobile, near transparent and glowing with a vivid light (often green or orange). They are frequently accompanied by a loud buzz or whistle.

Activities:
The strangest entities of all, they rarely engage in any kind of meaningful contact. They usually appear and vanish into thin air and seem more like two-dimensional images than living entities (although they resemble an advanced form of three-dimensional hologram). They are frightening in nature and have terrified many, from trained military personnel to guard dogs. They have never been associated with abductions.

Typical Case:
On 4 February 1973 three vehicles, passing on a lonely road near Kimba, South Australia, were involved. A large, orange oval was seen inside a clearing and projected in front of it was an entity described as being 7 feet tall and humanoid in outline. The various witnesses each saw something slightly different as they passed. An almost identical case occurred five years later at Worrall, South Yorkshire, when a dark, silhouetted being inside an orange ball floated towards a terrified couple, parked in a lovers' lane.

Physical Evidence:
Physical evidence is limited. In one case, from an army base in Spain, patrol guards fired volleys of bullets at a large, glowing figure as it floated near the wall. These bullets disappeared. In a Cyprus army barracks, a guard dog hid under the bed covering its ears, as the harsh whistle accompanying one figure was heard. The soldier in charge of the dog was found by guards, still clutching his speargun which was loaded to shoot at the entity.[115] One extraordinary photograph was taken by fireman Jim Templeton, while taking Sunday snaps of his daughter on Burgh Marsh near Carlisle. He and his family saw nothing, but the photograph depicts a white semi-transparent figure of large humanoid proportions, floating in mid-air. It has defied explanation.[116]

Number of Cases:
1950s – 8 per cent
1960s – 12 per cent
1970s – 14 per cent
1980s – 15 per cent
1990s – 10 per cent

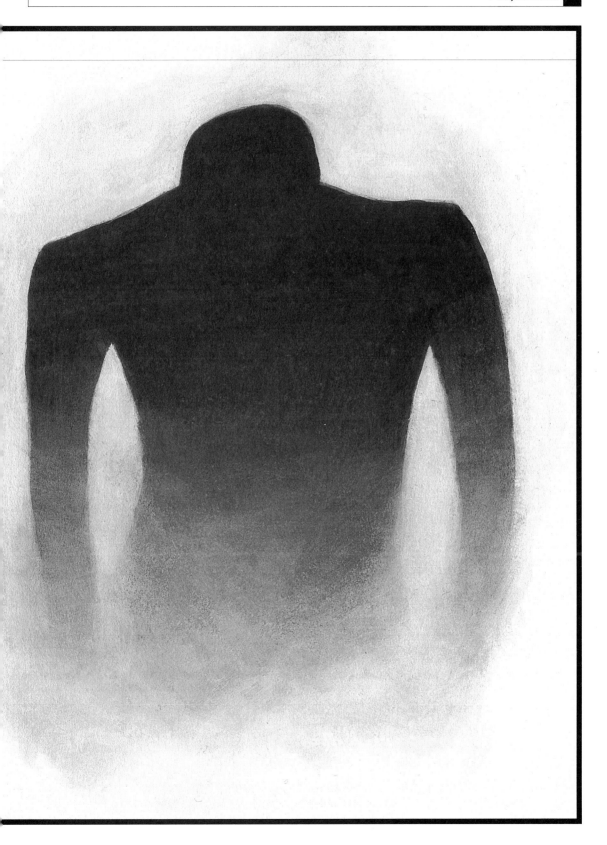

PART FOUR
ALIENS ON SCREEN

Before we can investigate the many theories proposed to explain abductions, it is worth looking at how fact and fiction weave the legends, myths and (perhaps) realities that we confront. Regardless of how real it may *seem*, this phenomenon is heavily influenced by the concept 'alien' held within our minds. We perceive all reality through stores of images forged by experience. To 'see' an alien we might have to visualise it through ideas generated by myth and science fiction. It is too simple to argue that fiction, as portrayed by Hollywood, *inspires* reality, or that movies are *based upon* real events. There is a process of osmosis which operates between the two. Here I look at some of the key movies and TV programmes that have shaped human imagination and the threads that link them together and with the 'reality' of contact and abduction.

IN THE BEGINNING WAS THE WORD

Jonathan Swift's *Gulliver's Travels* can be read in different ways, simply as a tale of adventure or, as was intended, as an allegory of Western culture to reflect our alienation in an era when new lands, and hence new cultures and ideas, were rapidly opening up to us through exploration and scientific endeavour. The same is true of the work of mathematician Charles Dodgson (Lewis Carroll). His 'Alice' stories can be seen simply as children's tales. But the motif of sudden transition into a bizarre, new reality populated by extraordinary beings is what we face with abductions – including the obviously human behaviour.

Mythic voyagers remain popular in twentieth-century literature. *The Lion, the Witch and the Wardrobe* by C.S. Lewis, where a doorway to another world opens up in a closet and, Frank Baum's stories popularised by *The Wizard of Oz* both offer examples. In the latter the move to another reality with strange beings (for 'grays' and Nordics read munchkins and wizards) is caused by a whirling cloud that 'abducts' Dorothy. Today Baum may well have used a

> *Escape to another reality clearly resonates with the human spirit.*

UFO, not a tornado, to make this transition, reflecting the 'Oz Factor' state that triggers real abductions.

Such literature is extremely successful – from Tolkein's *Lord of the Rings* and *The Hobbit* (voted most influential fiction of the twentieth century) to the incredibly popular works of Stephen Donaldson (abductions to Illearth). Escape to another reality clearly resonates with the human spirit. Are they examples of a good story idea that works no matter how you dress it up? Does their theme reflect some need within us that yearns to 'boldly go where no-one has gone before', to cite yet another hugely successful twentieth-century version? Or, we might wonder, is there more to it? Do they reflect an intuition – a knowledge that we possess at some unconscious level that other realities *do* exist? Perhaps these images are so strong in the minds of children because they have not yet learnt to distrust such innate knowledge?

THE ALIENS ARE COMING

Jules Verne's hugely popular novels undoubtedly had an effect on the mood of the late nineteenth century. They describe fantastic flying craft before these were invented. The airship waves of 1896 and 1897 were in many senses the first UFO sightings – but they were not reported as *alien* craft. They were cigar-shaped airships flown by real-life Robur the Conquerors or Captain Nemos as if Verne set the cue.

The British contemporary of Verne, H.G. Wells, put aliens on the agenda. His 1898 classic *War of the Worlds* portrayed an advanced civilisation that was not human and had insect-like propensities. They came to Earth intent on having their way with us, but had a sexless existence that made procreation difficult. These themes fit remarkably well with today's abduction stories.

During the early part of the twentieth century, the pulp-fiction comics and penny-dreadful novels picked up on this theme. Space was the next frontier now that the Wild West (which itself had replaced the 'dark continent' of Africa) was civilised. The aliens made great baddies to take over from 'gun-slingers'. Indeed, the choice of the phrase 'final frontier' to promote *Star Trek* in the 1960s was no accident. Creator Gene Rodenberry says he designed the series as *Wagon Train* in space.

Modern TV drama still adopts the theme. In late 1998, hit ITV series *Heartbeat* – set in the Pennines in the 1960s – involved a series of UFO encounters (inspired by a true case in my book, *The Pennine UFO Mystery*, solved as a gliding cargo plane). Aliens have become mainstream fiction in a big way.

REBIRTH OF SCIENCE FICTION

Possibly the strongest example of cross-fertilisation between science fiction and reality was in a 1930 *Buck Rogers* cartoon strip, unearthed by UFOlogist Martin Kottmeyer. The aliens have cat-like eyes, a feature of many recent cases. The story even follows the outline that Dr Thomas Bullard has traced for real abductions. So little variation is there in plot – from seeing a light, being captured, undergoing examination by the aliens and so forth – that Bullard suspects it may imply reality. Myths and stories often jumble the order in which they are told. But in Kottmeyer's view, the pattern Bullard found probably exists (as in the comic strip) because *this* is the right way to tell a story and not because abductions are real.[117]

Buck Rogers resurfaced in an abduction tale 50 years later, when West Yorkshire policeman Alan Godfrey described under hypnosis seeing robots making strange sounds (see page 44). He honourably reminded us that he had no way of judging the authenticity of his 'memories'. But on British TV at that time was the series *Buck Rogers in the 25th Century*, based on those comic strips. This strongly featured a little robot who made very similar noises. We might wonder if this was somehow lodged in Godfrey's subconscious and resurfaced, without him being aware of that fact, during regression. Fifteen years after Godfrey's own account was made public (in my book, *The Pennine UFO Mystery*) it too became the trigger for the story of a Yorkshire policeman being abducted during a British TV drama – from fiction to reality and back to fiction, via this remarkable process of cross-fertilisation. No wonder the aliens (by symbolism perhaps?) seem so fond of cross-fertilising species!

FLYING SAUCERS

There is little doubt that the early science fiction novels were read by a small, cult audience. They could *not* be what caused modern UFOlogy. Similarly, Hollywood did little to inspire such a mood. The serials of *Buck Rogers* and *Flash Gordon* were popular, but were not remotely like the real cases that followed. The heroes in these series flew in rocket ships that moved vertically with smoke and pyrotechnics. The aliens were slobbering monsters. Even their cat-like eyes in one comic are misleading. The rest of the entity bore no resemblance to a Nordic. It is too easy to see clues in what are really just coincidences.

From a cultural tracking point of view, the sudden appearance of the now ubiquitous saucer shape in 1947 had much to do with the tabloid press creating the name 'flying saucer' as a catch-phrase. Such hooks are vital when it comes to making an impact – ask any popular comedian or broadcaster. This cultural catch-phrase inevitably provoked hoaxes that inspired witnesses to see a

...the sudden appearance of the now ubiquitous saucer shape in 1947 had much to do with the tabloid press creating the name 'flying saucer'...

pattern behind ill-defined lights in the sky. Most UFOs *are* just lights or fuzzy balls. Specific shapes are reported in very few cases. Others are a product of our desire to see order in chaos. This effect meant that saucerlike craft were reported by many watching the skies for the first time, who probably saw something insubstantial. Human perception has constantly stamped an updated model onto lights and glowing energies to form the standard interpretation. In the 1890s it was Jules Verne's airships, in 1947 it became Arnold's misreported 'saucers'.

However, there is quite a problem. Witness sightings of 'flying saucers' provide no more than a tiny percentage of total reports. The vast majority of UFOs (over 90 per cent) never have been discs. Aside from a few dubious hoaxes, most photographs show lights and blobs.[118] This makes sense for simple sightings – the vast bulk of the mystery – but not when it comes to abductions. In far too many of *these* cases a structured craft *is* described. Unfortunately that craft tends to be one of these apparently illusionary saucers!

HOLLYWOOD SCARES

There can be no doubt that the saucer shape was first (mis)reported in real life and was only *then* adopted by science fiction and in particular by Hollywood. As its appearance coincided with early flights of our own rocket-shaped craft, some dramatically different image was needed to convey the impression of an alien vehicle. Until then rocket shapes had been sufficiently futuristic. Now they were mundane. The saucer shape was established by media stories as suitably alien and became the new model for unearthly craft. Once this pattern was reinforced endlessly by TV there was really no escape. The flying saucer was what any self-respecting alien would use to travel the universe.

Witnesses spacenapped by aliens still tend to see themselves as being 'picked up' by a flying saucer. Yet since the early 1990s there has been much attention focused on a new shape for UFOs – the triangle. This may be some new secret aircraft – possibly an updated version of a Stealth fighter. In 1997 as many as one-third of all UFOs were triangles. In the UK over 50 per cent were.

This is surely evidence that popular belief influences what people see. Something real *was* visible. The triangular shape was imposed upon that something because *this* was what people were currently led to expect a UFO to look like. Yet the mass-market programmes and movies that effect the zeitgeist still stand by the flying saucer. This suggests that Hollywood is more important as a moulding influence on abductions than it is on mundane sightings, where witnesses have quickly adopted the new model. In other words, UFO sightings and abductions are different – as we saw earlier for other reasons (see page 36).

SCIENCE FICTION, MOVIES AND TV – THE ALIEN YEARS

1950:

The first UFO books were published, proclaiming alien invasion and government conspiracy.

1951:

The Thing Based on a John Cambell story from 1938, the movie was quick to adopt the flying saucer shape for its alien craft, because of recent publicity. This in turn no doubt influenced some witnesses.

The Day the Earth Stood Still A classic movie in which a Nordic-like alien with a god-like nature, demonstrates superior technology without desire to cause harm. All electrical power on Earth is rendered useless. He more ominously threatens the Earth with mass destruction if we do not stop plans to export aggression into the universe. This remains one of the most singularly important movies for cultural tracking. Some of its ideas stem from UFO reality, where it had already been speculated that sightings 'began' in 1947 because the aliens had seen the building of our first rockets and atom bombs. This movie emphasised the trend during 1950s' contacts. Vital was the appearance of the 'car stop' or 'electrical interference' case which was not seen until after the film. Did our unconscious pick up on this 'good idea' and adopt it in real life? Or maybe real aliens saw the movie and *they* thought it was a good idea too!

1953:

Invaders from Mars With this, one of several movies to adopt the *War of the Worlds* theme of monstrous aliens bent on evil, Hollywood updated the horror movie into the UFO age. The craft were always saucers; the aliens blobs (although taking over humans to cut down on expensive make-up). Much was borrowed from UFO reality, but it did not reflect the friendly 'space brothers' or goblinlike 'little men' becoming dominant. However, some themes from it transferred *to* UFOlogy – such as the abduction of cars, 'sucked up' off lonely roads. There were also a few real 'monster' sightings in the mid-1950s.

1956:

Earth Versus the Flying Saucers A classic case of cross-fertilisation; the originator of the storyline (serious UFO writer Major Donald Keyhoe) allowed his 'factual' book to become an alien shoot-em-up movie. Hollywood seems to have played on the impact of saying 'this is real' and abused the phenomenon

Above: The Thing, 1951 – showing the tail of a flying saucer buried in the ice.
Below: The Day the Earth Stood Still, 1951.

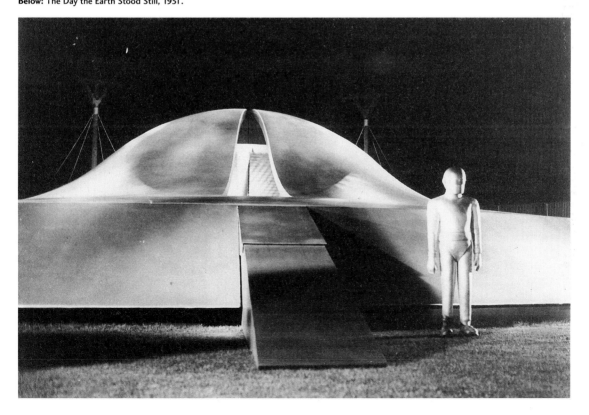

Above: Invaders from
Mars, 1953.

Left: Earth vs. the
Flying Saucers, 1956

to hype a movie that is otherwise undistinguished. Yet, interestingly, there was no resultant spate of real aliens zapping tanks and buildings.

1958:

Quatermass and the Pit This was the third outing for Nigel Kneale's scientist 'Quatermass'. Kneale had a staggering set of good ideas in this first serious UFO TV series – coincident with a book by psychiatrist Carl Jung.[119] A spacecraft is unearthed during work on a new underground line. This coincides with the sighting of imp-like aliens. Poltergeist attacks occur (as they do in real alien encounters – but nobody knew that in 1958). Quatermass (a sort of 1950s Fox Muldur) seeks the truth – that the craft crashed on Earth millions of years ago during a time when primitive man was surveyed by these beings. More fascinating is the idea that deep in our subconscious was the knowledge of this long-gone alien contact and in certain people at certain times the truth is awoken. Across the centuries, when a new well was dug, or railway line built, the shaking of the ground unleashed the energy. This triggered the psychic awareness in the minds of contactees and caused them to experience what were viewed as poltergeist outbreaks and sightings of 'demons'. Today, of course – we see aliens – when imp-like apparitions are unleashed from the unconscious. The location of the craft was associated with evil forces for centuries – as indeed have many real 'window areas'. This fascinating story reflects so much of what today is regarded as modern UFO thinking.

1961:

A for Andromeda Contrary to what might be expected there is antipathy between science fiction writers and fans and the UFO fraternity. Whilst some UFO researchers are fans of good science fiction (and some have even published in the field) the reverse is rarely true. UFOlogy is looked upon with less than enthusiasm, possibly because it is correctly assumed that the hackneyed media image – UFO equals spaceship flown by aliens saying 'take me to your leader' – *is* absurd. The 'more sophisticated' view came in this gripping serial by astronomer Sir Fred Hoyle. He conceived the receipt of a signal from space that when decoded served to 'educate' mankind. First it showed how to build a super computer that was then able to build an alien.

1963:

Village of the Damned/Children of the Damned These two interesting films are based on the John Wyndham story, *The Midwich Cuckoos*. The village of Midwich experiences a time-lapse/blink in reality and awakes to find all its women pregnant. The children are born looking normal but with alien traits and – indeed – as a sort of hybrid entity created by what we might consider a mass abduction. Wyndham also wrote *Chocky* – in which a youngster has telepathic rapport with an alien entity. This became a children's TV series in 1983. Two sequels were written, developing from Wyndham's original premise. These adopted some of the themes from current UFOlogy, either consciously or by coincidence. Indeed some of the imagery in *Chocky's Children* and *Chocky's Challenge* has obvious parallels with the contemporary true story of a family from Deeside in which young children had a series of friendly encounters with aliens of this type.[120]

1965:

The Night Caller Fascinating low-budget movie, in which an alien abducts women in order to conduct genetic experiments, as a necessity for his race to survive – exactly what abductees were to claim in reality soon after. The movie also shows vividly the difference between the subtlety of this understated British film and the decision to give it more impact in the USA. Here it was felt necessary to rename it, quite ridiculously, *Blood Beast from Outer Space*. In that one act we learn a lot about the cultural differences that operate in UFO terms between the 'gray'-obsessed, media madness of American UFO culture and the less blatant search for hidden meaning elsewhere.

1968:

2001: A Space Odyssey Based on a short story by Arthur C. Clarke (definitely no believer in UFOs, as he has told me) it came at just the right moment – when humans reached the moon and began space exploration. Its incredible photography, enigmatic quality and genuine alien nature struck a chord. The awe and inexplicability of how alien contact might happen is shown perfectly – a filmed version of the 'Oz Factor'.

1975:

Fade Out One of the first impressive alien contact novels by Patrick Tilley. The interplay between politics and an alien probe that effects the planet is superbly handled. Tilley told me that plans to make a movie of it were well advanced when Steven Spielberg got there first. I hope one day someone *will* film *Fade Out*.

The UFO Incident At long last, a movie based upon a real UFO case appeared. This low-budget American TV version of the Betty and Barney Hill affair (see page 29) was well done and told the story without hype. That the film was about a major abduction and was screened before such cases were well-known proved a problem. Indeed, within a few days of its transmission on US TV several new cases were reported, including the Walton abduction (see **1993** below).

Close Encounters of the
Third Kind, 1977

1977:

Close Encounters of the Third Kind The film that more than any other has influenced public thinking on UFOs is this early masterpiece by Steven Spielberg. One of the biggest box office successes, it won several Oscars. Easily the film most firmly rooted within UFO reality, Spielberg went to great lengths to portray the subject as it was. Dr J. Allen Hynek was chief consultant and appeared in trailers explaining his classification scheme for sightings, from which the odd title derives. Contactees are led to a mass landing site via a tele-pathic message from the aliens. There is an abduction scene, but in order to make it frightening (and in the process unrealistic) a spaceship lands amidst boiling clouds and kidnaps a young boy from a room set ablaze with pyrotech-nics. There was talk of Spielberg making *Close Encounters of the Fourth Kind* (a CE4 is UFOlogist-speak for an abduction). If so, one trusts that it will capture the weird blend of 'Oz Factor' unreality that is behind the abduction – not the UFOlogically absurd abductions that Hollywood loves. In terms of the impact that *Close Encounters* had on the public, this was intriguing. Many sceptics predicted a massive wave of contacts. This never happened. There was huge media interest and hot lines were set up to attract sightings. But these brought old cases and simple UFO sightings. Only one or two new abductions came to light. In fact, from 1979 to 1986 UFO sightings tailed off markedly. It was as if Spielberg fulfilled the dream for many and the mundane reality of boring lights in the sky just could not compete.

1978:

Miracle Visitors In my view the best novel about UFOs, it appeared just after the Spielberg film. Written by Ian Watson, who has penned other highly intelligent science fiction, it balances the altered states of consciousness and confusion that make alien contact baffling. Watson *knew* UFOlogy. He told me that UFO sightings 'dogged' him during his writing. Indeed, around publication, several abductions occurred in Northamptonshire near the village in which he then lived. These witnesses had never heard of Watson!

1980:

The Flipside of Dominick Hyde This superb BBC movie is a fictional presentation of UFOs as time-travellers. Filmed on a tiny budget, it is more about the people who fly UFOs. If the 'aliens' really are humans in craft from our future, then this may well be how the UFO phenomenon would be explained. A sequel followed in 1982.

1983:

V This was rather a throwback in some respects to the old-fashioned space monster movies (aliens come in peace but are intent on war). It is particularly interesting for showing aliens that are reptillian. At the time there were no such reports, but from the mid-1980s onward there have been quite a few – mostly from the USA.

1985:

A Secret Property This novel was penned by retired MoD under-secretary, Ralph Noyes, who supervised the UFO office in Whitehall for some years. Noyes set his story in the area with similar characters and events to the real life 1980 Rendlesham Forest case (see page 87). But it was not a direct fictionalisation. Instead, he speculated that alien contacts were the result of a covert experiment using a secret weapon. The weapon caused an interaction between the mind, psychic powers and Earth energy to trigger hallucinations with attributes of solidity.

1989:

Communion 1987 was a significant year for the abduction mystery with the massive success of horror writer Whitley Strieber's true abduction account. Two years later it became a movie, with Christopher Walken playing the writer, and is possibly the best fictional rendition of an abduction. He allows for an enigmatic presentation of the events, so that the viewer can puzzle how to interpret what unfolds. It is a testament to Strieber's awareness of the problems posed by the abduction phenomenon.

1992:

Intruders This American TV mini-series was based, loosely, on the real story of Indiana abductions (see page 43). It presented the 'grays' in their glory as never seen before on TV. It is interesting to compare the aliens in *Close Encounters*, from 1977, with those in *Intruders*, 15 years later. Both were carefully based upon real cases and they show how the little men with large eyes but friendly disposition (as portrayed by Spielberg) had evolved into the more sadistic 'grays'.

1993:

Fire in the sky The third real abduction film and, like the other two, it was also an American product. This movie tells the story of the 1975 abduction of forestry worker Travis Walton and his five-day disappearance, during which co-workers were suspected of murder! Rather disconcerting is the way in which the alien abduction scenes (shown in flashback at the end of the movie) are markedly different from how Walton actually described them. When in the UK promoting the movie, he said these changes were imposed late during production.

The X Files This American TV series has had a huge impact on popular concepts of alien conspiracies. It is rooted firmly in the paranormal and in UFOs in particular, openly borrowing stories and images rather than creating them. It began broadcasting at the height of the wave of interest stimulated by factual TV documentary shows that reconstructed real cases. In the USA there was *Sightings* and the UK *Strange but True?*. I had close association with the latter from its 1993 pilot and we achieved extraordinary ratings. Our film that reproduced the Rendlesham Forest encounters (1994 – see page 87) set a record of almost 12.5 million viewers. *The X Files* features two FBI agents charged with the task of probing cases with paranormal attributes. But the audience assumed that the fiction of *The X Files* was a mirror of the reality within UFOlogy. When some joined UFO groups and studied the real evidence, they found the truth was different. At the height of their success programmes like *The X Files* and *Strange but True?* brought thousands of new faces to the subject. In 1997 I lectured at the British 'X Files' conference alongside the actor who played 'Deep Throat' in the drama. Never was it more apparent that UFO reality is different from what science fiction fans expect.

1997:

Earth: Final Conflict An entertaining American TV series, it was based on a Gene (*Star Trek*) Roddenberry idea. Friendly, mystical aliens have arrived on Earth and seem to want to help, but why will they say so little about their real agenda? The aliens were more interesting than any on TV for a while (more Nordic than 'gray') and it will be fascinating to see if they effect the zeitgeist to add colour to real-life encounters.

Men in Black Based on genuine reports that, in the wake of close encounters, sinister strangers aim to silence witnesses through fear and intimidation,[121] these Hollywood 'Men in Black' are wisecracking, ray-gun-toting heroes who clear the Earth of interplanetary scum. The connection between UFO history and high farce in this enjoyable romp is superficial. It is worrying evidence that we still struggle to cope with the reality of alien contact. Serious debates about what is going on are few on TV or in the movies. Whilst the phenomenon is treated with levity or as the source of blood-sucking, monster-filled gore, it is unlikely that attitudes will change. And, of course, if there is cross-fertilisation between the fiction of these movies and the reality of alien contacts, then we reap the close encounters that we sow.

1999:

Taken Work began on a 20-hour TV mini series produced by Steven Spielberg to be aired in Autumn 2000. *Taken* will recount the alien abduction story via a fictional setting but through real UFO history. Its huge budget and obvious impact is set to alter our view of alien contact permanently.

PART FIVE
ALIEN ANSWERS

We now face a bewildering array of theories suggested to explain the alien contact mystery but cannot simply choose between lies, fantasies and alien kidnappers. Even so many of the solutions proposed are (sometimes highly tuned) variations on those themes! In compiling these status reports the use of words such as 'unreal' or 'imaginative' slip freely into the discussion, but tend to be destructive. Witnesses regard anyone who uses them with suspicion, because they wrongly assume that they challenge their integrity. So I have tried to come up with a way of looking at these various possibilities that do not make arbitrary judgements on questions of reality.

There will always be an event and a cause. For these events, I see two categories – internal and external. An event is termed 'internal' if the witness *experiences* it as real, but the majority of people *do not*. An event is termed 'external' if the consensus view is that most people *do* share the experience. In this way no judgement is made that one perspective is real and the other is imaginary. Both are simply different kinds of reality.

Theories also seek to explain these events as a result of various causes – either mundane or exotic. 'Mundane' causes are recognised as part of our accepted knowledge by science, whereas 'exotic' ones, at present, are not. Some of the exotic causes probably will become accepted. Others will remain unproven.

Any new theory that may be suggested should, I believe, find a place within this framework. The structure helps us to seek clues and patterns that will relate from one variation on a theme to another. Ultimately that may be the only way to resolve these issues since it is unlikely that there is only one way of explaining abductions. The trick is to find the right collection of answers that blend the most useful bits from each of these suggestions.

EXTERNAL EVENTS WITH MUNDANE CAUSES

MISPERCEPTION:

You might think that alien contacts could never be caused by a misperception of something mundane, but you would be wrong. UFOs are often the result of misperceived aircraft, balloons, stars, etc. More than 90 per cent of sightings start like this. Yet it is far more difficult to see how an alien contact could be the result of an honest mistake. Aircraft do not resemble little grey men.

It is improbable that more than a fraction will be misperceptions. But the percentage is not zero. There are instructive cases. I well recall on one frosty December morning in 1978 admiring Venus shining fiercely through an ice-filled sky. Within hours I was trying desperately to persuade the world that this was *not* an alien spaceship. Venus was, of course, doing nothing more than it often does when close to the Earth and very bright. But in such conditions the

UFO (Venus and lens flare) over Ruthin, Denbighshire, November 1996.

These days, it is tempting to think supernaturally and not logically...

ice in the atmosphere can act like a mirror causing a splendid sight. These days, it is tempting to think supernaturally and not logically in response.

The media had been alerted by some people in south Manchester who had seen Venus, just as I had, but did not know what it was. They pursued it across fields until blocked by the River Mersey, then called the police, who sent officers in time to see the faint 'star' 'going away'. It was, in fact, going nowhere but disappearing against the brightening sky. Within hours the story was on the radio, in the papers, and on local TV. An overexcited UFO group showed the witnesses identikit photos of spaceships from which they picked out the model of flying saucer that they believed they must have seen. Of course, they had only seen what I had – a white light in the post-dawn sky. But media expectation, cultural beliefs and the less than sensible tactics of this UFO group ensured that the story escalated.

By the time I was able to make a TV appearance explaining the truth, I faced absurd charges that I was a secret government agent out to hide the facts. All manner of 'clues' were brought in. Some cats had recently disappeared. Speculation descended into pure farce, with the idea that aliens in their flying saucer were abducting moggies for dastardly experiments. As I told the TV audience, 'Look outside at seven in the morning. If it's clear you will see the UFO, because I am afraid it was just Venus and it will be in more or less the same place again.' I suspect that most preferred to believe in cat rustlers from Mars.

In 1993 a video was taken in the West Country that clearly shows Venus in similar early morning opulence. What is impressive is the audio track, because you can follow the obviously sincere witnesses (an entire family driving to London for a day trip) coming to accept it as a UFO. Within two or three minutes these folk had reached the stage of near panic. One witness can even be heard saying that she has read that aliens kidnap people and perform medical experiments. Her terror was undoubtedly real.

To many people rationality has no business getting in the way of a good story. Dennis Stillings cites a case in which an abduction researcher received a call from a family in the USA who had seen 'aliens in yellow space suits' with 'flashing lights' nearby. Inexplicable? You judge. A check with the county highway department revealed that a work crew had been doing emergency repairs, wearing high-visibility jackets and using hazard lights to warn traffic – because of misty rain. Case solved, you might think. Except that, according to Stillings, the researcher 'categorically refused to accept the explanation'.[122]

We learn more from understanding solved cases than by ignoring them. To explain a case is a successful outcome, but many perceive it as a failure to find aliens. For example, at Bignall End in Staffordshire an elderly lady reported that she had seen a UFO and aliens. The UFO was a huge, orange ball outside her bedroom. It stopped her alarm clock at 2.45 am. Dark entities were moving about in front of the craft and her cat sat entranced. Her son also confirmed that he had seen the UFO (but not the aliens) on arrival home at 4.15 am. I suspected an explanation and the man who investigated on-site, Derek James, consulted a lunar astronomer. We thought the UFO just might have been the moon. Unfortunately this had set at 3.18 am – an hour before the son had seen the UFO. But was our trust misplaced? It was later established – to my satisfaction – that this was probably a set of chance events. The clock had stopped at 2.45 am. The sighting *was* likely to have been the setting moon. The son could have misread the time by an hour. The cat may simply have been attracted by the strong glow through windows etched with frost. And the aliens – well, there was a telegraph pole in line of sight just where the moon had set.

To many people rationality has no business getting in the way of a good story.

With such a case one is faced with a simple choice. The witnesses could be correct and a UFO with aliens could have landed, or the down-to-earth solution is more probable, even though it depends upon the acceptance of various 'maybes' that can never be proven. The honesty of the witnesses is not in question. But while we know that the moon, frost, telegraph poles and stopping clocks are real, the existence of aliens requires more to persuade us – or, at least, it should do. All too often cases provide witness testimony and nothing solid. We must accept that in some cases there will be terrestrial explanations for seemingly extraterrestrial events.

A report is filtered through many things – not least human memory. What the investigator seeks is the stimulus to that report. Tracking back through the quagmire of human perception is never easy. If a witness sees two lights and assumes that they were on the side of a craft, they may well submit a totally honest report of the craft that they believe was visible. But no successful interpretation will be possible if you only seek various types of craft in explanation. Take one step back and probe for potential lights. All too often this is all we can be sure that the witness *did* see.

A German newspaper hoax showing a crew member from a UFO which crashed in the 1950s.

INTERNAL EVENTS WITH MUNDANE CAUSES

HOAXING:

The only hope of resolving this sort of case is that the witness will admit the truth. But you can never prove a hoax, in the same way as you can never prove that aliens really did land. Although most researchers, and most sceptics, do not believe that hoaxing is the main cause of alien contacts, all are sure it has some part to play. Indeed, it is instructive to explore the reason why stories were invented.

Today fame and fortune are incentives that cannot be ignored. A well-told case of alien abduction can bring TV interest, newspaper money, book deals and even movie offers. It is far easier to make up an alien contact story that will be accepted by the gullible than it is to pick the winning lottery numbers. Such temptation must inevitably have got the better of some. UFOlogists and the media live too easily with lack of hard evidence. That you have no way of proving your story is rarely a problem.

Undoubtedly there are made-up cases with these motives. I would not dare to identify which ones I suspect. Hoax stories make money and telling the more mundane and confusing truth about aliens does not. Sadly the libel laws of the UK have been written on the maxim that you are *guilty until proven rich*.

Of course, just because somebody has seized the opportunity to gain fame and fortune from their story does not mean that it *is* a hoax. While most folk run from publicity rather than seek it, a few embrace the prospect. The idea of being famous can be attractive and some witnesses genuinely believe that they *should* tell their story so as to educate the world. There is also the nightmare scenario of the notorious spinner of tall tales who has the misfortune to truly meet an alien! But hoaxing is not always the result of a calculated plot. There can be many motives at work.

The only known photograph of an alien taken by an abductee (see page 110) was not hoaxed for any obvious reason – if it is a fake. I tried (unsuccessfully) with Peter Hough to find proof of trickery. The abductee has never been publicly identified, has shunned requests for interviews, assigned copyright in the photograph to Peter and made no effort to claim money from its use. Correctly marketed, as he knew (because I told him just to see how he would react!) a lot of money was on the table. If he hoaxed this case, then his reasoning is more complex. Both Peter and I considered the prospect that he was seeking to test the reaction of the UFO community to an amazing case. How would we write it up? This possibility galvanised the investigation. Eleven years have gone by and the witness still stands by his story.

Other pressures can be in play. As long ago as 1917 two young girls in Yorkshire claimed they had taken photographs of fairies near Cottingley Beck, in an effort to persuade their parents that they really were seeing them. Before long the photos were adopted by noted fiction writer Arthur Conan Doyle, who sadly did not emulate the skills of Sherlock Holmes. To him the photos were the proof he sought. Quickly the girls found themselves required to provide more evidence. They had lost control of their own story.

All the clues were there that this had started out as an innocent joke – the artistic skills of one 'witness', the fact that she had a book with suspiciously similar-looking fairies and that the girls needed to be alone in order to film anything strange. All this should have set alarm bells ringing. The cut-out imagery is in retrospect obvious. You can even see the hatpin used to prop up a gnome! But people sought fairies not answers. It was 60 years before the now elderly women admitted the truth. The photographs were faked using paper drawings carefully posed for effect. They had let the story ride when unable to disappoint the believers.

HALLUCINATIONS:

Once mistakes and hoaxes are removed from the picture the next port of call for the dedicated sceptic is the hallucination. It is used like a magic wand to dispel thought of real aliens.

Hallucinations can have two causes – pathological and natural. Pathological hallucinations occur as the result of some problem, perhaps a brain disease or illness such as schizophrenia. They can also be induced as a result of chemical changes in the brain brought on by drugs. Such matters have been extensively studied in order to assist in medical treatment. Any qualified psychologist should spot signs of psychopathology within a witness who claims alien contact. In the vast majority of witnesses studied professionally, no such cause was found. The overwhelming verdict of psychology is that witnesses are *not* suffering from any known pathological disorder. This has been repeatedly verified, but is at odds with quotes given to the media by sceptics who have rarely, if ever, studied the subject first-hand. It is easy to assume that witnesses must suffer from some trauma

The cut-out imagery is in retrospect obvious. You can even see the hatpin used to prop up a gnome!

that has caused them to hallucinate. Unfortunately, that tempting explanation is effectively denied by the evidence.

However, hallucinations do not only occur as a result of medical problems. They are a natural part of daily life, as images in the brain perceived to be occurring in the external world, but for which there is no corresponding outside stimulus. Sometimes an illusion can trigger a distorted perception of reality. At other times things are seen externally, when their true origin is within the mind.

One of the world's leading experts on hallucinations is Dr Ronald Siegel, who was a research professor at the UCLA School of Medicine. For years he has probed the experiences of people from all walks of life. An example he cites is of a Hollywood actress responding oddly to bright lights and of mountaineers seeing 'ghost climbers'. He notes that hallucinations are 'simply based on stored images in our own brains'.[123] They are common, occur as a result of brain activity and do not conjure up amazing things out of nowhere. They will always be consistent with our mental warehouse of images.

We can now reasonably deduce that an hallucinated alien contact will occur for a reason – possibly because of sensory isolation. And it will follow a pattern that might logically emerge from the mind of the witness. It will be represented by images that are already there – perhaps filed in the deep subconscious under headings such as 'alien' and coming from the bombardment of alien imagery that we confront in today's society. Witnesses would imagine 'grays' or Nordics because that is what other people have reported. Hallucinations would not feature flying, alien elephants, because nobody has yet claimed to have seen them. In fact, hallucinated alien contacts would be much like the cases in this book.

Siegel, conducting a survey in 1988, found that 79 per cent of ordinary people have had an hallucination. A third initially believed that what they were experiencing was a real event. They only realised that it was not when some impossible event occurred. From this it is easy to find abduction witnesses describing hallucinations. The Oxford, Maine case abductees (see page 39), speaking of their alien encounter, freely admit that they hallucinated floating cubes and snowflakes that were not really there. Police officer Alan Godfrey in Todmorden (see page 44) described under hypnosis a large, black dog in the UFO. It seems easier to accept that this image was an hallucination than to accept that aliens fly through the stars with big, black dogs.

The hypnotic state is known to be conducive to fantasy and involves dredging up hallucinated images. Normally we see these *inside* our heads and *know* that this is their true home. When regressed to an abduction memory, the intrusion of such an image will be much more difficult to assign. We are actively projecting memories on to the real world and may wrongly assume that is their origin.

In 1977 Alvin Lawson in California published new findings.[124] Volunteers with no UFO interest were regressed. Under hypnosis he asked them to *imagine* an abduction. There were similarities. Yet none of his subjects thought their hallucinations real. None described any obvious alien types. Also to some extent Lawson structured questions on real abduction cases.

I made an effort to expand upon this work for the MIT symposium (see page 49). I did not use hypnosis – just asked the witnesses to imagine vividly in a quiet environment what might happen. I tested 20 people who had not had a UFO sighting and professed no interest, against a sample who *had* seen a UFO or admitted to having gained some knowledge of the topic by reading books or watching TV programmes.[125]

> *The hypnotic state is known to be conducive to fantasy and involves dredging up hallucinated images.*

UFO-aware witnesses referred to typical entities and medical examinations found in real cases. The unaware subjects were different. None described 'grays' or Nordics or medical probes from abductions. UFO-aware witnesses imagined suddenly finding themselves on board the UFO with no recall of how they got there (the classic trait of 'doorway amnesia'). But the unaware sample (bar just two out of 20) gave a vivid account of how they were taken on board. This was often colourful – such as at the point of a ray gun.

The moment where the victim is abducted is, of course, an essential element of all good fantasy. When TV soap *The Colbys* had one of their cast abducted, they dramatised the kidnap scene, showing an entranced Fallon led aboard to face her medical examination. But real cases omit this part from memory in an overwhelming (98 per cent) majority. Does that argue against simply an hallucination? Common sense, TV experience and my MIT experiment all seem to show that it really ought to be one of the most visually dramatic scenes that we would choose to imagine. But it is not – so why?

FALSE MEMORY SYNDROME:

One intriguing clue has emerged about alien-contact witnesses. They have a very vivid recall of early life. Most people cannot remember events before the age of 3, partly because of changes around that age to the way the brain stores recall. So why is it that abductees claim to have vivid memories of periods long before – even as far back as their actual birth?

A complication is the discovery of False Memory Syndrome (FMS) by psychologists. There is evidence that children who sincerely describe being abused by their parents, especially with the 'help' of hypnosis, may be recalling a false memory that never happened. Through the process of hypnosis and investigation a memory emerges with such reality that criminal charges against parents are brought. When facts are checked these must be dropped, given no evidence that the memories are true. More generally it has long been known that people can honestly and with conviction recall all manner of events to the extent that they can pass a lie detector test. Yet a totally false memory of that experience has imposed itself upon their brain and taken on the status of reality.

Ulric Neisser tested this. In January 1985 his pupils watched the terrible explosion of the *Challenger* space shuttle live on TV. Next day he got his charges to write detailed accounts of their experience, describing what they saw. Psychologists know that emotive events provide a strong hook to memory. Like many I can recall the moment when news of the assassination of President Kennedy was received. Although just a child I have vivid recall of the scene in 1963, but could not tell you what I was doing on the same day last year.

In 1988 Neisser tracked down his pupils and got them to describe what they were doing when *Challenger* exploded. Two-thirds gave an accurate and vivid report. The others had equally detailed memories but when checked against their statements written immediately after the event, they were wrong in major respects.[126]

A dozen witnesses to a traffic accident will give a dozen different versions of the event immediately afterwards.

Recall is not a tape-recorded message or a video film. It is actively processed and edited with time to such a degree that it can become completely different. It is well-known to police officers and to psychologists that a dozen witnesses to a traffic accident will give a dozen different versions of the event immediately afterwards. Usually the differences are subtle, describing a blue car as green, for example, but sometimes they can be significant, such as referring to a second vehicle that simply was not there.

Psychologists have also established that the form of questioning can affect the answers given and that this in turn will *adapt* the memory. In one experiment witnesses observed two cars, both travelling at the same slow speed before an impact. When questioned carefully answers were reasonably correct. But if the questions were not well phrased serious problems occurred. Asking 'At what velocity was the speeding car travelling?' ensured that some people ascribed a much faster speed to one vehicle. 'When did the red car apply its brakes?' brought replies of time estimates for that very incident, even though neither car used any brakes at all.

When similar tests are carried out using hypnosis, even more difficulties emerge. In one case a witness, when asked to describe what they could recall happening during the night, at first quite clearly remembered nothing. After being subtly guided to the belief that a crime had occurred which they should have witnessed, a new memory of a gunshot was reported. Later the witness adamantly believed they *had* heard the gunshot and was stunned to see their original video testimony refuting the idea. But there was no gunshot because the crime that the witness was coerced into remembering was an invention.

Dr Elizabeth Loftus is one of the most experienced psychologists conducting such experiments. In 1993 she said (not of abductions, but certainly with relevance), 'We do not yet have the tools for reliably distinguishing the signal of true repressed memories from the noise of false ones. Until we gain these tools it seems prudent to urge care in how horrors on the other side of some presumed amnesic barrier are probed.'[127]

FMS amply justifies my stance on the need for UFOlogy to stop using hypnosis forthwith. Mike Wootten was a UFOlogist with BUFORA. In 1987 he was regressed to a November night and asked to describe what he saw. Wootten reported driving near Epping in Essex and seeing a white light tailing the car. The engine began to misfire, then died completely. As it did so, the light surrounded the car and Wootten had the urge to get out. He recalled walking through a field towards an object, then a memory jump and being inside a room on a table. Here small, shadowy beings were examining him. Then he was suddenly back in the car, with the UFO gone and able to drive away.

This regression is a classic account as provided by abduction witnesses. All who were present during the hypnosis confirm Wootten's real fear and tension as he relived the event. There is just one problem. He says 'Every detail of my hypnosis session is accurate. I can remember them very vividly and at the time felt as if it was really happening . . . The physical effects were obvious and very powerful . . . [but] I must firmly state that I am very certain that I have never been abducted, or in fact ever seen a UFO and I do not believe that the regression revealed any forgotten memories . . . It is obvious that the scenario that I related under hypnosis was gleaned from my studies of the UFO . . .'[128]

Clinical hypnotherapist, Debra Lindemann, writing for MUFON in 1997 aimed – as she termed it – to 'put FMS to bed'. While she made some valid points on its contentious nature, one of her arguments is worrying. She noted correctly, that 39 per cent of people with recall of child abuse did so without seeking hypnosis. Their memory surfaced in flashback and dream-image form. As she pointed out the same is true of abduction memories. But does that necessarily make them more accurate than hypnotic recall?[129]

Like Mike Wootten I was hypnotically regressed to a close encounter by a clinical psychologist. Unlike Mike I *know* that the starting point – a sighting of a bluish light in a Chester field – *did* occur. However, it was just a low-flying aircraft. I have never had reason to think myself an abductee. Yet under hypnosis I experienced 'new' alien memories that seemed real. I could check my recall of mundane features of my life at the time. The hypnosis recall of things like the day of the week was often wrong. Much of my 'memory' of alien contact here came to me in flashbacks and dreams after the hypnosis, just as real witnesses allege. This recall must be dubious given how wrong were the checkable 'facts' that I 'recalled'. I was not abducted. But under other circumstances it would be easy to think so. Most witnesses will find it impossible to judge the truth.[130]

Another important clue is how many abductions feature surgical procedures. We saw that some witnesses confused recall of real childhood medical treatment with later alien experimentation. Might not all on-board abductions feature false memories based on the true medical history of the witness? Why are no researchers pursuing this possibility?

ALTERED STATES:

Whatever the explanation for alien-contact stories, two inescapable conclusions arise. Firstly, the experience occurs during an altered state of consciousness. Many cases confirm that. Keith Basterfield shows this with statistical data that proves that the two most common environments are the bedroom late at night and when driving a car, often alone on a dark, isolated road. Both are havens of sensory deprivation.

All surveys agree that the majority of alien contacts occur between the hours of midnight and 5.00 am. Motorists driving on a busy highway in rush hour do not claim abduction. Yet any traffic survey proves that there are many times more potential witnesses driving in those circumstances than at 3.00 am on a back road in Devon. Of course, you might argue that 'they' (the aliens) deliberately choose not to put lives at risk by spacenapping victims from the M1. But it seems as likely that the sensory deprivation effect is absent when constant attention is needed on a busy road. The other major clue confirms this.

In case after case we hear witnesses describe the 'Oz Factor'. They tell of all environmental sounds fading, time stretching out and of a sort of inward tuning of consciousness where the external world temporarily disappears. This is without question part of the explanation. The 'Oz Factor' is a set of symptoms that indicate a switch in the state of consciousness. Like self-induced sensory deprivation to 'tune in' to an inner reality, it is needed to 'tune out' the external world. The 'Oz Factor' proves that alien contacts happen after the witness enters an altered state. And altered states can certainly occur with no intervention from little grey men.

Dr John Lilly was one of the pioneers of study in this field. A scientist investigating the workings of the brain, he decided from 1954 to 'map' inner space by conducting experiments upon himself. One way that he did this was to place himself in an isolation tank filled with water to cut out sensory input. He later expanded his tests to include taking drugs and hypnosis.[131]

During the tests, Lilly had numerous experiences involving 'contact' with two 'entities'. These seemed very much like the 'spirit guides' claimed by mediums who commune with the afterlife. They are also akin to aliens. Lilly conceded that they could be 'entities in other spaces, other universes than our consensus reality'. Indeed he shared numerous ideas about their nature – that they might be 'helpful constructs' or the 'communication of a civilisation way beyond ours, which is radiating information throughout the galaxy'. Of course, Lilly, like all the alien-contact witnesses that have been studied, simply did not know which explanation was correct. But he *did* know that he had these experiences because he had propelled himself into an altered state, via sensory deprivation and the 'Oz Factor', which acts like a sign on the door declaring entry into another reality.

After many months of experiment, Lilly told of how 'I went through dreamlike sequences, waking dreams as they are now called, in which I watched what was happening.' His control of this other reality was such that an entire drama was acting out of which he had become the observer. Yet, of course, his assistants saw no other entities and were well aware that he had 'gone nowhere'. He remained in his isolation tank. The analogy with how we have seen real-life abductions occur is surely obvious.

By 1964, Lilly was regularly able to slip into the 'Oz Factor'. This was marked by the sensation of floating out of his body. Many abduction stories start with this claim by the witness. Indeed in cases like the Aveley abduction (see page 40), the witnesses report the classic out-of-body experience image of seeing their bodies from some outside vantage point whilst they roam about with the aliens. Of his later treks Lilly said, 'There are entities in our universe that we cannot normally detect, but are there and have realities way beyond ours.'

> *His control of this other reality was such that an entire drama was acting out of which he had become the observer.*

A truly memorable encounter happened to Lilly when he found himself in a great space or room magically filled with light. Two entities communicated by telepathy. He felt a great sense of rapport and information was transferred into his mind at such a rapid rate that it overwhelmed him. Predictions about his future were offered. He was then given a choice as to whether to return to his body or not. If he did then an 'assignment' would be given. The beings planted information into his subconscious – 'They said I would forget it when I came back into the body until such time as (it) was needed. Then I would use it.'[132]

The comparisons between this self-induced 'contact' and reported abductions (or indeed with near-death visions) are stunning. There seems little doubt that these are the same phenomenon, and it is fascinating that Lilly progressed from initial assumptions that he was simply having hallucinations to the consideration that he might be in some sort of communion with a vastly superior intelligence.

FALSE AWAKENINGS:

Keith Basterfield was one of the first UFOlogists to see that many alien contacts begin within the bedroom late at night. He argued that they were extreme examples of what is known to psychologists as the 'false awakening'. In modified form this theory still holds some sway amongst cautious researchers.

Every human being must sleep. If deprived mental breakdown and death will follow. Sleep has two principle phases – REM and non-REM (NREM). REM sleep is characterised by the rapid movement of the eyes and research has proven that it is here that we dream. Bursts of REM begin at just a few minutes but grow longer as the night progresses and we all experience at least half a dozen spells a night. Even people who claim they rarely dream do so – profusely – every night. They simply do not recall their dreams upon waking, as they are not retained in long-term memory unless we consciously act to make that happen.

Although theories as to what dreams are remain controversial, most psychologists agree that dreaming is essential. If REM sleep and dreams are prevented, severe effects are noted – leading quickly to hallucinations (dreams intruding into the waking day) and major loss of bodily functions. When allowed to dream freely again after prevention, people do so for much longer than normal. Babies dream more than children, who in turn have more REM sleep than adults. After about the age of 35, the level of dreaming and its quality tails off. By comparison, we might note the finding that most abductees claim to have recall of many childhood experiences and even babyhood events (their vivid dreams possibly acting as memory hooks) but that witnesses older than 35 are far less common.[133]

In REM sleep the body has an in-built protection mechanism. It is easy to imagine that if one dreamt of jumping off a roof and then the body was able to act out this task the consequences might be disastrous. Therefore, in deep REM many motor functions of the body are paralysed. Those controlling breathing are not, for obvious reasons. Of course, we are deeply unconscious in REM sleep when this paralysis occurs so, even though it happens every night, we do not consciously remember it. It is worth noting here those many cases in which aliens use a beam to paralyse a witness. This paralysis seems selective, in that the breathing process is not effected. Is there a connection?

It is not simply a choice of either being awake or being asleep. The transition between these states can produce some odd effects. Dream images can intrude on the borders and appear to happen *within* the bedroom. A number of cases where apparitions and entities are seen briefly can surely be explained in this way. Normally we would not be aware of these fleeting images, because they would be absorbed into our dreams. But the common experience of waking with a start, sure that somebody has called your name, can result from this kind of hallucination.

The false awakening probably occurs when a person briefly wakes up without realising it and then falls straight back to deep sleep. If they immediately enter REM, then dreaming could adopt this theme. If so then a dream will be 'set' in the bedroom and involve the act of getting up – since this is what the mind would naturally expect to follow waking up. The person can then mistake this vivid dream of waking for true wakefulness and will not see their error until they actually do awake from the dream.

It is not simply a choice of either being awake or being asleep. The transition between these states can produce some odd effects.

In this state the dream can, of course, include odd events. Once I had to get up early on a cold, icy morning to see my boyfriend off to work on his motor-cycle. I did not want him to leave. When he did ride away, I sat back on the settee in front of a fire and moments later was aware that he *had* returned. Excited, I started to greet him and then 'awoke' still on the settee. I had clearly fallen asleep with my desire for his return uppermost, experienced a vivid dream of him doing just that, and then mistook it for reality because it 'occurred' in a perfect recreation of my living room. Here I could do a reality check and *prove* that my boyfriend did not come back. But without proof to the contrary, I might believe that he had.

For a moment assume that I had briefly awoken and seen a bright light through the window (the planet Venus perhaps). I might have returned to sleep with *that thought* dominant. Any realistic dream that followed might have included an alien encounter and I would have no way to judge its reality. If instead of my boyfriend I had seen a little, grey entity standing in my lounge, how could I have proven that this figure was not real? My boyfriend could tell me he did not return. You cannot interrogate an alien.

Equally, if my boyfriend had left at 7.00 am, I had fallen asleep, dreamt of this grey entity and awoken to find that it was now 7.45 am, would I suspect a time-lapse of three-quarters of an hour during which I was actually asleep? Would I seek hypnosis to try to find out what really happened? It seems improbable that hypnosis would reveal the truth – a false awakening dream – particularly if neither myself nor the eager UFOlogists egging me on were seeking that kind of resolution to such a seemingly exciting case.

In 1987 Michael Smith reported how a professional photographer called Barry, in Kidbrooke, London, had a vivid dream. It began with walking on Plumstead Common with police, when several humanoids appeared. In the dream a voice urged Barry to 'give yourself to us'. He then woke in his bed. Outside the window was a bright ball of light that disappeared. It resembled Venus. Noting that it was 3.00 am, Barry walked to the bathroom and then entered his parents' bedroom, something he would not normally do. The light was seen again, this time tilting to reveal itself as a saucer shape. It climbed vertically upwards in silence and was gone.

Barry's interpretation is interesting. His suggestion is that aliens in a craft above his roof were seeking to programme him as he slept, but by waking up he interrupted their plot. However, look at this slightly differently. What if Barry was having a typical muddled dream of police, aliens and odd voices from which he awoke. Shining through the window was a bright star. Immediately he re-entered REM sleep and a false awakening dream followed in which Barry 'got up and saw the UFO as a spacecraft'. This possibility is enhanced by the fact that he appears to have no further recall for that night after the UFO departed, other than of presumably falling sleep again. One imagines that if a dramatic close encounter occurred in a fully waking state, then one would be highly excited, or intent on documenting the incident, and would *not* instantly fall asleep. Does this suggest that Barry was never really awake?[134]

> *Any realistic dream that followed might have included an alien encounter and I would have no way to judge its reality.*

In one case from Derby, a witness saw a UFO from the bedroom, assumed an atom bomb had exploded and went straight back to sleep. This only makes sense as a false awakening where the witness clearly knew at some level that there really was no nuclear blast in his garden!

WAKING LUCID DREAMS:

Most of us experience flying dreams and nightmares about medical examinations. Of course, we tend not to regard them as alien in origin but as symbols teaching us things about the way that our subconscious works.[135] Lucid dreams are experienced by about one in three people during their lives. One in ten have them once or twice a year. If you have had a lucid dream, you will appreciate how no words can adequately describe it. They are literally another state of being – not like a dream and not like waking.

A lucid dream occurs when the sleeper becomes aware that they are dreaming and allows their conscious mind to take an active part in what follows. It is like being sat in a cinema and suddenly finding yourself inside the film, with the characters responding to your presence. While you do not control the scenery – the dream world just seems to be there – it is experienced with much-enhanced clarity. But you *know* that it is not real and that – being in a dream – if you want to fly, you can. If you want to walk through a wall, you can – as if you are doing it.

Theories about lucid dreams are still argued.[136] But we need to consider a spectrum of consciousness with a gradual transition from full-waking awareness to deep-dream sleep. Between the two are various altered states that share a mixture of waking and dreaming levels. False awakenings probably have about 50/50 – so they are set in the real world but with the dreaming mind equally active. Lucid dreams come somewhere closer to the dreaming end (possibly about 25 per cent waking and 75 per cent dreaming states). For balance there should be an experience that was 75 per cent waking and 25 per cent dreaming. I call it the waking-lucid-dream state.

From what we know of false awakenings and lucid dreams, we can predict the features a waking lucid dream would have. It would seem to occur within the real world, since the level of consciousness is closest to that end of the spectrum, but it would involve a healthy dose of internal imagery more appropriate to a dream. In a lucid dream, the conscious mind *enters* the dream and can control the dream reality. In the waking-lucid state, the dreaming mind *enters* waking reality to control its appearance.

In a lucid dream, the mind finds a boost of realism but accepts what is happening *as* a dream. With a waking-lucid state the person should accept what is happening as *reality* but with a sudden boost in dreamlike qualities. The 'Oz Factor' is exactly that and many images that unfold during an abduction resemble dream imagery briefly taking over the real world. Psychologists may not have recognised the existence of the waking-lucid-dream state because when it happens it appears to be supernatural in nature, perhaps as an alien abduction or near-death vision. Such claims are to most scientists abhorrent. I fear this could prove a fundamental mistake.

Many psychologists have reached the conclusion that dreaming is a process that never ceases. Professor H. Price said that dreaming 'goes on throughout our waking hours, and just occasionally we may catch a glimpse of it.'[137] Obviously we are more likely to do so when in a sensory-deprived location, such as the bedroom or in a car on a lonely road at night. This comes back to the *essence* of the abduction.

> **By entering the daydream state, you have foregone some features of the external world.**

The daydream is something we can pay attention to when we stop concentrating and it is quite easy to sit and relax for a few minutes, let your mind drift and have sudden images enter your head. If you try this subjectively only moments may appear to go by, but a look at the clock surprises you with the news that maybe half an hour has passed. By entering the daydream state, you have foregone some features of the external world.

SLEEP PARALYSIS:

Consider this case reported in 1995 by Scottish group SPI. It occurred in Grangemouth, within a high-rise flat that is home to a young family with daughters aged 4 and 2. For some weeks strange lights appeared in the sky and seem to have been the source of concern. But then 4-year-old Sarah started to report a 'monster' that came into her room at night. Of course, many young children have nightmares – partly because they have image-rich dreamlives but have yet to learn the boundaries of reality. However, here the extent and intensity of the episodes was too great and, connecting them with UFOs, this route was explored.

The descriptions and sketches of the 'monster' will not be a surprise. It is a small, spindle-bodied creature with long arms, an egg-shaped head and slanting eyes. Several would appear in the room. Sarah also experienced various sensations of people touching her. These events occurred on the edge of sleep. Indeed Sarah felt the 'monsters' tried to wake her up. Before long the mother and younger daughter were starting to share these sensations, but they stopped when the family moved to a relative's home.[138]

If aliens were trying to abduct Sarah, they seem a pretty incompetent bunch who were incapable of taking her from another nearby house. In fact, the experience reported by this girl is a remarkably common one and more often not interpreted as an alien contact. Dr David Hufford has studied centuries of reports of people – especially women – awaking in the middle of the night and finding themselves paralysed with a heavy pressure pushing down on top of them. There were sometimes senses of presence within the room and various other effects. The assumption long held was that some kind of monster was conducting an assault. In fact, this type of report was referred to in medieval times as the incubus and the succubus and was considered to be some kind of demon endeavouring to rape the helpless victim. The physical sensations can quite easily be interpreted in that way. Occult literature is full of stories of this so-called 'old hag' or 'night terror'. There seems an inevitable link with bedroom-visitor, alien abductions.

Psychologists still investigate demon-assault cases, although these have adopted media-inspired images such as 'randy ghosts'. In January 1999, one Derbyshire family tried unsuccessfully to prove to a judge that their home was haunted in this way, following repeated night-terror experiences. The story given by such witnesses is consistent – waking in the night, feeling this pressure, being unable to move, convinced that someone is on the bed and the assumption that a spectre is attacking you. Occasional reports of seeing the ghost follow, but visual sightings are less common than the physical sensations.

Old hags, randy ghosts and sex-mad aliens may be much of the same thing. David Hufford has taken an interesting approach, not attempting to explain the phenomenon but to record it. By 1992 he had established by survey in the USA that 17 per cent of the population were reporting the phenomenon. A quarter reacted positively when a connection with UFOs was inferred. One symptom that these witnesses often describe is an odd tingling/vibrating sensation throughout the body. This often occurs during alien contacts too.

Hufford is well aware that some of these problems result from the previously noted paralysis enforced on the body during REM sleep. A person waking unexpectedly could perhaps still feel the paralysis whilst regaining awareness. Similar feelings have been reported by patients when coming around from an anaesthetic after surgery. Drugs are used to stop them moving on the operating table but a patient can occasionally wake up before they wear off. If they are fully awake, yet still paralysed, it feels odd. But nobody ascribes what is happening to an alien attack. Of course a patient recovering from surgery might expect some unusual sensations. In your own bed at night, aliens may seem a better option.

Anthony Obanye conducted a series of experiments between 1991 and 1996 in which he attempted to train himself to experience this night terror. Knowing the physiology has not prevented him feeling the sensations or sense of presence. Nor has it stopped him from being projected beyond this experience into deeper visionary journeys – something Hufford has also noted in some patients. Indeed, after many experiences, Obanye is still unclear whether he really does go 'out of the body' or is experiencing some kind of dream state.[139]

Sue Blackmore argues that sleep paralysis is a key to the abduction. In her view the physical sensations are coupled with dream states and hallucinations to provide a wholly acceptable answer to this type of case. It is hard not to agree that this is part of the answer. Indeed, in an early letter to Budd Hopkins, some months *before* the observed abduction from her Manhattan tenement (see page 50), abductee Linda Napolitano reported a series of sleep disorders that one might perhaps connect with alien assaults. But equally they are akin to false awakenings, the sense of an unseen presence in the bedroom and a feeling of pressure and paralysis as she lay in bed. So were they natural, or supernatural in origin?[140]

NARCOLEPSY:

Narcolepsy has been considered an answer by several doctors studying abductees featured in this book. This condition occurs when a person effectively enters REM sleep suddenly from waking, because of a physiological problem with the part of the brain that triggers the sleep mechanism. It can be brought on by a period of routine activity such as driving a car. The period of unconsciousness is often short and may not be noticed. If it is up to 30 minutes long or more, the person may feel odd, drive to a stop, fall asleep and awake confused and uncertain. If they had a vivid dream, then memories of it might intrude into the discontinuous recall of the attack.[141] This idea is suggested by the experience of psychologist Dr David Gotlib.

He cites the case of a patient called Mike, from Ontario, Canada, who had a master's degree in science and had experienced numerous odd things during his life. These included several apparent time-lapses with strange associated memories that hinted at something deeper. After discovering the abduction phenomenon, Mike eventually found his way to Gotlib. Typical of what he had experienced was the meeting with a buffalo in the middle of the road on a drive home. This innocent event had caused him to be inexplicably two hours late. He wondered if it was a screen image for an alien memory.

There were other 'time-lapses' or periods of amnesia, dating back to Mike's childhood. Inevitably he connected scraps of associated dream imagery with various odd lights he had also seen in the sky. When treated by Gotlib, Mike was suffering migraine-like head pains and it turned out that he had already been diagnosed as having a sleep disorder, apnea, that affects the ability to breathe properly at night. Mike was sent to see a specialist. Genetic tests led to a new discovery. The patient had been a lifelong sufferer from narcolepsy. In the view of the specialist this was probably the solution to Mike's record of time-lapses and odd visions.

Narcolepsy has been considered an answer by several doctors studying abductees . . .

Once it was thought that sleep paralysis was a sign of narcolepsy because narcoleptics often experienced this problem. Now we know that the effect is simply remembered more by narcolepsy sufferers because they slip rapidly from wakefulness to REM sleep. But it is not unique to them.

Where it has been suggested as a cause, few medical tests have followed. Alan Godfrey, the Todmorden police officer (see page 44), is one witness for whom the idea was mooted, largely because he reported a number of time discontinuities during his life, usually of short duration and without attendant UFOs. These events have not, to my knowledge, been explored under hypnosis. But if abductees were routinely tested for this possibility, it might prove interesting. They often claim they were held in vicelike grips when on the table inside a UFO. Perhaps this is a dream image reflecting the physical sensation of sleep paralysis that their bodies are enduring?

TEMPORAL LOBE EPILEPSY:

A not dissimilar medical condition to narcolepsy is TLE (temporal lobe epilepsy). This is a sort of electrical storm within the brain that triggers short periods of unconsciousness but can also be presaged by an 'aura' in which the patient senses the oncoming effect. Certain conditions can induce TLE, for example, rapidly flashing lights or the moon flickering through trees as you drive past them on a straight road.

There may also be a connection with the far more common phenomenon of migraine. Often dismissed as merely a headache, migraine is in fact caused by chemical changes in the brain and can involve both an 'aura' and 'hallucinations' such as bright lights. Certainly many alien contact witnesses are migraine sufferers. In addition, witnesses often claim that after their encounter they are left with a severe headache and nausea that seems to resemble migraine.

Both the relatively rare TLE and post-abduction migraine attack suggest a connection between this phenomenon and changes in brain chemistry. Psychologist Dr Serena Roney-Dougal has investigated this idea and believes that two chemicals are particularly important in regulating the ability to experience altered states. One, serotonin, is a neurotransmitter that has a direct link in the brain with creativity and imagination and the regulation of emotion. The other chemical regulates sleep functions.[142] Abductees are known to have strong abilities at visual creativity. The problems linking cases to the sleep process have just been set out. And unexpected emotional reactions are frequently reported after alien contacts, such as bursting into tears as the aliens depart.[143]

Several doctors studying abductions have suggested problems with the temporal lobe. In 1967 Dr Paul Zeck proposed TLE as a possible trigger for the Mayanup, Western Australia case (see page 65) and we saw how the Anne Jeffries case from the seventeenth century (see page 13) featured suspicious signs of TLE. Psychologist Dr Moyshe Kalman further stated in 1997 that he has detected indications of TLE in British abductees.[144]

Dr G.N. Saxe found activity in the temporal lobe to be enhanced within people suffering from MPD (multiple personality disorder). In this condition, consciousness seems to split into several fragments with differing personalities. Neuropsychologist Norman Don claims to have measured increased activity in this part of the brain when studying mediums in a trance state, claiming to talk to entities in the afterlife. Patients suffering TLE have also been recorded as describing odd memory flashbacks akin to déjà vu. As a result, neuropsychologist Dr Michael Persinger set up experiments deliberately stimulating this region of the brain with electromagnetic energy. His subjects report out-of-body states and other 'Oz Factor' symptoms.[145]

FANTASY PRONE PERSONALITIES:

In 1983 Theodore Barber and Sheryl Wilson published a study of 52 highly intelligent women. This project set out to discover why half were excellent hypnotic regression subjects and the others were almost impossible to hypnotise. The psychologists found, to their surprise, that those easily regressed 'had a profound fantasy life', their fantasies often as 'real as real'. They also had remarkably vivid recall. Some 92 per cent could describe events before the age of 3, as compared with only 12 per cent of the normal population.

Unusual levels of visual creativity, rich dreamlives and particularly vivid early recall are *all* key factors to emerge independently from several studies of alien contact witnesses – including my sample of British cases. That these features so closely relate to the psychological profile of what Barber and Wilson defined as the 'best hypnotic regression candidates' cannot be coincidence.

Barber and Wilson termed the good regression subjects 'fantasy prone personalities' – or FPP. With more study, links with the paranormal began to develop. FPP often grew up believing they could see fairies or other elemental beings and a third still claimed to see them in adulthood. A staggering 58 per cent could describe in detail an imaginary playmate. In contrast only 8 per cent of non-FPP could do so. Over 90 per cent of FPP said they had at least once mistaken a fantasy for a real event. Their inner lives could be – as one put it – like 'being inside a 3-D movie without knowing the script'.

Moreover, FPP said that they had great difficulty driving at night because they had on occasions been forced to pull-over and stop when a figure crossed the road and vanished. Some assumed that it was a ghost, but nobody else could see it. Indeed, the lifelong track record of psychic experience by these FPP was every bit as notable as that reported by abductees – including (in descending order of occurrence to FPP) empathic rapport with loved ones, telepathy, pre-cognitive dreams, out-of-body states and near-death experiences. 92 per cent of the FPP sample reported some of these events – up to ten times the level described by non-FPP subjects.[146]

In 1985 a much more extensive test, involving men as well as women, was conducted by Susan Myers and Harvey Austrin at the University of St Louis. They found that men were *less likely* to be FPP, but some were excellent candidates. The overall figure for FPP in society was calculated as about 3 per cent However, these were people so strongly FPP that they were immediately obvious. Many others had limited FPP traits, suggesting that from time to time they would share some vivid experiences.

By 1987 more work by Steven Lynn (Ohio State University) and Judith Rhue (Toledo University) had found that FPP were also very artistic and creative, writing poetry or doing excellent artwork. This is yet another significant finding of studies into abductees. This creativity began in childhood as an escape mechanism, often because the child spent much time in their rooms alone – sometimes after personal trauma.[147] In 1988 Keith Basterfield, the Australian UFOlogist who had proposed a link with false awakenings, worked with sociologist Dr Robert Bartholomew to investigate this theory. They found strong hints that abductees might be FPP.[148] This fitted neatly with similar findings by other researchers – notably the ongoing anamnesis witness, life profile study begun by Ken Phillips at BUFORA. Indeed, in early 1999 Liverpool University also began to obtain stunning results from ESP experiments when focusing on creatively visual subjects, such as arts and drama students. This link seems now quite firmly established.

Basterfield and Bartholomew argued that the simplest solution was to assume that witnesses were having vivid fantasies that adopted the alien theme for no reason other than it was part of the creative process. The view of many UFOlogists was that FPP seemed to have problems. These centre on the physical evidence (such as alleged body scars on witnesses, the extraordinary consistency between cases and the lack of any rich array of colourful aliens). FPP should by definition be able to conjure up realistic adventures that involve all manner of entities doing all sorts of things.[149]

Unusual levels of visual creativity, rich dreamlives and particularly vivid early recall are all key factors to emerge from studies of alien contact witnesses.

By 1991 Dr Kenneth Ring was reporting FPP traits within people who experienced the near-death experience via his ongoing Omega Project. In 1995, noted Oxford researcher of the paranormal, Dr Charles McCreery (with Gordon Claridge), reported on a study of the personality profile of 450 people who had experienced an out-of-body state. Their findings contrasted with a control sample of 267 people who had never had one and revealed a correlation between out-of-body experiences and FPP traits. But it appears to occur as an inherent human ability. Moreover one question stood out – were the witnesses having such experiences *because* they were FPP, or were they FPP because of many 'psychic' experiences?[150] That is also true of abductions. Is an FPP prone to imagining alien contact or do they have enhanced abilities that can manifest in several ways such as dreams, NDEs or abductions?

There must be a connection since there are too many factors in common – artistic creativity, early life recall, lifelong psychic track records, hypnotic susceptibility etc. But exactly what *is* the relationship? Since much abduction data emerges via hypnosis and since from the start of work on FPP it was established that these people are the best hypnotic subjects, we have a problem. The data produced by abductees through hypnosis is by definition biased. Those without FPP traits would be less good at regression and less likely to produce the detailed recall that creates the abduction. This is another reason for ceasing the use of hypnosis, for while it is dominant we will never be sure what role FPP has in the abduction evidence.

Martin Kottmeyer further suggests that it is not FPP itself that is the issue, but the model of the world created by such people. He argues that in childhood we learn to categorise experiences as 'real' or as 'fantasies'. Because an FPP has many vivid experiences that straddle such a boundary, they may evolve without learning the distinction. Phenomena that most of us would regard as imaginary would be interpreted by FPP as part of reality. But are *we* correct to regard our visions as 'unreal' and FPP mistaken when judging them otherwise? Societies, such as the aborigines, live successfully on the premise that visions are valuable experiences and are not trivial imaginings.[151]

At the MIT symposium (see page 49) Basterfield presented his study on 152 UFO witnesses that showed a tendency towards FPP. Several other studies by psychologists were presented – with samples of up to 200 witnesses. The results were confusing. Some showed hints of FPP and some not. Even the study by Ring, while noting that witnesses had unusual psychological profiles, did not prove that they were FPP as such. The best that could be argued was that certain characteristics stood out – notably visual creativity. But Eddie Bullard argued that the witnesses most strongly FPP were what we would term contactees rather than abductees. He suspected that we might be linking two phenomena together when testing witnesses and that a strict definition of an abductee was needed. We had adopted too broad a series of psychic and altered states into aliens kidnap evidence. To some researchers these made the witness a contactee but not a victim of a proper abduction.[152]

Stockport clinical psychologist, Dr John Dale, with whom I worked on my own dubious recall, had an intriguing suggestion. He felt that the abduction mystery might be created by a few FPP with extreme abilities that emerge when they are regressed. They create the big cases and drag other, probably less FPP-orientated, witnesses along. Dale feels there is often one strong FPP personality who is readily hypnotised. Other witnesses can actively resist – perhaps because they fear that they would contradict the apparent reality of the experience. He noted several cases where witnesses 'prefer to forget' an incident, or need 'numerous sessions' before being forced into a supporting story. He wonders if they, without realising it, opt for silence to avoid contradicting the recall of a fellow witness – usually a loved one. As such any easily regressed FPP would most directly affect the subsequent detail of a story.

In 1994, Basterfield noted that while he recognises some cases have physical evidence and some UFO witnesses are not FPP, he suspects that alien contacts could be different. Some sort of psychological explanation has to be the most viable. It is hard to test or to falsify the presence of aliens.[153]

A remarkable study in 1980 by London psychiatrist Dr Morton Schatzman reported how a patient called Ruth demonstrated her ability to produce hallucinations that took over her life. There is no doubt these were not real images, because they featured living people (including the psychiatrist) who were provably elsewhere at the time. But the FPP abilities of Ruth gave them such reality that they became almost physical. In one test Ruth made an apparition stand in front of a flashing light, while she was wired up to a machine in hospital. This measured brain activity and proved that this person (invisible, of course, to her doctors) was sufficiently real to stop her brain from perceiving the light. But when asked to let the figure turn on a room light Ruth 'saw' that light come on but could not read anything put in front of her in the total darkness.[154]

EXTERNAL EVENTS WITH EXOTIC CAUSES

ENERGY FORMS:

Although much of the alien contact mystery suggests an explanation within 'inner' space, there are clear signs of physical reality – consistent reports that indicate that an energy form sets the encounter in motion.

Witnesses frequently refer to the sense of oppression or heaviness that pushes down on them from above (see page 29). They talk of a sensation like an electric storm in which the atmosphere feels strange and charged with static (see page 80). This book is filled with reports of electrical activity itself – including the tingling feelings on the skin, buzzing noises, arcing or sparking of the object and even witnesses gathering static charge that gives them electric shocks for hours after the encounter has ended. Other cases feature electric sparks being given off by clothes. The evidence is unmistakable.

We are almost forced towards the conclusion that some kind of energy form lies at the heart of the encounter – perhaps a floating, electrically-charged object of unknown origin. This physical energy is real by any definition we choose. Anyone who is present can see it or feel it. But what happens next is a different matter. In some cases this apparently real electrical force is witnessed by people who do not experience a close encounter. Alan Godfrey claimed that his police car was stopped by a rotating mass of energy (see page 44). This phenomenon was seen by police officers on a surveillance mission nearby, but they did *not* see the aliens. The electrified ball that terrified Harald in Sweden (see page 49) was witnessed, but nobody shared his later alien contact. In other words, we may need two distinct phenomena. While the details of the alien contact strongly imply it is subjective in nature and involves altered states of consciousness, some kind of rotating energy form may precipitate a close encounter and be very tangible.

Are there *two* UFO experiences – an objective event that anyone can see and a more subjective experience shared only by the gifted few? Alien contacts and abductions are rare. UFOs are not. Thousands of them are seen every year and while the vast majority are misidentifications, some are probably a more exotic energy form undefined by science. UFOlogists term these UAP (Unidentified Atmospheric Phenomena) as a way to avoid endorsing alien star ships while acknowledging some reality. But why are these two phenomena linked? Can this energy form *trigger* a deep level of alien contact in some people?

After the multiple car-stop events at Levelland, Texas, in 1957 the idea that ball-lightning or plasma might explain UFOs was considered.[155] The spread

Red sprite lightning photographed over the USA on 3 July 1994.

of similar cases brought speculation that this energy could create severe electrical disturbance. A team of scientists at Colorado University tested cars allegedly stopped by a hovering UFO. It was assumed that the magnetic signature imprinted onto the car body during manufacture would permanently alter thanks to any strong energy field. Tests revealed no such change.[156] But then one case featured grass seemingly 'cooked' by microwave radiation. In another a diesel-engined truck beneath a hovering UFO lost power to its lights but not to its ignition, whereas a petrol-driven car only feet away lost both engine and lights. This led to the idea that the energy within the UFO impeded the flow of ions in an electrical circuit.

By 1975 French researcher, Fernand Lagarde, noted that UFOs clustered around fault lines in rock strata and Paul Devereux developed the idea that the UAP created were what he called 'earthlights'. Electrical and chemical changes stimulated within the atmosphere could be triggered by the intense energies released from faulted rocks when put under strain. These concentrated in active areas, so-called 'windows'.

Canadian brain specialist, Dr Michael Persinger, reached similar conclusions from a different direction. He predicted that freely floating fields of electrical energy – which he called 'transients' – should exist within the atmosphere and stimulate a clustering of strange phenomena. Such was the energy in these invisible transients that they could trigger chemical changes inside the brains of susceptible witnesses and cause them to hallucinate a close encounter by stimulating the temporal lobe.

Persinger set about creating transients in his laboratory and proving that witnesses subjected to this high energy field *did* suffer altered states, out-of-body sensations and other curious symptoms, not dissimilar to the 'Oz Factor'. But what they did *not* report were alien contacts, let alone alien abductions.

In the meantime, Devereux established that earthlights could be reproduced in the laboratory – as tiny, short-lived, sparking lights. Of course, on the much larger scale of the landscape these lights could be long lasting and far grander in size. But there was still something of a gulf between theory and proven fact. Moreover, some of the arguments about the location of the hot spots where earthlights or transients seemed most in evidence came from statistical data on the UFO subject that was dubious. Because 95 per cent of UFO sightings are misperceptions (of stars, aircraft, etc.) there could be no conceivable link for them to rock strata or electrical energies.

It is certainly possible to envisage the transients that Persinger identified. Sometimes these would be undetected. Other times, witnesses would know of their presence by feeling the electrical effects, such as tingling and hair standing on end. Occasionally, the electrical charge could result in a glowing cloud forming from chemical changes in the atmosphere. This could drift around and trigger time-loss events (see page 98).

There are some comparisons between the theory that Devereux suggests for earthlights and the energy fields that Persinger describes. They would be far more common in locations where the environmental conditions were appropriate – so-called 'window' areas. The work in the mid-1980s that established the presence of floating plasma balls in the remote Hessdalen region of Norway was support for both concepts (see page 79). There is also some experimental work that backs up the existence of earthlights and transients. Evidence from the UFO mystery is strongly in favour of a free-floating UAP. And Persinger has proven that altered states can be induced in certain witnesses if they get too close to such a phenomenon.

Physicist, Dr Terence Meaden, whilst trying to find a solution to the crop circles that dotted the west of England during the 1980s, proposed a form of tornado as the cause. This 'plasma vortex' was a rotating electrified wind that he said could leave marks. Investigation by UFOlogists such as Paul Fuller revealed that a plasma vortex could in fact be more plausible as a meteorological trigger for electrical UFO encounters. Indeed the rotating dome shape seen

Can a full-blown abduction occur as a result of close proximity to one of these energy balls or plasma vortices?

by Alan Godfrey at the onset of his abduction (see page 44) seems a very good candidate for a plasma vortex.[157]

Can a full-blown abduction occur as a result of close proximity to one of these energy balls or plasma vortices? It is conceivable that some people would be unaffected by contact with such an energy and may only describe a glowing UFO. Others may experience chemical changes in the brain and report odd sensations of a physical nature. And perhaps a tiny few are extremely susceptible and experience a dramatic alien vision during the altered state/dream state/time loss that results from this.

These people may, or may not, be those who have problems with their temporal lobe, or who have other conditions such as narcolepsy, or are FPP, or some other undefined factor. But to my knowledge submitting repeater UFO witnesses or abductees in a controlled way to close proximity of artificially created transients or plasma vortices has yet to occur. It is not without risk but surely the next step.

PSYCHOTRONICS:

A favourite of science fiction writers for some years has been the idea of a mind-control device that can cause a person to suffer hallucinations. This is no longer speculation. It is actively being worked upon and may already be fact. Now that we understand the electrical and chemical basis of the brain and how when certain areas, such as the temporal lobe, are stimulated they can trigger frightening images, the prospect of doing this deliberately must be on the agenda of military intelligence.

Although it sounds like a plot from *The X Files*, the possibility that the alien contact mystery is part of a government experiment using 'psychotronic' weapons has been seriously debated. UFOlogist Martin Cannon was intrigued by Budd Hopkins's idea that aliens used mind control to make witnesses see them in more friendly terms (so-called 'screen imagery'). Cannon reasonably argued that it might be easier to believe in mind scrambling by humans. As he noted, the entities seem to know a remarkable amount about the witness and to behave in clearly human ways. To test the witness seems the main intention.

If such a prototype weapon were under development, the UFO mystery could have provided the perfect smokescreen. If your subjects believe they have been kidnapped by aliens then the phenomenon will dissolve into a mass of unproven assertions. Meanwhile, you can merrily conduct your tests.[158]

What is certain is that the US defence agencies have for more than 30 years experimented with 'behaviour modification'. The time-scale of this work seems appropriate to the way the abduction phenomenon has grown – almost as if the experiment uses the already widespread UFO mystery as a springboard for later abductions. Indeed, British researcher, Tim Matthews, has uncovered fascinating evidence that something similar apparently has occurred with secret aircraft. Projects have for years been test-flown in awareness that when seen they will be mistaken for UFOs. By allowing the UFO myth of alien visitors to flourish, authorities have had freedom to fly where otherwise not possible.[159]

We noted earlier in the book, how during the mid-1950s contactee stories were possibly manipulated by the CIA to inspire ridicule. Absurd as it seems, agents may have donned blond wigs and acted like the rather human-looking Nordics. Again, there are excellent grounds to suspect that the 'men in black' (MIB) are government agents, role-play acting to the mythology of UFOs. Clear signs of this appear in records. Indeed the USA even reportedly employed con-artists as intelligence agents in this role.[160]

There are also a number of UFO cases that hint at some sort of electronic weapon being developed nearby. Britain's most famous close encounter – at Rendlesham Forest, Suffolk, in December 1980 (see page 87) – was at a location where radar was perfected in secrecy. During the 1970s Orford Ness, right next to the UFO landing site, was used by the NSA (America's covert electronic intelligence network) as part of a controversial experiment to build a high-energy device. It was under control of intense military secrecy and there are reasons to suspect that this energy beam charged the atmosphere with intense electrical fields. It also may have been creating hallucinations as a side-effect. In fact, much about this case reads like an experiment using air force personnel as a test bed for mind-scrambling energies.

I reached this conclusion about the case after 17 years of extensive research.[161] But I am not alone. In the USA church minister and UFOlogist, Ray Boeche, was approached by two ex-CIA operatives, who said that their conscience demanded that they tell him the truth. According to these men, a psychotronic weapon had been under test near Rendlesham Forest. It had devastating effects on the mental health of people induced to see aliens and spaceships.

In addition, Ralph Noyes, former divisional head of an entire British MoD unit was well aware of (but could not openly discuss) the nefarious activities that the British government had allowed the NSA to get up to. Noyes cleverly suggested (through a novel) that the experiment used physical energies latent within the atmosphere, as shown by Devereux and Persinger. Once a massive energy field was in force it would trigger physical activity that would be witnessed as a UFO. People with certain abilities we term psychic

... a psychotronic weapon had been under test ... It had devastating effects on the mental health of people induced to see aliens and spaceships.

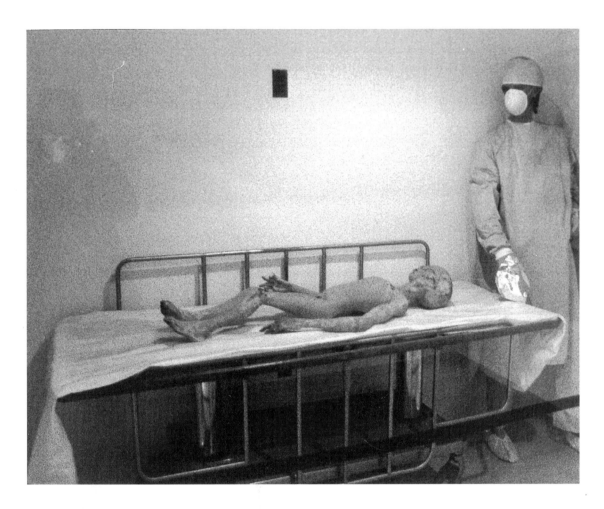

Model display showing dead alien autopsy at a UFO museum in Roswell, New Mexico.

were so affected by this massive energy, that they suffered deep-level close encounters. Noyes suspected that they actually unleashed some kind of poltergeist attack on the world.[162]

In truth, it is a chillingly logical progression, starting with the evident Cold War manipulation of UFO sightings by the CIA in the 1950s. Later research uncovered the way that the brain can be stimulated and UFOlogists then learned how natural UAP – such as earthlights or transients – could theoretically induce frightening close encounters. Given the massive public interest in UFOs, it is hard to imagine that some defence agency experiment did not seek to build a weapon out of this.

The US military lost a ground war in the jungles of Vietnam. But what if they had an energy beam that could power-up what resembled a UFO with huge electrical effects and that triggered vivid imagery of alien contact in some of the enemy troops caught by its beam? This would surely bring about such panic that victory would follow. It is even likely that to maintain this advantage, the myth of alien contact would be kept aflame by military intelligence. We might then see exactly what we *do* see in the current American UFO scene: dubious documents anonymously leaked out to UFOlogists that proclaim the reality of an alien crash at Roswell and a massive cover-up afterwards; seemingly official autopsy film fed out showing alien bodies; workers from government teams at covert sites trying to 'back engineer' spacecraft from crashed remains but telling their story to the world. Such a much-hyped saga would foster belief in aliens without acceptable proof. The UFO community is its own best advocate, its own worst enemy and the intelligence agents' greatest unpaid stooge.

TIME TRAVELLERS:

The idea that we might be visited by some real intelligence from 'out there' is why many people find the abduction mystery appealing. It is impossible to prove and hogs far too much attention. But the usual assumption is that the visitors come from another planet. In fact, the rather human appearance and behaviour of these entities is such that we might face a visit from ourselves!

This theory notes that time travel, long considered absurd, has in recent years been found by physicists not to oppose the nature of the universe. Quantum physics, which appears to describe how the universe functions, does allow for particles travelling faster than light and popping out of reality and reappearing instantly a long way distant. This is akin to some features of the alien contact mystery, where distortions of time are common and where apparent transport through time and space allegedly occurs. Indeed, in close proximity to UFOs, witnesses sometimes describe how the flow of time and space seems to break down. Moreover UFOs often allegedly just vanish rather than take off into space.

Serious research into time travel is being conducted by a number of physicists, for example, at Tulane University in the USA and Oxford in the UK. It is believed that transfer of information back through time using quantum physics may be possible. Physical time travel is another matter, but the transfer of images such as holograms through time is not improbable.[163]

Of course, many of the encounters in this book do appear to suggest a projected image rather than a physical craft and may fit the concept of a time travel device from our own future.[164] It is worth recalling that if time travel *ever* becomes a possibility in what we hope is the long future of mankind, then we ought to be aware of that fact. If, for example, someone finds a way to send a hologram back in time from the year 2099, that hologram might visit 1959 and 1989, and we could potentially be aware of these experiments since to us they have already happened.

Within the alien contact data what appear to be the same objects in every detail have appeared in different locations many years apart. It is almost as if one time-ship was going on a cruise through different eras. However, the time travel theory is the most contentious of all exotic solutions, since it depends upon a theory that is yet unproven and science that we cannot be sure can ever be performed.

It also might be hard to equate with the rich array of alien contact stories, particularly the abductions – unless this is a careful disguise to fit with expectations. Some theorists have suggested that our own descendants from an age when the human race is dying (then degenerated to a form that resemble the 'grays') are raiding human DNA from their own past in order to save the species. It is a fascinating idea, matching the tales told to witnesses, but must be pure speculation. On the other hand, if time travel does ever become possible, then this era would surely be of interest. If so, then there simply *have* to be time travellers around us today. By that logic if they are *not* flying in UFOs, then where are they?

EXTRATERRESTRIALS:

As we have continued to look for a solution to this mystery, the theories have become more extreme. Although most people usually assume that the ETH (extraterrestrial hypothesis) is the only option for alien contact, this is clearly not true. The ETH is a theory, just like others, and requires the acceptance of a lot of new science, but it is popular for two reasons. We would all find alien contact exciting. Paul Devereux neatly terms this desire 'the cry of a lonely species'. But the ETH is also the form that modern contacts usually follow, making it seem the most economic solution if some reality is accepted.

Enticing as these things may be, they are insufficient. The evidence shows that these phenomena have been around for centuries and perceived in different ways. The modern space visitor scenario may not be more true than previous guises. Moreover, the impact of human psychology, sociology, distortions of perception and cultural tracking show how the form that an experience takes – especially in an altered state of consciousness – is not the same thing as the form that the experience may fundamentally possess.

The universe is a vast place and there are trillions of stars, many of which are suns not unlike our own. Until very recently it was only possible to make informed guesses as to how many, if any, of these suns had planets orbiting around them. Without planets and atmospheres like our own, there could be no alien life. Modern space exploration – such as the Hubble Telescope in Earth orbit – has allowed us to detect a few planets around nearby stars. As of 1999, around 20 are known. None as yet seem much like Earth. Most are bigger than Jupiter and unlikely to be habitable. But so many seem to exist that the chances are high that there will be Earth-like planets out there in abundance.

Even if there are many other worlds, it is still unclear whether any would have life, let alone intelligent life. We know that there is little prospect of aliens on other planets circling our sun; although there are possibilities for microscopic organisms on Mars or on moons of Jupiter. Since we do not know how life evolves, we can only surmise that it is a natural process likely to occur on a percentage of worlds with favourable environments. If these guesses are correct, then the universe will teem with life. But there could conceivably be no life at all. We might be a special case.[165]

Most astronomers assume that there *is* life out there and that some is probably more advanced than ours. If so, then these lifeforms may have a method of crossing the vast distances involved in space. We cannot do this remarkable feat, because even at our fastest speed travel between stars would still take centuries. But faster methods are conceivable and there is nothing improbable about aliens having already achieved them. As far as science is concerned, this is a guessing game. Any option between no aliens at all and a veritable zoo could be the truth. The number of races that might have the ability to get here, varies in estimates between none and quite a few. But then most scientists begin to panic, for just one alien species, sufficiently advanced to chart the universe, ought

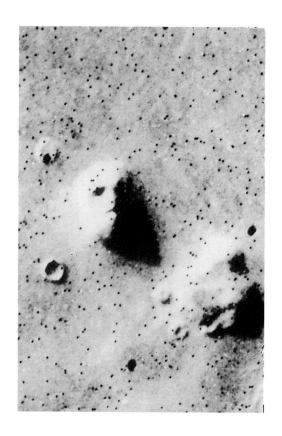

The 'Face on Mars' photographed by Viking 1 Orbiter, 25 July 1976. Images taken in 1998 using better cameras prove this is just a mountain and not an alien artefact.

to have made its presence obvious. The aliens should have left traces. That they seem absent is worrying – as is the apparent failure to detect radio or TV signals from them.

Unfortunately, all of this is a very Earth-centred view. We assume that aliens would *want* to come here – or, if they did, that they would say hello rather than observe without contact. We seek radio and TV signals because we know that we are spreading such communications ourselves, announcing our presence to thousands of new star-systems every year. However, if aliens are unlike us – as they may well be – then none of these assumptions are valid.

They may have passed us by as being too primitive. They may fear us as too war-like. They may study us covertly, as we would a fierce, jungle creature. Radio and TV may be a passing fad in the scheme of things. We have only had them for a century and any aliens trying to detect our presence in 1899 would have found a silent Earth. A century in the aeons-old history of any planet is a blink. It may take a civilisation from 1,000 years ahead of us to find a way to traverse space. To its inhabitants, radio communication might be the equivalent of trying to talk to each other using two tin cans and a piece of string! Any method they use could involve a science we have never conceived. Alien communication may be flooding all around us right now and we simply do not have the science to detect it.

Similarly, it is unwise to think that aliens will probably look and act like us. The diverse range of species on Earth shows the folly of that. Dolphins are a species known to have a social structure, a language and emotions. Their brain capacity is similar to our own. We know this because they live in the oceans and we have paid some attention to them in recent years. But if we only lived on the tops of mountains and shunned the seas, we would have no idea that dolphins exist. They communicate, they live intelligent lives and are right on our doorstep, but make no effort to 'contact' us. It is too easy to assume what an alien contact would be like. Chances are the truth will be quite different from what we anticipate. This is one of the reasons why science is not leaping about with excitement thinking that the abduction mystery *is* the long-sought communication from an alien race. These aliens seem far too human in their appearance and thought processes – in fact in everything. They are too much like we would imagine them to be and are inevitably suspect because of that.

When you study the internal evidence for the alien contact mystery, it is also awash with contradictions. Some of it is decidedly opposed to the ETH. In fact in many respects we appear to be visited by abstractions of ourselves not by real aliens.

There is also the huge problem posed by the lack of physical evidence – no alien DNA, artefacts, in fact anything that establishes a real visitation. It is hard to imagine how we could find aliens on a planet far from Earth and pay thousands of visits without accidentally leaving proof behind. And it is more serious than that, because solid evidence *does* exist for UFOs (in the form of photos, physical energy effects and so on) but not for anything clearly extra-terrestrial behind those UFOs. Some UFOs could be unknown energy phenomena, as we saw. The subjectivity of the alien contact where multiple witnesses can view different things, or some witnesses can see nothing at all when others have a full contact, plus the undoubted signs of altered states of consciousness in some cases, all argue against literal alien kidnaps.

In fact, at face value the ETH is one of the least supported theories under study. Yet it is the idea that grabs all the publicity! However, there is some positive evidence that is hard to explain away.

The cases studied display little trace of the 'Star Trek' effect – becoming outmoded with the progress of real science across several decades. We saw that the 1960s' *Star Trek* episodes now appear very dated and – if imagined – then real alien contacts should do so too. They do not. It is as if another reality is shared by witnesses with a consistent 'magical technology'. In addition, some cases provide scientific knowledge that seems ahead of our time – such as references to lasers and holograms before their discovery. Then there is the way that entities seem to have physical characteristics that match their planetary environment – large eyes on dark worlds, that cause them to avoid sunlight when on Earth.

There are also the subtle threads that link cases – such as the remarkable pattern displayed by the Wanderka (Austria) and Cook (UK) cases (see pages 24 and 25) – seemingly without any prospect of collusion between witnesses. The same is true of the many references to a two-tier propulsion system – an ion drive used in space and a magnetic field drive while in the atmosphere – allegedly because the former would be destructive to our atmosphere. This is especially intriguing given the way that they presage fears about damage to our atmosphere through abuse of science. And we have to wonder about the hints of some sort of plan behind the evidence. The way in which the October/November 1957 wave tied together with our first foray into space via Sputnik, and links between demonstrations of superior car-stop technology and the sites of the first and the most recent atomic bomb blasts. This is incredibly strange. It is hard not to see some intelligent design.

The way that the stories about genetic experiments weave together is equally chilling. We can trace the pattern from the Villas Boas and Hill cases (see pages 26 and 29) through many more obscure reports that fit together like a jigsaw. On the other hand, there would surely be easier ways to get human DNA than mass kidnaps! Why not raid a science lab or use alien science to clone humans after just one abduction?

More than one witness has told me that it was a profound experience and that during its occurrence they came close to grasping the meaning of life.

We also have cases where cultures not versed in space technology see aliens and interpret them differently (for example, as tribal spirits) and yet still describe them in a way that we instantly recognise (see page 60).

What do we make of all of this? There have been few attempts to find a way to solve the dilemma posed by the gap between the lack of proof that aliens are really coming here and the suggestion that some genuine contact is occurring. Leo Sprinkle has argued for a sort of 'education programme', where aliens may be seeking to display themselves in ways that we can accept, setting us puzzles to try to raise the level of our awareness. Jacques Vallee argues an almost religious theory, that the aliens might be a sort of universal control system that regulates the behaviour of our species – in a way almost the visible manifestation of God, although I am not sure that Vallee intended that.

I wonder if aliens might not be able to come here physically but are communicating with us through an advanced science built around the nature of consciousness. Certain people who are able to 'tune in' to this alien message beamed from 'out there' would be the focus of attention and undergo repeated contacts throughout their lives, during periods when they are in some sort of altered state. For in that altered state they 'tune out' the normal world and 'tune in' to the message.

If so, then the witness inevitably perceives this contact in personal ways, using images from their mind and following the rules of cultural tracking. They create a drama that 'acts out' the message being picked up. This message will *be* real and so there will be links between diverse cases and signs of intelligence, because the true essence of the contact seeps through. But the drama itself would be a waking, lucid dream. If a passerby saw an abductee having such a vision, they would see them in a trance state, having physically gone nowhere as no alien presence is actually on Earth. But the witnesses would be communing with it in some way. In other words, an alien species talks to us through those few among us with the ability to listen. Such people are overwhelmed by the contact and assume that they are 'taken away', but in fact are facing a more sophisticated and subtle form of communication.

Perhaps this communion – as witness Whitley Strieber aptly termed it – is with another intelligence and has been going on for centuries, but our minds have had to interpret it as best we can. Perhaps the aliens are not from space, as such, but from some other level of reality that we cannot fully comprehend given our present depth of knowledge. Is this why more than a few witnesses describe the awe and the spiritual nature of their encounter? More than one witness has told me that it was a profound experience and that during its occurrence they came close to grasping the meaning of life. Is that the key to it all?

INTERNAL EVENTS WITH EXOTIC CAUSES

SPACE AGE FOLKLORE:

Although we know some things about the human mind there is much still to be explored. As a result exotic mind-based theories have been suggested to try to explain alien contact. Possibly the easiest to define is the image of space age folklore developing within what psychiatrist Carl Jung calls the 'collective unconscious'. Indeed it is no coincidence that Jung is one of the few psychiatrists to write a book on UFOs.

When comparatively little was known and there were no abductees, Jung made a remarkably good attempt to understand what was happening.[166] Think of the depths of the Pacific Ocean. Individual minds are like floating icebergs, with each conscious mind visible above and the unconscious levels out of sight below. We can seek to understand individuals by studying their minds, but this will ultimately fail if it does not take account of the common things we all share deep down at the bottom of that ocean.

To Jung the collective unconscious was a storehouse of myth, symbols and imagery. It is here that folk tales and common dreams have their roots. They can pop up in many different ways, varied slightly according to cultural differences, but in essence will share the same symbolism because at heart they all come from one species. Jung noted many features of folklore within the alien contact. He was talking about the friendly aliens involved in contactee tales, with evident similarity to the wise magician that features in folklore from dozens of cultures. Time has not diminished the impact of his ideas. Indeed, the 'grays' may be mythic goblins.

Hilary Evans argues that the alien contact follows such a pattern simply to make its mark. As Jung noted, it is easy to produce a visionary experience that is convincing to someone who often has visionary experiences. But if some kind of message is trying to impress you from the depths of your unconscious, then it needs to take a very dramatic form to attract a typical sceptic. So it borrows images from the collective unconscious, draws up a myth that has modern relevance and projects it as a drama to the startled witness. Because it is using the same building blocks that we all use, the cases all seem remarkably similar.

Evans adds, 'If a witness is to believe in his own story (and, of course, he must, if it is to have the psychological effect – which is why he is having the experience at all) then others must believe in it also: and the way to make them believe his story is to present it as part of an accepted pattern.'[167] He feels it is 'irresponsible and wicked' to allow a witness to believe that they have had a real abduction if their experience is a projection of a myth. That myth was catapulted into the life of the witness for a very important reason. Waving it away as some unavoidable act of abuse by outside forces abrogates responsibility from the one person upon whom that responsibility must be placed.

This theory is hatefully regarded by witnesses who see it as an attempt to brand them as facing delusions. Most find the idea that aliens are sexually abusing them much more comforting – bizarre as this may seem. It is tempting to regard aliens as intergalactic cavalry riding to the rescue of Earth. Sadly, if there are no aliens, just ourselves, able to put things right, then we have to wake up to that fact very quickly indeed. Cultural tracking may offer support for this prospect.

The promotion of minor story items (like cinnamon-smelling aliens or 'grays' themselves) clearly alters the phenomenon. The collective unconscious adapts with time to a new version made evident through the next batch of visions. More recently, *Magonia*'s Peter Rogerson (see page 177) likened the mystery to a 'collective work of art' – *folk literature*. The phenomenon of crop circles, known to be largely the result of hoaxing, has a continued major impact on many people because it is an equivalent *folk sculpture*.[168]

> *It is tempting to regard aliens as intergalactic cavalry riding to the rescue of Earth.*

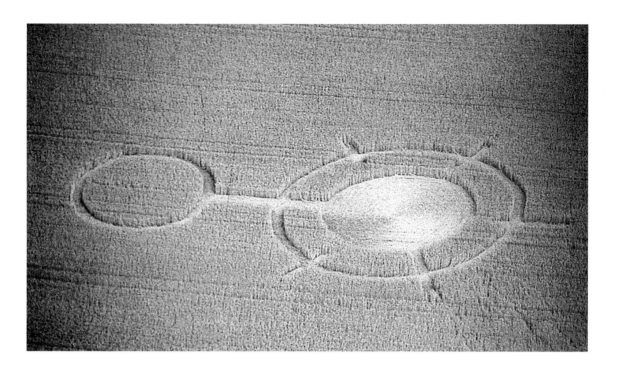

A mysterious crop circle photographed in Wiltshire in 1989. Most of these are hoaxes inspired by the huge publicity for aliens, but many strongly believe thay are messages from outerspace warning of an ecological disaster.

For Rogerson alien contact *must* emerge – not from some other intelligence but from deep within ourselves. That is because no case has ever produced an alien *idea*. It is one thing having no hard evidence, such as DNA samples, alien artefacts or discarded ray guns dropped in haste by fleeing ETs. Far more significant is that nobody has ever had a contact with an alien that has revealed a truly different way of looking at the universe. The conversations with these visitors are every bit as banal as the chats had with dead people via mediums. Here we find spiritual inanity and mindless chit-chat about supermarkets in heaven![169] 'Zog' from 'Alpha Centauri' also tells us to love one another, stop using atom bombs and so on. Rogerson feels, and one can sympathise, that the communications are not what real contact with a non-human civilisation would offer. Of course, the problem is that nobody knows what an alien race would actually be like. Any creation from our collective unconscious would inevitably follow this pattern. Unless and until we have a *real* alien intelligence to judge from, we cannot know if Rogerson is justified in these doubts.

The obvious links between the NDE and abduction also have to be reconciled. Both involve lights, contact with wise beings and changes to the lifestyle of the witness afterwards. Yet one is viewed as a trip to heaven and the other as a voyage on a UFO. Both begin with altered states and out-of-body visions and may be different takes on the same phenomenon. If so, are they real 'spiritual' journeys or variations on a theme of inner self-discovery?

One of the few UFOlogists best able to judge this debate is folklorist Dr Thomas Bullard. He started off suspecting that abductions were folklore, tested this theory for a decade against almost 1,000 cases and has concluded that it just does not work. He says the evidence fails to follow the major rules. Although mythology uses stereotyped characters, all studies of how it develops show wide variations. The Cinderella story crops up all over the world and you can recognise it in a British pantomime or in a Native American legend. But it is also very different in how it is told each time. Abductions just feature the same aliens doing the same things in the same way with such monotony, that they stun folklorists.

One argument I might raise against Bullard's stance is that folklore tends to develop slowly across many years, passed by word of mouth and written tradition. There has never been anything like the space age myth of alien abductions. This has had vast and near immediate global publicity, through markets perceived as reporting truth not mythology. This different mode of story-telling could have changed the rules. Bullard claims that modern urban myths reveal that our mass market does not affect the basic rules. But few other phenomena can claim such global significance as a result of mass-media intervention. Intriguingly, crop circles are one possibility – being 'invented' in the 1980s and still holding massive cultural sway despite the huge evidence for trickery.[170]

Yet even Bullard recognises a significant barrier. With typical clarity he says, 'If I truly believed that aliens could seize me, I would spend my life in the company of a hundred others . . . I do not; therefore deep down I do not believe. A literal reading of abductions clashes with common sense and learned good sense alike, but that reason in itself gives me licence to question but not to close my eyes. The evidence as I see it, shows me a puzzle that I cannot solve with reference to conventional phenomena known to me, nor have the alternatives offered by psycho-social advocates proved adequate to the task.'[171]

WINDOWS TO ANOTHER WORLD:

There is no doubt that sincere witnesses have genuinely puzzling experiences and that research into 'inner space reality' has provided vital insights. But what status should be ascribed to these visionary experiences? It is tempting to assume that if one person sees these things and a dozen others do not, then that phenomenon is unreal. But the experience of Dr Schatzman's patient Ruth (see page 155) showed that her hallucination was both real and unreal according to which experiment you tried.

There is no doubt that witnesses choose to ascribe what happens to them as an alien contact after a personal decision. I have investigated many cases where the incident could just as easily be a ghost, or a near-death or an out-of-body experience. Including a case in any study of alien contact is always subjective. But events rarely happen in isolation. They come amid a long track record of paranormal phenomena.

At times it is as if the witness simply has a special way of viewing the world and sees many things that you or I do not. Some mediums who commune, they believe, with the afterlife have also claimed alien contact. Doris Collins is one example. Psychics like Uri Geller have had encounters too.

In the reverse direction Sue, one of the witnesses to the Aveley abduction (see page 40), became a direct-voice medium when I spoke to her during hypnosis. She replied to me as if relaying the words of the aliens. I gather from other UFOlogists that similar things have occurred in their cases from time to time.

In another case, a woman living in moorland Yorkshire told me that she had experienced a bizarre sequence of encounters. These included poltergeist activity and precognitive dreams. But she also claimed to be able to pick up a household object, like a vacuum cleaner, and see images in her mind such as the replay of conversations. These, she believed, were the words of factory workers who had built the device or shopkeepers who had sold it.

Alien encounters also featured in her story – with entities landing in an egg-shaped object next to an electricity pylon. But she had failed to integrate all these experiences and UFOlogy was the latest port of call in her quest to find why she was so different. Her best hope came when she discovered spiritualism. It was suggested that she train to be a medium. The last I heard she was no longer seeing aliens or getting messages from her domestic appliances, but was having friendly conversations with dead souls.

It may seem tempting to laugh, but that does not answer the questions posed. This case suggests that the alien contact might be a symptom of a broader ability that some people have. They can manifest this ability in many ways and the alien contact is an appropriate mode of expression today. If so, then could someone suffering from frightening alien kidnaps 'cure' themselves by attempting to transform the way that their ability manifests? Could they find a more amiable mode of expression?

I have taken to advising witnesses that they try automatic writing (sitting in front of a sheet of paper and entering an altered state, then letting the words just flow). Automatic artwork is another possibility, especially given the creative potential of many abductees. If they are able to switch the mode of expression of the phenomenon, they may find that the aliens go away and are replaced by some kind of probably more benign contact.

I already know of several abductees who claim to have painted pictures and written novels that vent their inner feelings. Meanwhile the little, grey men have gone off to bug someone else. One woman from Northamptonshire discovered that she could now perform psychic healing, particularly on animals. Perhaps abductees are closet psychics who need to make their mark. Indeed many alien contact witnesses have reported being left with a 'gift' from the aliens and this is often some sort of latent psychic ability. Researcher John Spencer has studied some of these cases.[172]

Other witnesses felt a psychic intuition that an experience was about to happen. Some, after the encounter, had contacts in the form of channelled voices. Jessie Roestenberg is a case in point (see page 23). Perhaps what is happening is that these people – whether we call them mediums, FPP or abductees – are gifted at something that the rest of us are not. We might assume that this is some mental outlet and it may be. But for centuries mankind has believed that the mind can serve as a doorway to other realities.

... a woman living in moorland Yorkshire told me that she had experienced a bizarre sequence of encounters. These included poltergeist activity and precognitive dreams.

For a long time psychics have stared into crystal balls seeking glimpses of these other places. Psychologists have realised that the glass probably acts as a focal point and itself does nothing. It simply helps a potentially 'psychic' person bring out their inner visions. Lately researchers have been getting people to stare into mirrors – which are bigger versions of a crystal ball. Remarkable results have been alleged with subjects claiming to see strange figures and even undergo contact. Because they are guided on the premise that they might encounter dead loved ones, this is the form that the experience usually takes. It would be interesting to see what might happen if other kinds of contact were encouraged.[173]

It might also be worth asking ourselves whether this form of self-induced vision is not at work accidentally during alien contact. I have investigated a number of psychic visions where witnesses claimed to see distant events (for example, a car accident) acted out on some real-life screen before their eyes. Typical is the kitchen window when the person chances to be in altered state, perhaps idling away as they wash the dishes. Alien-contact witnesses appear to enter altered states. Most involve locations filled with potential substitutes for the crystal ball. The bedroom has windows and mirrors, and the car a large windscreen in front. Do these act as the screens onto which alien visions are projected? Are abductions simply a technological form of 'scrying'? Do witnesses find themselves having space-age visions of other realities, via the medium of such objects?

Wherever we look there are questions and some answers, but always more questions appear. There are theories and ideas, some sensible, some rational and others quite bizarre. Nobody *knows* what the truth is, but one thing seems clear. We *will* learn something – perhaps something more than trivial – when we finally unravel the alien contact mystery.

Alien Hunters

Basterfield, Keith
PO Box 1894, Adelaide, South Australia 5001
A social services worker, born in Staffordshire but resident in South Australia, Basterfield has investigated alien contact reports for 25 years. In 1980 he published, through the Australian Centre for UFO Studies, a major report on Australian entity cases. He developed what was called 'the image hypothesis' in 1981, which tried to see abductions in terms of abnormal states of consciousness, and has made a particular study of false awakenings. He teamed up with psychologist, Dr Robert Bartholomew, to conduct a number of detailed studies on witnesses, bravely seeking physical evidence that might dispute his original theory. He has published extensively in the British journal *Magonia* and through *International UFO Reporter* for the Dr J. Allen Hynek Center for UFO Studies (CUFOS). He was the only Australian participant in the 1992 MIT symposium, arguing for 'false memory syndrome' – an idea that witnesses might have vivid creative imagery that makes it difficult to tell fantasy from reality. He has worked hard to test this hypothesis and been brave enough to publish data that appears to be opposed to the conclusion. He publishes regular updates on Australian cases and in 1997 his book containing an annotated catalogue of Australian entity cases appeared.

Blackmore, Dr Susan
Psychology Department, University of the West of England, Bristol
This British psychologist developed her interest in 'psychic' matters gradually and as a consequence of first-hand research became more sceptical. Her main fields are ESP and – in particular – the topic of 'out-of-body' experiences (OOBEs). Through research and experiment she has come to believe the OOBE is an illusion, forged by a temporary breakdown in the brain's ability to formulate mental models. She extended her work to the near-death experience (NDE), explaining this visionary state by a combination of physiological and psychological processes she terms 'the dying brain hypothesis'. Although sceptical of any important new science, she is one of the most open-minded sceptics. She has often taken part in conferences – including the BUFORA conference in 1992, where she gave her first major paper on UFO-related events. A key member of the SPR (Society for Psychical Research), she is frequently seen on TV programmes. In 1994 she was invited by the BBC to make a documentary assessing the arrival on the scene of abduction researcher **John Mack**. This *Horizon* special stirred much controversy – focusing as it did only on American abduction data. She subsequently apologised for having done this programme as a novice, but has since conducted research into her theory that many abductions are the result of sleep paralysis and has begun to publish material expressing this point of view.

Bullard, Dr Thomas
517E University Avenue, Suite 2, Bloomington, IN 47401, USA
The academic who has had most impact on serious abduction research in the recent past, Bullard is a doctor of folklore at the University of Indiana. He came to the field with an open mind but a suspicion that much of what was happening would relate to modern folklore. However, to his great credit, he did not run and hide when his extensive research failed to vindicate that prospect. Instead he discovered that the alien contact mystery was far deeper than he had imagined and much harder to explain. He was initially interested in the way that waves of sightings developed by the interaction of social forces and made a particular study of the airship cases of the late nineteenth century. His decision to probe abduction reports produced a series of major

works that have compiled statistical breakdowns of cases. In 1985 he first put together a study of 300 abductions. Using a grant from FUFOR (Fund for UFO Research) he published this in more depth (1987) and later expanded the cases studied to almost three times the initial number. In 1995 he produced a comparative study conducted with the assistance of a number of leading abduction investigators. All but two were from the USA. He wanted to compare the data found by each researcher and see if their culture, belief systems and individual methods affected the outcome. The result was Bullard's conclusion, that he defends steadfastly and with great thought in the UFO literature. That view – at least for now – is tinged with reservations due to both national and temporal variations. But he argues that the abduction follows a precise pattern that shows so little change that it appears not to be folklore but to possibly reflect some underlying reality. This honesty, unquestioned depth of research and conversion from scepticism (but not to any dogmatic belief) has won admirers from all sides of the debate.

Devereux, Paul

c/o The Ley Hunter, Box 180, Stroud, Gloucestershire, GL5 IYH
Although not the founder (French researcher Fernand Lagarde was in 1975), there is no doubt that Devereux is the man who established the 'Earth energy' theory for UFOs. This began around 1976 with a statistical analysis of lights in the sky across the East Midlands. From these he deduced patterns and that they appeared to concentrate near locations such as mines, quarries, fault lines and towers. By 1982 he had developed the concept of 'earthlights' – generated by tectonic forces in the Earth, leaked into the atmosphere as energy and triggering processes that evolve glowing lights. His work since has increasingly diverged from UFOlogy into his love of Earth mysteries. He edited the magazine *The Ley Hunter* for many years and is still a chief consultant. Earthlights were found to occur all over the planet and could

be reproduced in laboratory experiments (filmed with high-speed cameras in the UK and USA). Devereux now seeks a bridge between natural phenomena and close encounters such as abductions. From personal experience he suspected that the energy has a component that is almost intelligent and can interact with human consciousness in altered states. He has gone on to research trance states and psychedelic-induced phenomena and make documentaries for Channel 4 (1995–8) on earthlights, altered states and drug-induced consciousness experiments.

Evans, Hilary

c/o 59 Tranquil Vale, London SE3 0BS
A highly erudite commentator, Evans is a Cambridge don with a passion for social history who also operates a respected picture library. In 1982 he was one of several members of the SPR (Society for Psychical Research) who branched out to create a new organisation called ASSAP (Association for the Scientific Study of Anomalous Phenomena) with the intention of investigating more spontaneous cases. The SPR has long had little time for UFOs and alien contact stories, which Evans considers an error of judgement. Although he rarely does field investigations, he has authored a number of sweeping literary surveys of altered states and psychological theories regarding the abduction. He is one of the pioneers of what is known as the psycho-social hypothesis. Strong in Europe but derided in the USA, this seeks to find a solution to the mystery within the bounds of human consciousness. In this work he has explored a number of pre-modern-day cases of what might today be considered alien contacts. This research has established new frontiers. Few have expressed this difficult (and to many highly sceptical) concept better than Evans. His books, though not numerous, are each well argued. He rarely writes articles but has compiled as editor two mammoth books aimed at marking the fortieth (1987) and fiftieth (1997) anniversaries of the birth of the UFO mystery. These, more than any other source, bring to the general reader papers by

many non-British or American UFOlogists whose work is sadly not seen very often beyond their native lands.

Fowler, Ray
c/o MUFON, 103 Oldtowne Rd, Seguin, TX 78155, USA
Fowler is one of the world's most prolific investigators on the alien contact subject, with numerous books to his credit; although he has had both a full-time job (in technology) and a part-time career running an observatory and astronomy centre for school-children. He has investigated hundreds of cases in the USA (being born in the remarkable 'haunted' town of Salem, Massachusetts). He is one of the most experienced UFOlogists and has brought this expertise to bear as the Director of Investigations and as author of the field investigator's manual for MUFON – the world's largest membership group. He has been the driving force behind and has thoroughly documented some of the best-known abduction cases in the USA, such as the Andreasson Affair and the Allagash multi-witness encounters. He has been a staunch supporter of the 'unknown machines in our airspace' theory for many years and argues his case through the evidence that he has painstakingly accumulated. Having experienced a number of strange things within the abduction field, he is also one of the few UFOlogists to have published his own memoirs.

Hind, Cynthia
Postbox MP, 49 Mount Pleasant, Harare, Zimbabwe
Cynthia Hind is a marvellous ambassador for both her country and her continent. Having the fortune to be able to move freely around the world, she spends half the year researching local close encounters, often in remote villages, and the rest of the time travelling to give lectures to the UFO community. More than anyone she has opened up to view the way in which the alien/UFO mystery is experienced and perceived by native cultures (just as in Australia where Bill

Chalker has revealed a hidden dimension to aboriginal beliefs through his study of shamanism). Hind is one of the most popular lecturers on the UFO circuit and always has new tales to tell with gusto. She publishes regular updates through her own journal (in English) – *UFO Afrinews* – and while she has only published one book, her papers in the literature are numerous and most are based on case studies. She has a strong belief in an alien reality.

Hopkins, Budd
Intruders Foundation, Box 30233, New York, NY 10011, USA
Hopkins is the best-known abduction researcher so far as the public is concerned. A respected New York artist, he has since 1987 become guru to thousands of witnesses who look to him for advice. His conversion to a cult figure was not immediate. During the 1970s he quietly investigated cases with Dr Aphrodite Clamar and believed that he had uncovered a pattern using hypnosis. The first recognition of the prevalence of 'grays' appeared this way. Hopkins argued that hypnosis could lift the drawbridge and let out the knowledge of a hidden abduction from where it was blocked behind missing time or just an innocent-looking sighting. He defined the concept of 'cover stories' imposed on the memory to block frightening, alien, medical experiments. By 1983 he had a major case that involved multiple witnesses, repeated abductions and clear evidence of an alien genetic experiment. Hopkins was exploring hundreds of cases first-hand. A naturally, amiable man and skilled communicator, his work was taken to heart and he set up the Intruders Foundation and through the massive, international success of his books and a resulting TV mini-series was never out of demand. Quickly besieged by people wanting to tell their stories and requests for media appearances, by 1989, he was involved in another 'big one' – a case that Hopkins felt might revolutionise the subject. This was the kidnap of a witness from a Manhattan high-rise, witnessed by people on the ground –

including (allegedly) a world-leader statesman. Hopkins seems firmly convinced that real aliens are abducting many people, many of whom are unaware of that fact.

Hufford, Dr David

College of Medicine, University Hospital, Hershey Medical Center, Hershey, PA 17033, USA

Hufford has a PhD in folklore and spent four years (to 1974) conducting fieldwork in Newfoundland, Canada, developing his speciality 'widely-held beliefs'. Hufford explored for the first time the centuries-old tradition known as 'the old hag' – a ghostly visitation in the dead of night in which people are said to be attacked, paralysed and probed by unknown entities. Physiologically these are clearly tied to **Sue Blackmore's** subsequent adoption of the 'sleep paralysis theory' to explain abductions. Hufford identified this pattern years before abductions were properly recognised by the UFO community. He is willing to consider all options regarding the reality of the event. But it is the beliefs that develop from it that interest him. He feels that he has proven that abduction-like stories have occurred in other cultures for centuries and been interpreted in non-alien ways, thus the historical antiquity of the abduction experience needs to be addressed by all who theorise about it. To take it out of context by only considering modern-day, alien incidents is not to do the phenomenon justice.

Jacobs, Dr David

Department of History, Temple University, Philadelphia, PA 19122, USA

Of all UFOlogists, Jacobs has made perhaps the most interesting transition. As a professional historian he wrote one of the seminal works of the field, describing the political and social factors that created the first half of UFOlogy's twentieth-century history. He was also able to get his academic university course accredited, teaching UFOlogy to students. He began working on the mammoth second volume of his historical thesis, but then became converted to the

importance of the abduction mystery. In the past decade, he has devoted much of his time to investigating witness stories via hypnosis. Although he still writes more broadly on UFOs than counterpart, **Budd Hopkins**, Jacobs has seen the abduction as a key to the mystery. Yet his approach to the subject is more forthright about the genetic experiments and hybrid babies. He considers reports of nice, humanlike beings to be either deliberate covers for more frightening events or actual use of hybrid human/alien entities by the UFO abductors. Whilst there are many similarities between the findings of the two American abduction leaders, there are sufficient differences in the style of report and subtleties of interpretation to pose interesting questions.

McClure, Kevin

3 Claremont Grove, Leeds, LS3 1AX

Kevin McClure was at college with **Sue Blackmore** and has also developed interest in the paranormal. His work in social security sees him used to seeking out strange claims and he has brought this to bear well on abduction stories. McClure has made a particular study of the interaction between belief and religious phenomena, focusing on anomalous events that today would be interpreted as UFOs. They accompanied nineteenth-century apparitions of the Virgin Mary and early twentieth-century religious revival fevers in Wales, during which strange lights appeared. McClure has in recent years become deeply perturbed by the rising tide of abductees, the over-dependence on hypnotic regression and the way in which lives may be irrevocably altered by acts of selfish UFO buffs. He has mounted something of a campaign to try to curb the excesses, in 1997 launching one of the only magazines devoted specifically to abductions and almost certainly the most rational of them all. He says that he will not write a book expressing his doubts over the abduction evidence and the too literal way it is interpreted, because this would only further inflame the passions of a subject that needs damping down. McClure looks set to be an important sobering influence.

Mack, Professor John

PEER, 1493 Cambridge Street, Cambridge, MA 02139, USA

Mack created a sensation in 1992 when he publicly entered the field. As a professor of psychiatry at the prestigious Harvard Medical School, his association, particularly when not dismissing the reality of alien involvement (although with a more sophisticated view of the interaction with humanity at times), was viewed with shock. It saw him hailed a hero by abductees, who now had a champion that the media could not easily ridicule. At the MIT symposium, with which he was closely involved, he received a lengthy standing ovation from witnesses. At that time Mack was still learning the subject, but had interesting perspectives. He had made studies of the effects of things like global ecological problems and the nuclear arms race on the human psyche. That he was now probing seriously into abductions was viewed with optimism by many UFOlogists, especially as a book was promised and Mack had already won a top literary award. Sadly he offered no real breakthroughs and it was, I suspect, written too early in his quest for illumination. He came into some professional criticism for his research methods (again using hypnosis) and for a time this was under review. But he escaped the threat of censure and his integrity is not in question. He has also brought to the American UFO scene a touch of European cross-fertilisation from broader areas of consciousness. Possessing an awareness – previously only present beyond the USA – that changes to the lifestyle of a witness created by the events are crucial, Mack's future work should be of interest.

Magonia

5 James Terrace, Mortlake Churchyard, London SW14 8HB

Magonia is not a person, but a collective effort. It is a quarterly magazine that for over 25 years has presented the finest literary debate on philosophical and psychological issues behind the UFO mystery. Behind it have been several individuals, but its chief contributors over the years have been librarians John Rimmer and Peter Rogerson – Rimmer editing, Rogerson writing many in-depth assessments of the so called psycho-social hypothesis. Many leading researchers have written for *Magonia* across the years. Aside from these two men, regular writers of perceptive and thought-provoking commentaries are John Harney, Martin Kottmeyer and Peter Brookesmith (author of several fine books). Some regard *Magonia* as being so introspective and wordy that it can be impenetrable without a classics degree and there are times when that is true. American UFOlogists often dislike its unrelenting non-alien (even non-anomalistic) approach, viewing the subject purely as a form of psycho drama. But it can be at its best a great champion of this defensible viewpoint and should be read by all abduction researchers.

Ring, Dr Kenneth

Department of Psychology, University of Connecticut, Room 107, 406 Cross Campus Rd, Storrs, CT 06268, USA

Ring is a psychologist and was the first scientist to establish a link between the near-death experience (NDE) and the abduction. He did this by way of a mammoth experimental project (with Christopher Rosing) during the late 1980s/early 1990s. They found that certain people with a specific psychological profile were prone to both the NDE and abduction and that both phenomena shared similar features and also provoked similar changes in lifestyle within the subject afterwards. He called these people Omega people and began to suspect that there was an evolutionary shift within mankind of which these cases and witnesses were symptoms. Whether this was internally or externally generated was open to debate. To Ring it may simply be prevailing circumstance and the way in which an event is interpreted that determines whether an Omega person is considered an abductee or to have had a brush with death. As to deciding whether these events are real or imaginary, Ring instead proposed the 'imaginal' realm. This is not either extreme of reality but a cross between both, allowing for real experiences of an imaginative nature to take place.

Sprinkle, Professor Leo
Department of Psychology, University of Wyoming, Laramie, WY, USA
Leo Sprinkle was the first in a long line of abduction researchers. In 1967 he was called in by the ultra sceptical 'Condon Report' at the University of Colorado to probe the abduction of a policeman. They were not impressed by the results of his pioneering hypnosis sessions. Sprinkle was. As a counselling psychologist and university professor, he became fascinated and has since then worked with 300 abductees – probably more than any one person. It is regrettable that he has written little, for his views are certainly different from those of **Hopkins** and **Jacobs**. He regards what is happening as much less threatening and shuns an interest in physical aspects or what aliens look like or how they act. Instead he thinks there is a kind of 'consciousness conditioning'. He sees an alien intelligence setting us role-play exercises and mind games with a view to attempting to increase our awareness of the interface between reality and spirituality. Indeed, he believes that his own research was triggered by a childhood abduction in which Nordics 'educated' and prepared him for the task that he was to do. To this end he has for some years staged the Rocky Mountain Convention in which abductees and contactees spend time together in a retreat, hoping to 'tune in' to better understanding. Indeed, almost alone amongst UFOlogists, Sprinkle feels that one day the contactees from the 1950s will be rehabilitated in this way and that we will come to see little difference with the abductees.

Vallee, Dr Jacques
*1550 California, *6L, San Francisco, CA 94109, USA*
In Steven Spielberg's alien contact movie *Close Encounters of the Third Kind,* the person in charge of the American UFO team is a Frenchman who talks of social forces. The reason is simple. This character is based on the work of CUFOS and Dr J. Allen Hynek. Hynek's closest colleague was computer scientist, Jacques Vallee. Hynek appears in the movie (meeting aliens near the end) and Spielberg built a key character around Vallee. Consistently different amongst the American UFO community, not least in the fact that he has never really been a part of it, he once told me that nothing of any importance ever gets done by a committee. The computer scientist has lived by that philosophy, only occasionally entering the field to contribute some thought-provoking ideas or a new book. He is also an award-winning, science fiction writer. Indeed one would imagine that had the other J.V. (Jules Verne) lived 100 years later, his career might not have been that different from Vallee's. In the 1960s, with his wife Janine, Vallee wrote the first scientific books. He championed the links with folklore, writing of the fairy world 'Magonia' and its alternate reality. As part of what Hynek called an 'invisible college' of scientists for years, this led ultimately in 1974 to the creation of CUFOS. Vallee has said that the UFO mystery is like a thermostat and changes according to social patterns, almost as if it were regulating the 'temperature' of our culture. Possibly this concept was too soft for the growing American interest in real aliens and genetic experiments, something Vallee has struggled to take on board. As might be expected, his ideas have always found more favour in Europe, where he is often described as the best UFO writer there has ever been. His dissociation from the media-obsessed world of American UFO culture has made him something of an outsider. A trilogy of books between 1988 and 1991 set out his ideas more clearly, indicating that the force behind the 'control' might be ourselves, our collective consciousness or just perhaps something truly alien. He has worked on some of the most extraordinary close encounters, such as the Dr X case and the Trans-en-Provence landings. What he has to say tends to set new paths of thinking, but these can take some years to win over the often rather sluggish UFO sub-culture.

REFERENCES

1 See, for example, *Missing Time*, Hopkins, B. (paperback edn, Ballantine, New York, 1988)
2 *Human Memos*, Loftus, Dr G. and E. (Halstead Press, USA, 1975)
  Memory Observed, Neisser, U. (ed.) (W. H. Freeman, USA, 1982)
3 *The Emergence of a Phenomenon 'CE 3 1901–1959'*, Clark, J. (ed.) (Omnigraphics, Detroit, 1992)
4 *A Dictionary of Fairies*, Briggs, K. (Allen Lane, London, 1976)
  Fairy Tales, Cooper, J. C. (Aquarian Press, Northampton, 1983)
5 *The Secret Commonwealth of Elves, Fauns and Fairies*, Kirk, R. (Sterling, New York, 1933)
6 *Passport to Magonia*, Vallee, Dr J. (Regnery, Chicago, 1969)
7 *Country Folklore*, Hartland, E. (Gloucester, 1982)
8 Reports submitted direct by Ahmad Jamaludin (1983/4)
9 *An Account of a Meeting with Denizens of Another World*, Langford, D. (St Martin's Press, New York, 1981)
10 *The Oz Files*, Chalker, W. (Duffy & Snellgrove, Australia, 1996)
11 *The Truth about Flying Saucers*, Michel, A. (Criterion, New York, 1956)
12 Rose told her account in French as *Meeting with the Extraterrestrials* (Rocher, 1979)
13 *The Coming of the Saucers*, Arnold, K. and Palmer, R. (Private, Boise, ID, 1952); see also *The Complete Book of UFOs*, Randles, J. and Hough, P. (Piatkus, London, 1997), ch. 5
14 Study by Bullard, Dr T., FUFOR (Maryland, USA, 1987)
15 *UFOs*, Basterfield, K. (Reed, Australia, 1996)
16 *The Complete Book of UFOs*, Randles and Hough, op. cit., chs 9, 10 and 11; see also *The Truth Behind the Men in Black*, Randles, J. (Piatkus, London, 1997), ch. 3
17 *Flying Saucers Have Landed*, Adamski, G. and Leslie, D. (Werner Laurie, 1953; new edn, Spearman, 1970)
18 Case investigation by Dr Jacques Vallee
19 Personal interview with Jessie Roestenberg, 6 August 1987
20 Letter to me dated 12 August 1978

21 *The Complete Book of UFOs*, Randles and Hough, op. cit, ch. 14
22 *The Lubbock Lights*, Wheeler, J. (Award, New York, 1977)
23 *The International UFO Reporter* (CUFOS, July/Aug 1988)
24 *The Complete Book of UFOs*, Randles and Hough, op. cit., ch. 15; see also *High Strangeness*, Clark, J. (Omnigraphics, Detroit, 1996)
25 *The Interrupted Journey*, Fuller, J. (new edn, Souvenir, London, 1980)
26 Valensole in *Flying Saucer Review (FSR)* 11:6 (1965)
27 San Pedro de los Altos in FSR 15:2 (1969)
28 *UFOs*, Basterfield, op. cit., p. 211
29 *The UFOnauts*, Holzer, Dr H. (Grafton, London, 1981)
30 *Scientific Study of UFOs*, Condon, Dr E. (ed.) (Bantam, London, 1969)
31 *UFO Trek*, Smith, W. (Signet, New York, 1975)
32 *The Psychology of Perception*, Vernon, Dr D. (Penguin, London, 1971)
33 *Terror Above Us*, Kent, M. (Tower, USA, 1967)
34 *Memory and Hypnotic Age Regression*, Reiff, Dr R. and Scheerer, Dr M. (IUP, USA, 1959)
35 Details of my own experiments are in *Star Children*, Randles, J. (Hale, London, 1994)
36 *UFOs*, Basterfield, op. cit.
37 Pascagoula in *FSR* 20:6 (1974)
38 Reports by Raynes, B., Fickett, S., and Schwarz, Dr B. in *FSR* 22:2 (1976)
39 UFOIN case file by Andy Collins and Barry King (1979)
40 *Life After Life*, Moody, Dr R. (Bantam, New York, 1975)
  Life At Death, Ring, Dr K. (Coward, McCann & Geoghegan, USA, 1980)
41 *Time Travel*, Randles, J. (Blandford, London, 1994)
42 *Missing Time*, Hopkins, op. cit.
43 'The Neglected Science of UFOs' Randles, J. and Warrington, P. in *New Scientist* (February 1983)
44 *Science and the UFOs*, Randles, J. and Warrington, P. (Basil Blackwell, Oxford, 1985)
45 *The Pennine UFO Mystery*, Randles, J. (Grafton, 1983)

46 *Communion*, Strieber, W. (William Morrow, New York, 1987)

47 *Intruders*, Hopkins, B. (Ballantine, New York, 1987)

48 *UFO Abduction: A Dangerous Game*, Klass, P. (Prometheus, Buffalo, 1989)

49 *Witnessed*, Hopkins, B. (Bloomsbury, New York, 1997)

50 *Alien Discussions*, Pritchard, M., et al (eds) (North Cambridge Press, Massachusetts, 1994); see also MIT Conference, *Close Encounters of the Fourth Kind*, Bryan, C. D. (Weidenfeld & Nicolson, 1995)

51 Unusual personal experiences, Roper Poll Organisation (1992)

52 *UFOs*, Basterfield, op. cit., pp. 123–9; *Oz Files*, Chalker, op. cit., pp. 9–16

53 *Skeptics UFO Newsletter* 39 (1995)

54 Case 68 in files of Cynthia Hind

55 Mesnard in *FSR* 19:3 (1973)

56 Humcat Catalogue, Bloecher, T. (New York) – an ongoing unpublished database

57 *UFO Afrinews* 4 (1991) and 8 (1993)

58 'Escorted by UFOs' in *FSR* 21:1 (1975) and 21:2 (1975)

59 See 'The Very Strange Cloud' in *Abduction*, Randles, J. (Hale, London, 1988)

60 Randles and Whetnall in *FSR* 24:2 (1978); see also Hough, P. and Randles, J. in *Scary Stories* (Futura, London, 1991)

61 The Dong, P. book is not available in English, see Creighton in *FSR* 28:6 (1983) for a summary

62 *Oz Files*, Chalker, op. cit.

63 See Kaikoura cases in *Something in the Air*, Randles, J. (Hale, London, 1999)

64 *The Mystery of the Min Min Light*, Kozicka, M. (Boston Imprint, Australia, 1994)

65 Retrospective investigation by Keith Basterfield

66 See Basterfield in *International UFO Reporter* (May/June 1990 and Sept/Oct 1992)

67 *Something in the Air*, Randles, op. cit.

68 *Strangers in Our Skies*, Dykes, M. (Lower Hutt, USA, 1981)

69 Lagarde (in French) in *Lumiers dans la Nuit (Lights in the Night)* 118 (1972)

70 Cattiau, Gayral and Lacenal in *Lumiers dans la Nuit* 153 (1976)

71 Michel in *FSR Special* 3 (1969)

72 Creighton in *FSR* 15:5 (1969)

73 *Munich Mercury* (14 April 1980)

74 Conti in *FSR* 18:5 (1972)

75 UFOIN case file by Maurizio Verga

76 Liljegeren in *FSR* 16:6 (1970)

77 Hessdalen reports published c/o AFU, Box 11027, 600 11 Norrkoping, Sweden

78 Creighton in *FSR* 9:4 (1963)

79 Frederickson and Liljegeren in *FSR* 16:5 (1970), 16:6 (1970), 26:3 (1980) and 26:5 (1980)

80 *Aura Z* 1 (1994)

81 *UFO Retrievals*, Randles J. (Blandford, London, 1995), pp. 18–25

82 Ibid., pp. 85–7

83 Lina in *FSR* 24:1 (1978)

84 Humcat, Bloecher, op. cit.

85 *UFO Crash Landing*, Randles, J. (Blandford, London, 1998)

86 *Ipswich Star* (21 September 1965)

87 *Derby Evening Telegraph* (22 September 1965)

88 Finch in *FSR* 11:6 (1965)

89 *Abduction*, Randles, op. cit., pp. 119ff

90 Musgrave in *FSR* 22:6 (1976)

91 Allan in *FSR* 20:6 (1975)

92 Detailed case reports submitted by Lorne Goldfader of UFORIC, Canada

93 *San Francisco Examiner* (20 August 1949)

94 *Lorenzon in The Humanoids*, Bowen, C. (ed.) (Spearman, Suffolk, 1969)

95 *Life After Life*, Moody, op. cit.

96 Bloecher and Schwarz in *FSR* 20:2 (1974), 21:3 (1975) and 21:4 (1975)

97 CUFOS case file (1977)

98 Fowler, R. in *MUFON Journal* 300 (1993); see also *The Allagash Abductions*, Fowler, R. (Wildflower Press, USA, 1993)

99 *Ohio UFO Newsletter* 15 (1998)

100 *La Razon* (Buenos Aires, 10 April 1950)

101 Further teleportation cases described in *Time Travel*, Randles, op. cit.

102 *FSR* 12:2 (1966)

103 *Lumiers dans la Nuit* 129 (1973)

104 Case file by Pedro Romaniuk

105 *Confrontations*, Vallee, Dr J. (Ballantine, New York, 1990)

106 *Flying Saucer Occupants*, Lorenzen, C. and J. (Signet, 1967)

107 *FSR* 7:5 (1961)

108 *FSR* 21:3 (1975)

109 *FSR* 35:4 (1990)

110 *FSR* 5:2 (1959)

111 *The Mothman Prophecies*, Keel, J. (Dutton, New York, 1975)

112 A detailed analysis of the case is in *The Complete Book of UFOs*, Randles, op. cit.

113 See *The Truth Behind the MIB*, Randles, op. cit., ch. 1

114 *Light Years*, Kinder, B. (Atlantic Monthly Press, New York, 1987); for much more sceptical coverage see *Spaceships of the Pleiades*, Korff, K. (Prometheus, Buffalo, 1995)

115 *Aliens – The Real Story*, Randles, J. (Hale, London, 1993)

116 A full case study is in *The Truth Behind the MIB*, Randles, op. cit.

117 *Magonia* 35 (1990)

118 *UFO Revelation*, Matthews, T. (Blandford, London 1999)

119 *Flying Saucers: A Modern Myth*, Jung, Dr C. (Routledge & Kegan Paul, London, 1959)

120 *Alien Contact*, Randles, J. (Sterling, New York, 1997)

121 *The Truth Behind the MIB*, Randles, op. cit.

122 *Magonia* 35 (1990)

123 *Fire in the Brain*, Siegel, Dr P. (Dutton, New York, 1992)

124 *MUFON Journal* 120 (1978) and 121 (1978)

125 My experiments are described in MIT proceedings *Alien Discussions*, Pritchard, op. cit., pp. 394–5

126 *Promises and Disappointments* 2 (1994)

127 'You Must Remember This – Or Do You?', *Washington Post* (27 June 1993)

128 *UFO Times* 9 (BUFORA, 1990)

129 *MUFON Journal* 346 (1997)

130 *Star Children*, Randles, op. cit.

131 *The Centre of the Cyclone*, Lilly, Dr J. (Calder & Boyars, London, 1973)

132 Ibid., pp. 64–5

133 *Night Life*, Cartwright, Dr R. (Prentice Hall, New York, 1977)

134 'Did a UFO Engineer Man's Dream?', *Anomaly* 4 (ASSAP, 1987)

135 *The Secret Language of Dreams*, Fontana, Dr D. (Piatkus, London, 1997)

136 *Lucid Dreaming*, LaBerge, Dr S. (Ballantine, New York, 1986)

137 *Brain and Mind*, Smythies, J. R. (ed.) (Routledge & Kegan Paul, London, 1966)

138 *Enigmas* 41 (SPI Scotland, 1995)

139 *Naro Minded* 8 (NARO, Manchester, 1998)

140 Harney in *Magonia* 59 (1997)

141 *Bulletin of Anomalous Experience (BAE)* 4:4 (1993)

142 *Introduction to Psychology*, Atkinson, R. and R., Smith, E. and Benn, D. (Harcourt Brace, USA, 1993)

143 See Walsden, West Yorkshire case in *Star Children*, Randles, op. cit.

144 *The Truth About Alien Abductions*, Hough, P. and Kalman, Dr M. (Cassell, London, 1997)

145 *BAE* 3:5 (1992)

146 Wilson, S. and Barber, T. in *Imagery*, Shekh, A. (ed.) (Wiley, USA, 1983)

147 *Journal of Personality* 51:2 (1986) and 55:1 (1987)

148 Basterfield and Bartholomew in *International UFO Reporter* (CUFOS, May/June 1988)

149 *International UFO Reporter* (CUFOS, July/Aug 1988)

150 *Society for Psychical Research Journal* (London, Jan 1995)

151 *Magonia* 32 (1988)

152 *Magonia* 34 (1989)

153 *MUFON Journal* 309 (1994)

154 *The Story of Ruth*, Schatzman, Dr M. (Penguin, London, 1981)

155 *UFOs – Identified*, Klass, P. (Random House, New York, 1968)

156 *Scientific Study of UFOs*, Condon, op. cit.

157 *Crop Circles: A Mystery Solved?*, Fuller, P and Randles, J. (Hale, London, 1993)

158 *MUFON Journal* 270 (1990)

159 *UFO Revelation*, Matthews, op. cit.

160 *The Truth Behind the MIB*, Randles, op. cit.

161 *UFO Crash Landing*, Randles, op. cit.

162 *A Secret Property*, Noyes, R. (Octagon, London, 1984)

163 *Timescape*, Benford, Dr C. (USA, 1980)

164 *Time Travel*, Randles, op. cit.

165 *We Are Not Alone*, Sullivan, W. (McGraw-Hill, New York, 1964); see also *Is Anyone Out There?*, Drake, Dr E. and Sobel, Dr D. (Delacorte Press, New York, 1992); and *Are We Alone?*, Davis, Dr P. (Basic Books, New York, 1995)

166 *Flying Saucers*, Jung, op. cit.

167 *Wild Places* 1 (1990)

168 *Magonia* 52 (1995)

169 *Life After Death and the World Beyond*, Randles, J. and Hough, P. (Piatkus, London, 1996)

170 *Crop Circles*, Fuller and Randles, op. cit.

171 *Magonia* 37 (1990)

172 *Society for Psycyhical Research Journal* (London, April 1996)

173 *Gifts of the Gods*, Spencer, J. (Virgin, London, 1995)

ALIEN HUNTERS – SELECT REFERENCES

Basterfield, Keith
UFOs: The Image Hypothesis (1981), updated as
UFOs: Australian Encounters (1997), both Reed,
Australia. Also several papers on Australian cases
and fantasy prone theory in the MIT proceedings.
Articles worth checking: *IUR* (Mar/Apr and May/June
1988) on fantasy proneness; (Jan/Feb 1992) on
implants; (May/June 1992) on witnessed abductions.

Blackmore, Dr Susan
Beyond the Body (Heinemann, 1982); *Adventures of a
Parapsychologist* (Prometheus, 1988); *Dying to Live*
(Grafton, 1993). Her unpublished manuscript
Abductions by Aliens or Sleep Paralysis? (1997)
achieved much comment. Articles worth checking:
The Skeptic 11 : 1 (1996) on sleep paralysis.

Bullard, Dr Thomas
On Stolen Time (private paper); *UFO Abductions: The
Measure of Mystery* (1987) and *The Sympathetic Ear:
Investigators as Variables* (1995) both published by
FUFOR. Articles worth checking, all published in the
CUFOS annual *Journal of UFO Studies*: vol. 1 (1989)
on how hypnosis varies data; vol. 3 (1991) on
abductions as folklore; vol. 6 (1996) assessing the
MIT symposium.

Devereux, Paul
Earthlights (Turnstone, 1982); *Earthlights Revelation*
(Cassell, 1989); *UFOs and UFOlogy* with Peter
Brookesmith (Blandford, 1997); *The Long Trip*
(Penguin, 1997). Articles worth checking: *New
UFOlogist* 1 (1994) on altered states, psychedelic
chemicals and abductions.

Evans, Hilary
The Evidence for UFOs (1983), *Visions, Apparitions,
Alien Visitors* (1984), *Gods, Spirits, Cosmic Guardians*
(1986), *Altered States of Consciousness* (1989) all
published by Aquarian Press. His edited
compilations, for which he also wrote sections are:
UFOs: 1947–1987 (Fortean Times, BUFORA, 1987)
with John Spencer; *UFO: 1947–1997* (Fortean
Times, John Brown, 1997) with Dennis Stacy.

Fowler, Ray
The Andreasson Affair (1979), *Casebook of a UFO
Investigator* (1981) and *The Andreasson Affair. Phase
Two* (1982) all Prentice-Hall; *The Watchers* (Bantam,
1990); *The Allagash Abductions* (1993) and *The

Watchers II (1995) both Wild Flower Press. Articles
worth checking: an article on the Allagash case
appears in *UFO: 1947–1997*, Evans and Stacy, op.
cit.

Hind, Cynthia
UFOs: African Encounters (Gemini, Zimbabwe,
1982). Articles worth checking: MUFON Conference
annual proceedings (1981 and 1987); an updated
feature on her cases to 1996 appears in her article in
UFOs: 1947–1997, Evans and Stacy, op. cit.

Hopkins, Budd
Missing Time (Merak, New York, 1981); *Intruders*
(Random House, 1987); *Witnessed* (Bloomsbury,
1997). Articles worth checking: *IUR* (Sept/Oct 1987)
for his views on the alien presence; *MUFON Journal*
(Sept 1996); also several detailed papers in the MIT
symposium proceedings.

Hufford, Dr David
The Terror that Comes in the Night (University of
Pennsylvania Press, 1982). Articles worth checking:
detailed report on his updated findings in the MIT
symposium proceedings.

Jacobs, Dr David
The UFO Controversy in America (Indiana University
Press, 1975); *Secret Life* (Simon & Schuster, 1993)
published as *Alien Encounters* (UK edn, Virgin,
1994). Articles worth checking: *MUFON Journal*
(Mar 1997) on the Manhattan transfer/'Witnessed'
case; also many pieces in the MIT symposium
proceedings.

McClure, Kevin
Stars and Rumours of Stars (self-published, 1980);
The Evidence for Visions of the Virgin (Aquarian
Press, 1983). Articles worth checking: several issues
of *Abduction Watch* (produced from his address) each
with cogent criticism of specific cases or the
phenomenon in general; also see an article on his
views in *PSI Researcher* (SPR, May 1995) and a crie
de coeur in *UFO Times* 42 (BUFORA, 1996).

Mack, Professor John
Abduction (Scribners, 1994). Articles worth checking
for his views *IUR* (July 1992).

Magonia
The Evidence for Alien Abductions, Rimmer, John

(Aquarian Press, 1984); *UFO: The Complete Sightings Catalogue*, Brookesmith, Peter (1995), *UFO: The Government Files*, Brookesmith, Peter (1996), *UFOs and UFOlogy*, Devereux, Paul and Brookesmith, Peter (1997), *Alien Abductions*, Brookesmith, Peter (1998) all published by Cassell. Articles worth checking: *Magonia* 60 (1997) on aliens as modern folklore.

Ring, Dr Kenneth

The Omega Project (William Morrow, 1992). Articles worth checking: *Journal of UFO Studies* 2 (CUFOS, 1990) on his theory (with Christopher Rosing).

Sprinkle, Professor Leo

A lengthy chapter on his work appears in *Flying Saucers Occupants*, Lorenzen, Coral and Jim (Signet, 1967). Another major paper, based on a study of a Wyoming abductee, appears in *UFOs and the Behavioural Scientist*, Haines, Dr Richard (ed.) (Scarecrow Press, New Jersey, 1979).

Vallee, Dr Jacques

Anatomy of a Phenomenon (1965) and *Passport to Magonia* (1969) both Regnery, Chicago; *Challenge to Science* (Spearman, Suffolk, 1966); *Messengers of Deception* (And/Or Press, Berkeley, 1979); *Dimensions* (1988), *Confrontations* (1990) and *Revelations* (1991) all Souvenir Press. Articles worth checking: proceedings of the conference of the Society for Scientific Exploration, University of Colorado, Boulder, CO (1989) – five arguments against the ETH.

Readers wishing to discuss any experiences (in confidence, if preferred), who would like to be directed to a more local, creditable research centre (please send an SAE for reply) or receive details of the magazine *Northern UFO News* (which she has edited for 25 years) can contact the author: c/o 1 Hallsteads Close, Dove Holes, Buxton, High Peak, Derbyshire, SK17 8BS or e-mail nufon@currantbun.com

USEFUL ADDRESSES

BUFORA (British UFO Research Association): publishes *UFO Times*
16 South Way, Burgess Hill, Sussex, RH15 9ST
CUFOS (Dr J. Allen Hynek Center for UFO Studies): publishes *International UFO Reporter*
2457 West Peterson Avenue, Chicago, Illinois 60659, USA
IUFOPRA (Irish UFO & Paranormal Research Association)
PO Box 3070, Whitehill, Dublin 9, Eire
IUN (Independent UFO Network) www.iun.org
MUFON (Mutual UFO Network): publishes *MUFON Journal*
103 Oldtowne Road, Seguin, Texas 78155, USA

NARO (Northern Anomalies Research Organisation): publishes *NARO Minded*
6 Silsden Avenue, Lowton, Warrington, WA3 1EN
OVNI Presence
BP 324, 13611 Aix-en-Provence, Cedex 1, France
SUFOI (Scandinavian UFO Investigation)
Postbox 11027, S-600 11, Norrkoping, Sweden
UFORA (UFO Research Australia)
PO Box 1894, Adelaide, South Australia 5001
UFORIC (UFO Research Investigation Centre Canada)
Department 25, 1665 Robson Street, Vancouver, British Columbia V6G 3C2, Canada

MAGAZINES

Abduction Watch 3 Claremont Grove, Leeds, LS3 1AX
Bulletin of Anomalous Experience (BAE) 614 South Hanover St, Baltimore, MD 21230–3832, USA
Flying Saucer Review (FSR) PO Box 162, High Wycombe, Bucks HP13 5DZ
Lumiers Dans La Nuit 5 Rue Lamartine, 91220 Betigny sur Orge, France
Magonia 5 James Terrace, London SW14 8HB
Ohio Notebook Box 162, 5837 Karric Square Drive, Dublin, OH 43016, USA
Skeptics UFO Newsletter (SUN) 404 N Street SW, Washington DC 20024, USA
SPR Journal 49 Marloes Rd, London W8 6LA
UFO Afrinews PO Box MP 49, Mount Pleasant, Harare, Zimbabwe

Further Reading

The books listed below represent most of the major works that have appeared about the alien contact and abduction mystery, but there are sure to be some omissions. I do not include general titles on UFOs; although two or three important books are added and will help to put the alien contact story into a broader perspective. The brief annotations describe the main purpose of the book.

1953
Flying Saucers Have Landed, Adamski, George and Leslie, Desmond (Werner Laurie)
Pioneering book by a contactee claiming friendly encounters with Nordic-style aliens.
1954
Flying Saucer From Mars, Allingham, Cedric (Muller)
First British contactee and possibly one of the first alien contact hoaxes.
1956
Report on UFOs, Ruppelt, Captain Edward (Ace)
USAF UFO investigator launches the now famous phrase and provides the best early set of data.
1958
Flying Saucers and the Straight Line Mystery, Michel, Aime (Phillips)
French UFOlogist's report on the world's first wave of serious alien contacts.
1959 *Flying Saucers: A Modern Myth*, Jung, Dr Carl (Routledge & Kegan Paul)
Famous psychiatrist investigates beliefs, dreams and cultural images of the new UFO craze.
1965
Anatomy of a Phenomenon, Vallee, Dr Jacques (Regnery)
First study by a scientist who analysed the data statistically and cross-comparatively.
1966
The Interrupted Journey, Fuller, John (Putnam; updated edition, Souvenir, 1980)
The first documented abduction – comprehensive account of the Betty and Barney Hill case.
1967
Flying Saucer Occupants, Lorenzen, Coral and Jim (Signet)
Husband and wife who ran then top UFO group, APRO; catalogues first 20 years of alien sightings.
1968
UFOs – Identified, Klass, Philip (Random House)
Sceptic and aviation journalist seeks to explain cases

as misidentifications and plasma energy balls.
The Humanoids, Bowen, Charles (ed.) (Futura)
Based on a *Flying Saucer Review* special issue, articles by many top researchers surveying alien cases.
1969
Passport to Magonia, Vallee, Dr Jacques (Regnery)
The first book to link fairy lore with alien contacts and find a continuum between such cases.
Scientific Study of UFOs, Condon, Dr Edward (ed.) (Bantam)
A 1,000-page report on the two-year survey by many scientists – with minimal coverage of alien contacts.
1970
Operation Trojan Horse, Keel, John (Putnam)
A journalist suggests that alien contacts and monsters are an intelligence deliberately deceiving mankind.
1972
UFOs: A Scientific Debate, Sagan, Dr Carl and Page, Dr Thomton (eds) (Cornell University) Many scientists, believers and sceptics, present papers from a weeks debate into the evidence.
1975
The Unidentified, Clark, Jerome and Coleman, Loren (Warner)
The first serious theory book on the collective unconscious idea; since disowned by Clark but intriguing.
1976
Space-Time Transients, Persinger, Dr Michael and Lafreniere, Ghyslaine (Nelson-Hall)
Trailblazing book that links strange phenomena with electrified energy fields.
1977
The Eighth Tower, Keel, John (New American Library)
Theory that an energy/radiation spectrum produces both physical UFOs and alien contacts.
Abducted, Lorenzen, Coral and Jim (Berkley)
The first case book devoted to alien abduction cases, primarily from the USA.
1979
Messengers of Deception, Vallee, Dr Jacques (And/Or Press)
An investigation of cults and cultural belief built around the alien contact, leading to the 'control' theory.
The Andreasson Affair, Fowler, Ray (Prentice-Hall)
Case study of a New England abduction (story

continued in *Phase Two* – same author/
publisher, 1982)

1980

Beyond the Light Barrier, Klarer, Elizabeth (Timmins)
African witness describes her amorous adventures
with an alien.

The UFO Handbook, Hendry, Allen (NEL)
Possibly the best introduction to UFOs; by CUFOS
investigator with a fully objective look at sightings.

1981

Missing Time, Hopkins, Budd (Merak)
The now famous abduction guru and his first
unassuming look at a handful of American
abductions.

*An Account of a Meeting with Denizens of Another
World*, Langford, David (St Martin's Press)
Spoof alien contact from the nineteenth century,
written (as William Loosley) so well it fooled some
UFOlogists.

1982

Alien Contact, Randles, Jenny and Whetnall, Paul
(Spearman)
Report on a series of alien contacts involving an
entire family from Deeside, North Wales.

1984

The Evidence for Alien Abductions, Rimmer, John
(Aquarian)
Britain's first abduction book – a sceptical summary
by the *Magonia* editor of the psycho-social theory.

Visions, Apparitions, Alien Visitors, Evans, Hilary
(Aquarian)
Cross comparisons between diverse 'entity' sightings
seeking a link within altered states. Followed in 1986
by part two from the same author/publisher: *Gods,
Spirits, Cosmic Guardians*.

1987

Communion, Strieber, Whitley (William Morrow)
The US horror fiction writer's first-hand true life story
of how he recovered alien abduction memories.
Followed with several update books: *Transformation*
(Avon, 1988); *Breakthrough* (Harper, 1995)

Intruders, Hopkins, Budd (Random House)
Multiple abductions to an Indiana family that brought
to light 'wise baby' and genetic experiment cases.

1988

Abduction, Randles, Jenny (Robert Hale)
Detailed study of 100 British alien contacts, placed
into context with the evidence from elsewhere.

Dimensions, Vallee, Dr Jacques (Souvenir Press)
Vallee's first look at alien contacts and abductions in
the post-Strieber and Hopkins era, attempting to fit
his ideas into the new pattern of sightings.

Phenomenon, Evans, Hilary and Spencer, John (eds

for BUFORA) (MacDonald/Futura)
400 pages of progress reports compiled from 30
leading global researchers, some writing in English
for the only time. Includes Devereux, Hind, Hopkins,
Hough, Keel, McClure and three chapters from
myself.

1989

Earthlights Revelation, Devereux, Paul (Cassell)
The best expression of the theory that energy forms
can trigger altered states that provoke alien contact.

UFO Abduction: A Dangerous Game, Klass, Philip
(Prometheus)
Best expression of debunking, seeking to demystify
abductions as hoaxes, deception and misperception.

1990

Confrontations, Vallee, Dr Jacques (Souvenir Press)
A first-hand search for alien contact cases where
physical energies might have deadly consequences.

The Watchers, Fowler, Ray (Bantam)
Leading American UFOlogist reports his own
discovery of family-related contacts and abductions.

Perspectives, Spencer, John (MacDonald/Futura)
A look at abductions from a witness-centred
perspective, calling for a broader-based approach to
study.

1991

Looking for the Aliens, Hough, Peter and Randles,
Jenny (Cassell)
The approach of scientists, science fiction writers,
UFOlogists, the church and society towards aliens.

Angels and Aliens, Thompson, Keith (Addison-
Wesley)
Folklore, modern mythology and the content of alien
contacts – a modern-day Carl Jung-style vision.

Mind Monsters, Randles, Jenny (Aquarian)
Theory linking aliens, apparitions, monsters and
quantum physics with a form of projected
hallucination.

1992

Into the Fringe, Turner, Dr Karla (Berkeley)
College lecturer explores a family saga of ongoing
alien contacts and abductions.

The Omega Project, Ring, Dr Kenneth (William
Morrow)
Psychologist and NDE expert cross-compares after-
effects of these events with claims of alien abductees

Hidden Memories, Baker, Dr Robert (Prometheus)
Sceptical look at hypnosis, regression and alien
contact evidence from a psychological approach.

The UFO Encyclopedia Project, Clark, Jerome
(Omnigraphics)
A stunning, award-winning work. Three enormous
and very expensive encyclopedia on every conceivable

aspect of UFOs and alien contacts – compiled as a five-year, full-time project by Clark. Published as *Emergence of a Phenomenon – to 1959* (1992); *UFOs in the 1980s* (1994); *High Strangeness – 1960 to 1979*, (1996). In 1998 a revised 'combined' volume was published with over 1,000 pages and a million words.

1993

Secret Life, Jacobs, Dr David (Simon & Schuster)
Personal study conducted by US history professor of a number of American abductees seeking patterns within their sightings. In Britain this book was published as *Alien Encounters* (Virgin, 1994).

1994

Gifts of the Gods?, Spencer, John (Virgin)
Cases where abductees have been given alleged ability or psychic power in the wake of their encounter.

Star Children, Randles, Jenny (Robert Hale)
Alien contact witnesses who believe they have psychic bond with aliens, possibly even being alien children.

Abduction, Mack, Professor John (Scribners)
Harvard medical psychiatrist reviews abductees and finds in favour of some sort of alien encounter.

Dark White, Schnabel, Jim (Hamish Hamilton)
Sceptical journalist's view of alien contact that is a good outsiders view of what the fuss is about.

Alien Discussions, Pritchard, Mack, et al (eds) (North Cambridge Press)
Phenomenal 700-page proceedings of the 1992 MIT symposium, featuring dozens of papers by leading researchers, psychologists, abductees etc, examining numerous facets of the abduction. Includes all Question & Answer sessions after each paper. Very expensive but immensely valuable for serious researchers.

1995

Close Encounters of the Fourth Kind, Bryan, C. D. (Wiedenfeld & Nicolson)
One of the few journalists allowed to attend the MIT event reports on his week there probing abductions.

Spaceships of the Pleiades, Korff, Karl (Prometheus)
Well-argued, sceptical report on a modern contactee, the colourful character of Swiss man, Billy Meir, who met and filmed many UFOs and aliens – including a very terrestrial-looking, blonde woman from the planet Erra! A gentler treatment of the case is in Gary Kinder's *Light Years* (Atlantic Monthly Press, 1987).

1996

Witnessed, Hopkins, Budd (Pocket Books)
The story of the Manhattan transfer 'observed abduction' case, involving Linda Napolitano in New York.

Fire in the Sky, Walton, Travis (Marlow)
Abductee tells his true story from a 1975 Ariziona encounter, released as a fictional movie of the same title.

UFOs, Basterfield, Keith (Reed)
Australian perspective on cases, notably ones involving aliens, abductions and altered states.

Alien Impact, Craft, Michael (St Martin's Press)
Interesting survey of the impact of beliefs in alien contact on society in the USA.

1997

The Uninvited, Pope, Nick (Simon & Schuster)
British MoD civil servant who collated UFO files 1991–1994 gives his pro-ETH views on abduction data.

The Truth about Alien Abductions, Hough, Peter and Kalman, Dr Moyshe (Cassell)
Despite the naff title, a fine set of UK case studies with perceptive views as to what they might mean.

1998

UFO Crash Landing? Randles, Jenny (Blandford)
Investigation of the Rendlesham Forest close encounters, where physical evidence and altered states meet.

Alien Abductions, Brookesmith, Peter (Cassell)
Glossy general survey of alien claims, with emphasis on the USA, but sensible criticism of excess theories.

Electric UFOs, Budden, Albert (Cassell)
Theory linking UFOs to effects of electromagnetic pollution, also possibly triggering visionary abductions.

Cosmic Test Tube, Fitzgerald, Randall (Moon Lake Media)
Idiosyncratic project aims to study progress in ideas on alien contact by selecting over 100 'seminal' books on ancient astronauts, UFOs, aliens and the search for extra-terestrial life. These are tied together in date order by giving a précis and brief review of each title, as well as explaining how it furthered progress.

1999

Alien Investigator, Dodd, Tony (Headline)
Yorkshire police officer tells story of his own case studies and first-hand alien contacts.

Index

Also available from Piatkus

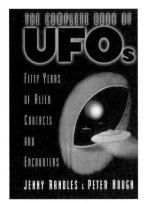

The Complete Book of UFOs:
Fifty Years of Alien Contacts and Encounters
ISBN 0-7499-1711-3
£6.99

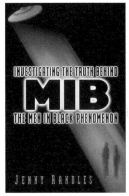

Men In Black:
Investigating the Truth Behind the Phenomenon
ISBN 0-7499-1721-0
£9.99

The Paranormal Source Book:
The Comprehensive Guide to Strange Phenomena Worldwide
ISBN 0-7499-1884-5
£9.99

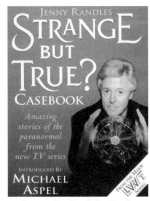

Strange But True? Casebook:
Amazing Stories of the Paranormal
ISBN 0-7499-1558-7
£10.99

The Afterlife:
An Investigation into the Mysteries of Life After Death
ISBN 0-7499-1804-7
£6.99

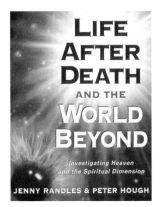

Life After Death and the World Beyond:
Investigating Heaven and the Spiritual Dimension
ISBN 0-7499-1802-2
£10.99

Other books by the same author

UFOs and How to See Them
The Unexplained: Great Mysteries of the 20th Century
Aliens: The Real Story
The Paranormal Year
Time Travel

and with Peter Hough

Strange But True? Stories of the Paranormal
Spontaneous Human Combustion
Looking for the Aliens
Mysteries of the Mersey Valley
Encyclopedia of the Unexplained